HOUSES BY MAIL

HOUSES BY MAIL

A Guide to Houses from Sears, Roebuck and Company

KATHERINE COLE STEVENSON

H. WARD JANDL

THE PRESERVATION PRESS

The Preservation Press
National Trust for Historic Preservation
1785 Massachusetts Avenue, N.W.
Washington, D.C. 20036

Printed in the United States of America
90 89 88 87 86   5 4 3 2 1

Library of Congress Cataloging in Publication Data

Stevenson, Katherine Cole.
   Houses by mail.

   Bibliography: p.
   Includes index.
   1. Prefabricated houses—United States.
   2. Architecture, Domestic—United States—Designs
and plans.   3. Sears, Roebuck and Company.   I. Jandl,
H. Ward.   II. Title.
TH4819.P7S74   1986   728.3′73   86–3186
ISBN 0–89133–120–4

Designed by Marc Meadows and Robert Wiser, Meadows & Wiser, Washington, D.C.
Edited by Gretchen Smith, Associate Editor, and Diane Maddex, Editor, The Preservation Press.
Composed in Cheltenham with Peignot and Park Avenue display type by Carver Photocomposition, Inc., Arlington, Va., and printed on 70-pound Warren Patina by Collins Lithographing and Printing Company, Baltimore, Md.

Cover: The Preston, from the 1918 Sears Modern Homes catalog.

CONTENTS

ACKNOWLEDGMENTS

This book is dedicated to the memory of William H. Brabham, our friend and colleague in the National Park Service.

The preparation of this book would not have been possible without the invaluable assistance of many people. Above all, Lenore Swoiskin, Archivist, Sears, Roebuck and Company, and Vicki Cwiok, her assistant, helped familiarize us with Sears's archives and willingly shared their extensive knowledge. We are grateful to Sears, Roebuck and Company for allowing us to research its Modern Homes catalogs and make the needed photographs, which totaled more than 500. Most of the photographs, floor plans and drawings in this book, except as otherwise noted, are from the catalogs in the Sears archives. John Alderson photographed more than 500 pages from the original Modern Homes catalogs in the Sears archives, including the cover photograph.

We are also indebted to Louis Wall and Ken Weinstein, who loaned us hard-to-find catalogs in their possession; Sabra Clark, of the Chicago Historical Society, who provided useful information about several architects of Sears homes; Thomas J. Schlereth, of the University of Notre Dame, who contributed important research on Sears's Modern Homes operation; Laura Muckenfuss, of the Georgia Institute of Technology, who provided information about vernacular housing in America; and Lee H. Nelson, FAIA, of the National Park Service, who gave us the benefit of his knowledge of construction technology.

The Avery Architectural and Fine Arts Library, Columbia University, which in late 1985 added a 1924 Modern Homes catalog to its collection, provided prints of the house styles found only in that catalog—the Delmar (page 134), the Princeton (page 179), the Monterey (page 286) and the Double-Duty (page 345). Marsha Lederman made watercolor illustrations and Stanley Bandong redrew the floor plans of three house styles—the Melrose (page 54), the Laurel (page 141) and the Sherwood (page 193), of which only photocopies were available—from the 1929 Modern Homes catalog, now missing from the Library of Congress. Richard J. Vitullo, of Darrel Downing Rippeteau Architects, P.C., created the logos for the 15 house types.

Our appreciation also is extended to Diane Maddex, Editor, the Preservation Press, who first suggested that the National Trust publish *Houses by Mail* and oversaw its development and production; and to Gretchen Smith, Associate Editor, whose thorough and careful editing aided considerably in making the book the useful guide it is. The appropriate period design for the book is due to the high standards of Marc Meadows and Robert Wiser of Meadows & Wiser, and their staff Alan Pitts, Mary McCoy and Terri Brand. The manuscript was typed by Cecelia Dickerson of the Preservation Press and Sherry Fauth.

Finally, we thank our families and friends for their moral support during this four-year effort.

Katherine Cole Stevenson
H. Ward Jandl

RECOLLECTIONS

Modern Home No. 167 as advertised in the 1909 Modern Homes catalog. The house sold for $753 that year. (Gail Mooney)

*M*y Sears mail-order house—Modern Home No. 167, later named the Maytown—was built in 1909. It is unabashedly American, the kind of house you see in movies about the good old days when virtue triumphed and the nice guy won the girl, usually while sitting in the front porch swing. Visitors often comment that there is something vaguely familiar about the house, which is quite true. They have seen versions of it all over America, in small towns and old suburbs, along streets lined with maple and elm trees.

Modern Home No. 167 is straightforward and unpretentious yet without dowdiness. Its turret and porch columns and spindles lend a certain elegance that easily matches the gingerbread and more elaborate architecture of its turn-of-the-century neighbors. Inside, the rooms and hallways are large and airy. There are high ceilings, protruding bays, paneled doors, soft pine floors and oddly shaped closets for children to hide in. The third floor, once the attic, provides a quiet hideaway, a place where model trains can be left up all year long, a spot from which you can look down at the treetops and watch squirrels building nests.

Living in Modern Home No. 167 is not without its challenges. It is hard to heat on cold January days no matter how high the thermostat is set. It is almost impossible to find house painters brave enough to tackle the exterior. Plumbers shake their heads and make ominous sounds about impending floods. One electrician sat down and chuckled, and a roofer wouldn't even get out of his truck to give me an estimate when the steep, gabled roof needed repairs. Replacing broken porch spindles meant a special order to a Colorado firm, not the local Sears store. But at 75 everything and everybody has a few mechanical problems.

My Sears house allows me to connect with the past, to a time when the century was new and the country was optimistic, idealistic and still innocent. Teddy Roosevelt was leaving the White House to William Howard Taft, and millions of immigrants, including my grandparents, were pouring into the country. Sometimes at night I "listen" to the house and try to imagine what life was like when the house was the new place on the block. Did the first owners notice how the rain tumbles from the turret onto the porch roof? Did their children practice their first steps holding onto the porch spindles as mine did? Did they see the circus train roll by on its way into Washington? Did they put their Halloween pumpkins on the porch? Did they cut holly from the tree in the backyard to make a wreath for the front door at Christmas? And did the window on the second-floor landing stick even then?

Mary Anne O'Boyle, 1985
Takoma Park, Md.

*M*y father, J. S. Hogue, purchased our home—Modern Home No. 146, later named the Saratoga—from Sears, Roebuck in Chicago in late 1912 or early 1913. He saw the finished house on the firm's lot, liked it and had it shipped precut on the Frisco Railroad to Chelsea, Okla. None but our immediate family has occupied this home. It was the first house in Chelsea to have electric lights. We are using the original plumbing and wiring. The redwood siding holds paint remarkably well. The floors and the woodwork, including the ceiling beams, are all solid oak. There has been no change in the walls or floor plan; it is truly a compliment to Sears, Roebuck.

Erskine Hogue Stanberry, 1981
Chelsea, Okla.

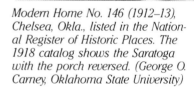

Modern Home No. 146 (1912–13), Chelsea, Okla., listed in the National Register of Historic Places. The 1918 catalog shows the Saratoga with the porch reversed. (George O. Carney, Oklahoma State University)

The Cornell, a four-square house, shown in the 1928 Modern Homes catalog.

*O*ur home, the Cornell, was built in 1928. My dad did the carpentry and subcontracted the masonry, electrical and plumbing work. I recall the times during my folks' later years when my mother suggested they sell and buy a retirement home at the Jersey shore. My dad's reply was always the same: "I built this house. I know where every nail is. It's a good, solid house, and I'm not leaving it." And neither of them did.

Richard Ferguson, 1981
Linden, N.J.

*W*e started the foundation of our Sears house on December 4, 1934, digging it out with a team of horses and a scraper. Our supplies and lumber were trucked in from Newark, N.J., as needed. We bought the whole package, which included the plumbing and electric wiring. We bought our furnace a few years later as we had to conserve money. The only changes we made were to add two more windows to the kitchen and put up a stone chimney instead of brick. We finished it in April 1935, and it was beautiful.

We love our home and through the years have had many compliments. People stop and take pictures of it; some people call it a gingerbread house or fairyland house. It was the best investment of our lives, and all materials were far superior to anything we could find locally and saved us money. We have kept it up in good shape, and it has withstood the heavy winds and weather remarkably well. We have enjoyed our home as we have struggled along through life and hope to enjoy it for a few more years.

Kenneth and Marjorie Bailey, 1982
Kiamesha Lake, N.Y.

The Dover (1934–35), seen in 1938, Kiamesha Lake, N.Y. (Courtesy of Kenneth and Marjorie Bailey)

The Maplewood, shown in the 1932 Modern Homes catalog.

*I*n 1933 we built a Sears home, an English-style four-room house, the Maplewood. We are still in it and love it. It has held up very well, and we found the materials of excellent quality.

You may be interested to know what the house cost us—the materials were $2,300, the contractor was $1,500, and two extra contractors for a break-fast nook and back porch came to $900. It was hard work as the property is rocky and was partly swampy at that time.

We live on a hill just outside the village of Pleasantville, and there were so many Sears houses up here that it was known as Sears, Roebuck Hill. We were sorry to hear that Sears gave up selling homes.

W. Stephen and Beatrice Bordeaux, 1982
Pleasantville, N.Y.

Modern Home No. 105, pictured in the 1913 Modern Homes catalog.

*B*y the use of your blueprints my carpenter was able to work without mistake or delay. By the use of your bill of materials I was able to order just what I needed for my house and no more. By the use of your catalog and low prices I had my home complete, plaster, paint and all, before cold weather came on. I saved as much as 60 percent on some of the finishing lumber. If I build another home, my millwork will come from Sears, Roebuck and Company.

Bartlett D. Dickson, 1913
Cowley, Wyo.

The Rembrandt (1926), built by Earl Goekeler, Merchantville, N.J., seen in 1936. (Courtesy of Carl and Carol Breitinger)

*T*here is no better house in town, and it is admired by all. This you may think is putting it pretty strong, but it is nevertheless a fact.

N. E. Noblet, 1918
Halifax, Pa.

*T*he principal reason I elected to build a Sears, Roebuck house was not to save money. I know present-day lumber, and it was my intention to have a house built in the same old-fashioned construction that we saw before the war. I wanted high ceilings, I wanted quantity, and, last, I wanted to be sure of it. Whether I saved any money or not I don't know and I don't care. I got exactly what I wanted, and I'm entirely satisfied. I cannot speak too highly of the treatment I received from Sears, Roebuck, and I am particularly grateful for their valuable suggestions and interest in my home. I can say no more than this: If it were necessary for me to build another house, I would do it exactly the same way.

Earl Goekeler, 1927
Merchantville, N.J.

The Magnolia (1927), South Bend, Ind. The Magnolia was first featured in the 1918 Modern Homes catalog, which advertised it for $5,140. (John Helmer)

As an Air Force family, we have lived with our four children in many strange, wonderful and not-so-wonderful houses, large and small, throughout the world. In 1969, on retirement from the Air Force, we purchased our dream house in South Bend, Ind., a two-story neo-classical structure built in 1927. We were very happy with our purchase, our first real home, and named it April House. We planted several magnolias in front.

We did some redecorating but left the kitchen as it was, with its blue and white tile floor. We are both cooks, and the kitchen became the heart of our home. It was the place for our cooking classes (Gourmet 101, Indiana University at South Bend) and where the Notre Dame Cook Book *was born. Holidays, graduations, weddings and christenings were all an important part of the kitchen activities.*

In 1982 we discovered that our house was the Magnolia, a Sears Honor Bilt house. We were quite excited and very proud—we felt the house was true Americana. The magnolias in front had more meaning than ever before, and we planted several more along the side. And even though the children are gone, our dream house is still full—with students, family and friends.

Francis A. and Florence G. Yeandel, 1986
South Bend, Ind.

THE ATTLEBORO..
• SIX ROOMS—BATH AND LAVATORY

The Attleboro (1933), State College, Pa., built with its chimney turned, a departure from the style as pictured in the 1937 Modern Homes catalog. (Abby Dochat)

*O*ur Attleboro was built in 1933, and we are the third owners. The Maurice S. Gjesdahls, who built the house, hired a landscape architect on the faculty of Pennsylvania State University to develop a landscaping scheme. They planted such a variety of shrubs, flowering trees and shade trees that Penn State botany professors brought their students to this property to demonstrate identification methodology and how landscaping can enhance private homes. The second owners, the Nelson McGearys, made major structural alterations to accommodate their growing family, including extending the dining room, making a bedroom over the garage and converting the garage to a partially paneled and beamed library. We restored the landscaping, did some interior remodeling and updated the house for energy efficiency.

The evolution of this property indicates that this Cape Cod style has adapted extremely well to the changing needs of several families and has maintained its exterior appeal for more than 50 years. The house reflects the quality of the original plan and materials of the Sears Modern Homes program. The contractor who has kept the house in shape for 15 years stoutly observes that "houses today are just not built like this one."

James D. and Marion I. Hammond, 1985
State College, Pa.

*A*t the foot of the Buffalo Peaks in south central Colorado, at an elevation of 8,600 feet, lies the Pine Creek Ranch, first settled around 1880 by German immigrants. In front of the original ranch buildings of hewn logs stands a 1929 Sears house, facing the spectacular view of the Collegiate Peaks rising beyond the Arkansas River. The materials for the house were delivered by rail and then transported over the river to the homesite. Used as the main house for the owners of the ranch (we are the fourth), it is solidly built and shows no sign of structural deterioration. Nestled into the Ponderosa pines on the mountainside, it fits quietly into its setting and looks exactly as if it belongs there.

Mr. and Mrs. Robert A. Ferris, 1986
Buena Vista, Colo.

The Westly (1929), Buena Vista, Colo., and shown in the 1918 Modern Homes catalog. (Robert A. Ferris)

*M*y house has attracted a good deal of attention and favorable comment and has been visited by people from quite a distance, farthest being 120 miles. Everybody is surprised at the quality of millwork, nothing like it being obtainable here for natural wood finish. Saved $419 on lumber, net.

A. A. Ward
Coldwater, Kans.

he materials used to build the Crescent were excellent. All materials, weighing 27 tons, were delivered by freight and trucked eight miles to the building site. About 18 years later I added two roof dormers and finished off two bedrooms in the attic and also added a half bath. The cost of the completed home was less than $4,000. One of my sons and his family are living in the house now.

Kenneth H. Mayne, 1985
Norwich, N.Y.

I wish to acknowledge the receipt of the ready-made building. The house is all right in every respect and has saved us labor and money. I would recommend its use to anyone going to a new country as we did. Having the house on the train with us, we were able to have it up and move into it two days after we reached Powell. We now have as nice a little house as anyone.

Irvin E. Cameron, 1918
Powell, Wyo.

The house I built according to your plan is fine, and as soon as I get the curtains up I will have a picture taken for you. Someone is here every Sunday looking at it. They call it the Sears, Roebuck house. Some that built before I did wish now they had sent to you for the material.

William Gregg, 1913
Abbeyville, Kans.

The Crescent, Norwich, N.Y., seen in the early 1930s shortly after it was built. (Kenneth H. Mayne, Sears, Roebuck and Company)

Modern Home No. 55M118, a Simplex Sectional four-room portable house.

Modern Home No. 264P151 (1917), Ray City, Ga. In the 1918 Modern Homes catalog the style was labeled the Avondale. (Connell Studios)

*I*n 1917, after living in a two-room log cabin for 12 years, William and Mollie Lee, my grandparents, moved into their newly constructed Sears Modern Home No. 264P151, near Ray City, Ga. It was a large house—with seven rooms, 25 glass windows, 12-foot ceilings, heart pine floors and plaster walls—and they needed the room, because the family grew to include seven children, various relatives and the teacher from the nearby schoolhouse.

The materials for the house were presumably transported by rail to the depot at Ray City and then by mule and wagon to the building site. The mantel and interior columns were purchased at the Sears, Roebuck store in Valdosta, Ga. Electricity was not available in south Georgia when the house was constructed. Sometime in the late 1930s a gasoline powered dynamo, or "light house," was obtained, and a primitive electrical system was installed. Some years later, following passage of the Rural Electrification Act, south Georgia and the Lee family entered the electric age, and the dynamo was retired.

At some point, the rear of the house was extended to enlarge the kitchen and two rear bedrooms. A porch on the right side of the house has been enclosed to make a sun porch or Florida room.

Over the years the house became a social hub for this sparsely settled area of rural south Georgia. A clay tennis court was constructed near the house, a number of school proms and church socials were held there, and at least three weddings have been performed at the house. William and Mollie lived in their Sears home until they died, William at age 86 and Mollie at age 96.

The house is still in the family. In January 1983 my wife, Brenda, and I purchased the house and the 110-acre farm from Mollie Lee's estate.

Michael C. Lee, 1986
Ray City, Ga.

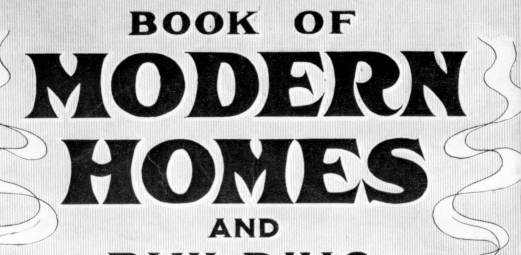

BOOK OF
MODERN HOMES
AND
BUILDING PLANS

SEARS, ROEBUCK & CO.
CHICAGO

INTRODUCTION

From Pleasantville, N.Y., to Coldwater, Kans., from Philadelphia, Pa., to Cowley, Wyo., and beyond, 100,000 families turned to Sears, Roebuck and Company earlier in this century for one of their most important purchases: their homes. Between 1908 and 1940 Sears was the place to find not only everything to fill an American home; it also manufactured and sold the houses themselves—approximately 450 ready-to-assemble designs from mansions to bungalows and even summer cottages. Ordered by mail and sent by rail wherever a boxcar or two could pull up, these popular houses were meant to fill a need for sturdy, inexpensive and, especially, *modern* homes—complete with such desirable conveniences as indoor plumbing and electricity.

Thousands of these well-built houses survive in small towns and big cities throughout the country. Most present owners, however, are unaware of the mail-order origins of their houses. Until recently the existence of these Sears houses was not widely known and, thus, there was little interest in them. But beginning in the late 1970s, as the supply of affordable and restorable Victorian houses dwindled, young homeowners started buying and re-habilitating houses built in the first decades of the 20th century. In so doing, many of them discovered a common thread: A large percentage of the houses could be traced to the Modern Homes Department of Sears. Feature stories on surviving Sears houses around the nation began to appear in publications such as the National Trust's *Historic Preservation* magazine, daily newspapers and the popular press. This discovery of historical interest in what only recently had been thought to be ordinary bungalows or colonial-style houses has led to nationwide concern for studying, saving and restoring Sears houses.

Sears was not the only American company to manufacture or sell houses through mail-order catalogs, nor was it the only company to sell house designs. The late 19th and early 20th centuries were ripe for entrepreneurs who sold architectural plans as well as the houses themselves. The Hodgson Company, Alladin Homes and Montgomery Ward all had their start in the housing business between 1895 and 1910. Sears, however, was the largest: Its sales reached 30,000 houses by 1925 and nearly 50,000 by 1930, more than any other mail-order company. In fact, its 1939 homes catalog claimed that "over one hundred thousand families, or approximately half a million people, are living in Honor Bilt Modern Homes today." In its three decades of operation, Sears set an impressive record, making substantial contributions to 20th-century housing in America.

One of the reasons for the popularity of Sears houses was that they consciously reflected popular American taste of the period; designs were selected for their broad appeal and acceptance. Boris Emmet and John E. Jeuck, authorities on the history of Sears, have written: "Sears, Roebuck's merchandise line during the years since 1925 has generally been typical of its line in all other periods in one basic respect: the company has almost never been an innovator in products" (*Catalogues and Counters*, 1950). Another reason for Sears's early success in the housing market was its reputation for quality at a reasonable price. Sears was committed to and took great pride in the products it manufactured and sold. A 1918 Sears-produced history stated that "the customer must *be satisfied for a lifetime* for every house we sell is a standing advertisement for Sears, Roebuck and Company" (P. F. Holden, "Building Materials Department D/664: A History"). A third reason was the speed and ease with which Sears houses could be constructed. Sears provided precut lumber at a time when power tools were almost unknown, as well as a complete set of specifications and instructions to aid in construction. Because owners were directly involved with design selection and actual construction, they were especially proud of their Sears houses once they were erected.

Right: The Mae Novelle home (the Matoka), Medford, N.J., soon after the shingled bungalow was built, about 1912. (Sears, Roebuck and Company)

Below: Pages from the 1917 Modern Homes catalog announcing, in Sears's inimitable way, the number of houses sold within nine years.

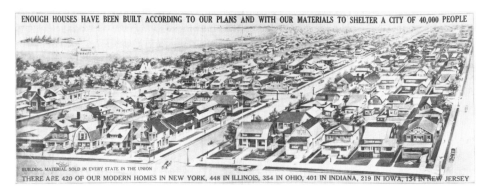

ENOUGH HOUSES HAVE BEEN BUILT ACCORDING TO OUR PLANS AND WITH OUR MATERIALS TO SHELTER A CITY OF 40,000 PEOPLE

BUILDING MATERIAL SOLD IN EVERY STATE IN THE UNION

THERE ARE 420 OF OUR MODERN HOMES IN NEW YORK, 448 IN ILLINOIS, 354 IN OHIO, 401 IN INDIANA, 219 IN IOWA, 134 IN NEW JERSEY

THE MODERN HOMES PROGRAM

The creation of what ultimately became the Modern Homes Department can be traced to the years between 1895 and 1900, when Sears began to sell building materials from its mail-order catalog. Success in the building materials area was slow in coming; in fact, in 1906 Sears considered closing the unprofitable department and reassigned the manager of the china department, Frank W. Kushel, to do so. In short order Kushel decided that he could make the department pay and took on the challenge to transform the department into a money maker. By 1908 the first catalog devoted exclusively to mail-order homes was issued. Entitled *Book of Modern Homes and Building Plans,* it featured 22 styles priced between $650 and $2,500. These prices included plans, specifications and most materials down to the nails. In addition, Sears provided cost estimates for such work items as labor and excavation so the customer would have a good idea of the overall construction price.

The idea of mail-order homes quickly caught on. Sears expanded its holdings between 1909 and 1912 by purchasing a lumber mill in Mansfield, La., in 1909, a lumber yard in Cairo, Ill., in 1911 and a millwork plant in Norwood, Ohio, in 1912. The plant at Cairo was a 40-acre establishment strategically located on a rail line at a rate-breaking point, which allowed Sears to receive, store and precut the lumber cheaply before forwarding it to customers (F. K. Wheeler, "Recollection of 36 Years with a Fascinating Lumber Plant").

Sears's success in selling houses was tied, in large part, to its attractive financing plans. Although initially Sears did not offer financial assistance for the purchase of the houses it sold, by 1911 it had begun to offer loans. By 1918, after some rocky times, Sears was able to offer credit for almost all the material and, sometimes, to advance a portion of the capital required for labor. Loans typically ran for five years at 6 percent interest, with regular monthly installments. Alternative plans, extending monthly payments for up to 15 years, were also available. Sears would loan customers money for the lot as well, and down payments could be as small as one-fourth of the total value of both the lot and the house.

Although most of its business was with individual homeowners, Sears also dealt directly with organizations and corporations. During World War I Sears supplied hospital buildings to the Red Cross. These were ready made, shipped in sections and ready to bolt together and use. Sears also sold houses to companies for company towns near their factories. In the 1919 catalog, Sears illustrated the 192 houses purchased by the Standard Oil Company and erected for workers in Carlinville, Ill., in 1918 at a reported cost of $1 million. After an inspection trip covering all the mining towns in Illinois, Oscar Hewitt of the *Chicago Tribune* wrote that Carlinville had the reputation for having the best mining houses in Illinois. Another corporate customer was Bethlehem Steel, which erected houses in Hellertown, Pa.

Although mail-order catalogs were produced throughout the history of Sears's Modern Homes program, sales offices were able to offer customers personalized service. Customers were always able to modify the floor plans and materials of the basic models at the time their orders were placed, and sales offices facilitated this service. Sears established its first Modern Homes sales office in Akron, Ohio, in 1919. Six years later there were sales offices in nine other cities: Cincinnati, Cleveland, Columbus and Dayton, Ohio; New York; Washington, D.C.; Chicago (downtown and Central Park Avenue); Pittsburgh; and Philadelphia. By 1930 Sears had 350 salespeople working in 48 sales offices, all east of the Mississippi and north of the Mason-Dixon line. Office locations included Elgin and Rockford, Ill.; Gary and Mishawaka, Ind.; Canton, Lorain, Painesville, Warren and Youngstown, Ohio; Ann Arbor, Flint and Pontiac, Mich.; St. Louis; Albany; Trenton, N.J.; and Bridgeport, Conn.

The postwar housing boom coupled with the creation of the sales offices boosted sales from about 125 units a month in 1920 to more than 250 units a month in 1929 at the Cairo plant alone. In one particularly busy month, May 1926, the plant at Cairo shipped 324 ready-cut houses. This demand resulted in Sears's opening another 40-acre lumber mill in Newark, N.J., in 1925, aimed specifically at the increasing East Coast sales. Although

A glimpse into Sears's mass production process, its factories and lumber yards, seen in the 1937 catalog.

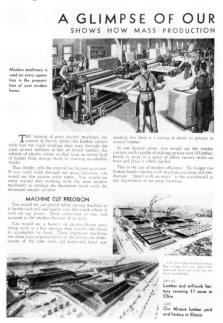

An invitation in the 1925 catalog urging potential customers to visit one of Sears's regional
offices for a first-hand look at the Honor Bilt
ready-cut system of home building.

The Standard Addition, Sears houses built for
Standard Oil Company employees in Carlinville, Ill., in 1918 and still home to a thriving
neighborhood. (© 1985 Gail Mooney)

eastern sales increased, the sales from Cairo began to lag, and the factory there supple-
mented its Modern Homes sales by fabricating and shipping buildings to more than 50
Civilian Conservation Corps (CCC) camps nationwide.

After the stock market crash of 1929, Sears continued to increase the number and
amount of loans offered to customers, liberalizing its loan policy to include actual
construction costs. Although the high point of sales came in 1929 with a volume of
$12,050,000, nearly half of that figure—$5,622,000—was in mortgage loans *(Catalogues
and Counters).* By then some 49,000 houses had been built.

Despite the depressed state of the national economy, in 1930 Sears began to supervise
the construction of its homes, either by hiring the labor directly or subcontracting to local
firms. The eastern sales manager reported that in 1931 in the New York area the demand
had become so heavy "that we have decided to establish separate building loan facilities in
New York City . . ." ("Sears Home Construction Gains in 1930," *Chicago Tribune,* January
22, 1931). By 1933, however, the depression was beginning to take its toll: The company
reported that it was preparing to stop midwestern sales of ready-cut houses, and mortgage
financing and construction supervision were eliminated for the most part. The company's
1934 annual report tersely announced: "About $11,000,000 in mortgages were liquidated
during the year, and the Modern Homes Department was discontinued."

This decision was short-lived, for in 1935 Sears reentered the housing business, this
time selling only houses (not lots or financing), fabricated especially by General Houses,
Inc., of Chicago. This arrangement resulted in a new line of 30 prefabricated houses with
steel framing members, steel roofs and plywood walls. That association apparently ended,
however, before the 1940 *Book of Modern Homes*—the last catalog—was issued. (Before
the discovery of this catalog in late 1985, it was thought that the last catalog was published
in 1939. The 1940 catalog is basically the same as the 1939 catalog, with no new house
styles added. Because the text for *Houses by Mail* had already been typeset when the 1940
catalog was discovered, the data for 1940 are not included in the entries.) The housing

Streetscapes of Sears-built workers' housing from the 1921 catalog: the Standard Addition (top), Carlinville, Ill.; houses at Schopper, Ill. (middle), constructed for the Standard Oil Company; and houses at Plymouth Meeting, Pa. (bottom), built for the American Magnesia Company.

market rebounded slightly in 1935, and sales of houses tripled over those in 1934. Despite Sears's decision not to finance houses, a 1936 internal document reported that "there is considerable sales resistance in the policy of selling material only and letting the customer arrange his own financing and contracting. Customers generally prefer a complete proposition." The financing for the Newark factory's homes came from local banks and later the Federal Housing Administration. By 1936 sales were approximately $2 million; in 1937, $3.5 million; and in 1938, $2.75 million.

Despite the substantial figures, profits were insufficient to keep Sears in the home building business, and in 1940 it sold the lumber plant at Cairo. Sears apparently intended, however, that the fabrication and sales of homes would continue. Speaking at the 1940 Sears convention in Chicago, a top company official reported that the plants at Norwood and Newark and 20 branch offices staffed by more than 150 salesmen were still operating; moreover, "additional offices will be established as salesmen can be trained and prospects for profits warrant. . . . The executives of the company are watching this fast-growing department of the organization with a great deal of interest" (D. M. Wilson, "Sears New Way of Selling Houses"). These predictions notwithstanding, the Modern Homes Department did not revive.

MARKETING SEARS HOUSES

*S*ears, of course, made its name with the mail-order catalog, and it was with the catalog that Sears initiated the sale of houses, supplementing it with other methods only much later. Sears, founded in 1886, began its general mail-order business that same year; it issued its first catalog, 80 pages devoted exclusively to watches, in 1888. The business boomed. By 1907 Sears had produced 65 special catalogs devoted to such diverse articles as baby carriages, farm wagons, tombstones, washing machines and millwork. From this last specialty item and related products—such as

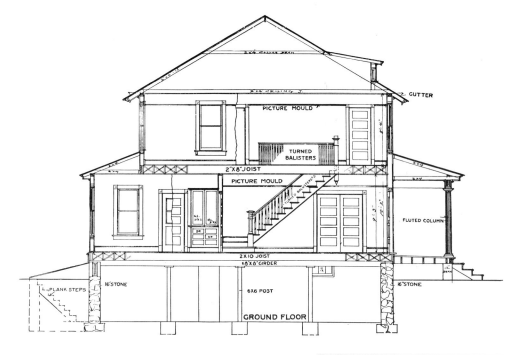

Above, right and bottom: Longitudinal section, blue-print of sectional detail drawing and front elevation drawing of Modern Home No. 102, from the 1908 catalog. Sears provided these three types of drawings with each set of house plans.

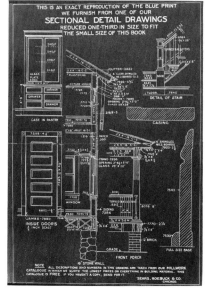

Cover of the 1918 Modern Homes catalog, featuring the Magnolia, the grandest house Sears ever offered. The house cost $5,140 that year.

Sears's reproduction of Mount Vernon, illustrated in the 1933 Modern Homes catalog.

Federal Hall, the first U.S. capitol, shown in the 1933 catalog.

roofing, gutters, downspouts, doors and windows—the origins of the Modern Homes Department can be traced.

The 1908 Modern Homes catalog, only 44 pages long, drew heavily on Sears's reputation for reliability. The first pages refer to two banks that testify to the company's integrity and credit. With its characteristic knack for self-promotion, the catalog trumpets cost savings and ease of construction in its slogans: "Build now as prices are greatly reduced." "Our low prices for building these houses have amazed everybody in the building line." "Our plans are more complete and simple than you can get from ordinary architects." "Any carpenter or ordinary workman would understand them perfectly." "A home, residence or building, built according to our plans and specifications, will make you a splendid investment which will bring you large returns." The catalog then went on to laud and illustrate examples of Sears millwork specified with the houses; a reproduction of a blueprint was included as further testimony to Sears's thorough attention to detail.

By 1911 the house catalog contained testimonials from happy customers and photographs of erected houses and for the first time included owners' names and locations in an effort to inspire customer confidence. By this time catalogs were being printed in spring and fall editions. The 1911 and 1912 catalogs contained a further enticement—illustrations of the interiors of several houses, providing the opportunity to visualize daily life inside these model homes. Also illustrated, for the more curious customer, were the extensive saw mills, lumber plants and yards operated by Sears. By 1912 the catalog had grown to 118 pages, increasing to 124 pages in 1913 and peaking at 146 pages in 1918. Although the number of houses sold in each year is not available, the 1916 catalog claimed that "enough houses have been built according to our plans and with our materials to shelter a city of 25,000 people." The 1925 catalog boasted: "Over 30,000 houses sold, every customer satisfied."

In the 1933 catalog, Sears illustrated four models that amply displayed the expertise and reputation Sears had gained by that date. Built surely for advertising as well as patriotic purposes, these four buildings included a "dream home" built by Warner Brothers Picture Corporation in Pittsburgh; two reproductions of Mount Vernon, one for the U.S. government at a 1931 Paris exposition and the other for the Washington Bicentennial Celebration in Brooklyn, N. Y.; and a reproduction of Federal Hall in New York City, also for the Washington Bicentennial Celebration. To promote sales Sears erected an exhibit house using its highest-quality materials and furnished it for the Century of Progress world's fair in Chicago, where it was exhibited from May to October in 1933 and 1934.

Sears attempted to make ordering a home as easy as ordering an automobile, radio or piece of furniture. Typically, prospective customers would visit a sales office, peruse the latest Sears Modern Homes catalog and select a design that suited their space needs, design sensibilities and pocketbook. The catalogs contained everything from modest two-room cottages to eight-to-10-room residences, in a range of colonial, English, Spanish,

Right and center: Dining room and living room of Modern Home No. 146, shown in the 1911 catalog, complete with clear oak paneling, double French doors and beamed ceilings of the latest Craftsman design, finished in a rich silver gray.

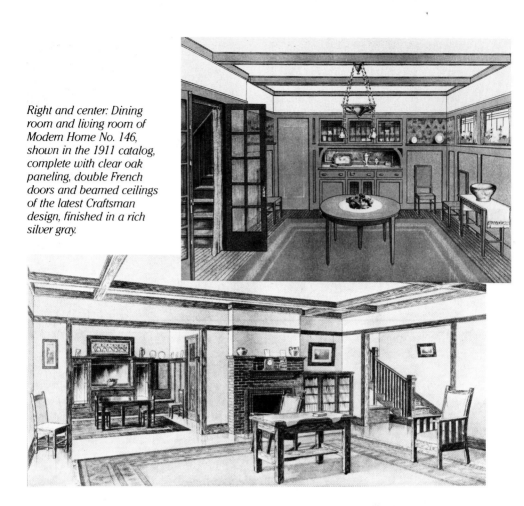

Doors, window and Craftsman oak buffet specified for Modern Home No. 146, in the 1911 catalog.

*Left, above left and right:
The covers of the 1911, 1920
and 1937 Modern Homes
catalogs, reflecting the popular house styles during these
years, from four-squares to
California-style bungalows
to Cape Cod cottages.*

*Right: A typical page from the Modern
Homes catalogs, featuring an illustration of the exterior of the house, several paragraphs of advertising copy
about the model, floor plans and ordering information. This page, from
the 1924 catalog, shows the Princeton.*

Right: Sales model of the Puritan, two feet high, used for selling Sears houses. (Sears, Roebuck and Company)

Below: Sears house (1930) customized by William T. Dettman, St. Louis, Mo., and his father, a carpenter, for his family's needs. They adapted the room arrangement and substituted a full second floor for the half floor in the original plans. (Sears, Roebuck and Company)

Right: Form for an estimate for Modern Home No. 3406, the Honor Bilt house Sears exhibited at the Century of Progress world's fair. Potential customers could also request an estimate of the cost of furniture to fill the house.

Below: The Honor Bilt line specified clear cypress on all window and door frames, double plates around the door and window openings, gutters and downspouts of galvanized steel and the finest electrical fixtures.

"HONOR BILT" 100 · POINT SPECIFICATIONS
MAKE PERMANENT ECONOMICAL HOMES

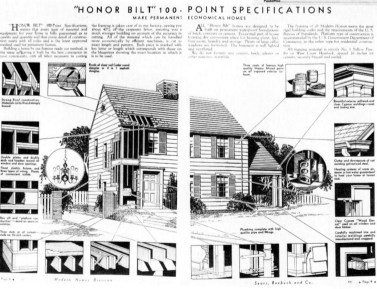

Norman and other architectural styles. But customers were not bound by the existing plans on file with Sears; they could bring their own plans and have Sears build the house and furnish the necessary materials. Similarly, Sears catalogs stressed that almost any frame house it offered could also be built of brick or have a reversed floor plan.

In addition to the catalogs, salespeople used sales kits, photographic displays and models to sell houses. The sales kits consisted of photographs of houses purchased and built by customers as well as models specifically constructed by Sears to promote sales.

CONSTRUCTION

Once a customer selected a house model and placed an order, an efficient system was placed in action. A service representative assigned to the customer wrote to confirm general instructions, provided a construction manual and enclosed a shipping schedule and origin sheet noting from where materials were being shipped, along with specific instructions for plastering, electrical work, plumbing and heating. Also enclosed was a paint catalog from which the owner was to select body, trim, shingle stain and sash paint. The certificate of guarantee was sent either with this package or separately, stating that the Modern Homes materials would be sufficient in quality and quantity or Sears would pay all shipping costs and refund the purchase price.

The construction manuals, some as long as 75 pages, were written for both the owner and the contractor and included detailed instructions for every phase of construction. The blueprints consisted of elevations, floor plans and a foundation plan drawn to a one-fourth-inch scale and framing details drawn to a three-eighths-inch scale. On each blueprint was printed a list of materials required for each portion of the design. Letters on the prints corresponded to the key letters on the precut lumber, the number of pieces, length of material and purpose.

With the exception of Sears's concrete block or brick houses and cottages, traditional wood platform frame construction was used for every Sears home until 1935. Every piece of framing lumber was precut to size and numbered at the factory for assembly on site. In 1935 Sears began using steel framing members and roofs and plywood walls, a practice that continued during its association with General Houses.

Sears offered three categories of houses. The Honor Bilt houses were Sears's finest-quality homes. Specifications called for joists, studs and rafters to be spaced $14\frac{3}{8}$ inches apart. Walls were lined with high-quality wood sheathing and outside siding. Cypress siding and cedar shingles were used on many Honor Bilt homes. Flooring and inside trim were clear grade (free of knots), of yellow pine, oak or maple, depending on the room. Of lesser quality were Sears's Standard Built houses. Studs and joists were spaced further apart, and at least one Sears catalog noted that "Standard Built houses do not make as warm houses as Honor Bilt houses." Not surprisingly, Standard Built houses were recommended for warmer climates. Typically, lumber for these houses was not cut or fitted at the factory. Many Sears designs were offered with both Honor Bilt and Standard Built specifications. The third category was the Simplex Sectional cottages. These modest, one-story houses were built for summer use, were lightly framed and usually were not plastered on the interior.

The following materials and products were usually provided by Sears in the sales price as part of the total house package: millwork, cabinetry, lath, roofing materials, flooring, siding, building paper, downspouts, doors, window sash, shutters, hardware (in a variety of patterns), nails, paint and varnish. Not included was the cost of bricks, concrete blocks, cobblestones, plaster or other masonry products, even though these were shown in the designs and listed in the specifications. Optional materials and equipment that could be obtained from Sears at extra charge were screens, storm windows, plasterboard and plumbing, heating and electrical fixtures.

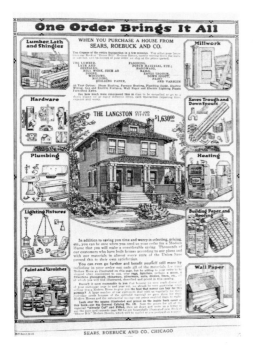

Left: Page from the fall 1919 general catalog advertising Sears's ready-cut homes and the materials provided for complete assembly.

Below: Certificate of Guarantee ensuring sufficient material, safe delivery and a complete refund if the customer were not satisfied with the materials. (Sears, Roebuck and Company)

Although Sears used conventional construction techniques and materials, it popularized the use of sheet plaster or plasterboard, the precursor of today's drywall, by offering it as an extra-cost option on many models. Sears also introduced a "crushed slate" siding to be used on the exteriors of the more modest houses. Another brand product was Stonekote, a cement stucco plaster offered as a decorative alternative to shingles or clapboards. Asphalt shingles, known in the catalogs as Oriental Slate Surfaced Siding, were available as an extra-cost option on virtually all models and came with a 17-year guarantee.

All shipping was done by rail; consequently the largest concentrations of Sears houses are in the Northeast and Midwest, which were served by more rail lines. The shipping schedule sheet showed from what point each type of material was shipped and the approximate date of the shipment. The construction manual instructed the owner to make a record of each shipment, including the number shown on the seals on the railroad car doors, and an inventory of each piece as it was unloaded. A typical Sears house, unassembled, could fit into two box cars.

Shipping dates were staggered to allow the materials to arrive about the time they were needed. The first arrivals were building paper and nails, lumber and frames; the last arrivals, about a month later, were the millwork and laundry tub. The number of separate parts, not including nails or screws, averaged about 30,000 in an ordinary house.

Beginning in 1929, in communities covered by sales offices, Sears engaged local building contractors and supervised all construction from start to finish. In some cases, however, customers hired their own contractors; even then Sears was available to supervise construction. Owners skilled in construction also could assemble their own houses and have the value of the work credited as part of the down payment. Sears used conventional construction techniques and materials, so most contractors experienced no problems in erecting a Sears house. In fact, Sears estimated that, because of its precut lumber and detailed instructions, a small house could be built in 352 carpenter hours compared to 583 hours for a conventional house, an impressive 40 percent savings in labor. Simplex Sectional cottages could be built even more quickly—some in eight hours.

Above and right: At 7:45 a.m. the floor, wall and roof sections of Modern Home No. 55MP22, a three-room Simplex Sectional cottage, lie on the ground ready for assembly. By 9:30 three sides of the building and some of the interior partitions and floor sections have been set in place.

Left and below: By 11:00 all walls and partitions are in position and all doors and windows in their frames. Iron bolts are used to fasten the roof sections to the ridge pole, and iron straps connect the roof sections with the side walls. After eight hours, the job has been completed.

*L*ittle is known about the architects of most Sears houses, but this much is certain: Sears houses followed rather than set architectural styles. The 447 designs documented here clearly show that there is no such thing as a typical Sears house. Sears designs included traditional two-story center-hall colonial-style houses, Craftsman and Spanish-style bungalows, asymmetrical Queen Anne farmhouses, Cape Cod cottages, split levels and even a few Prairie Style and Modern houses. Sears's designers were adept followers—rather than leaders—of fashion; they were more comfortable adapting popular designs and styles and making them widely available, and this is one of the many reasons for Sears's success in the housing business. Rarely did Sears become involved with the modern styles; notable exceptions, however, include the Aurora and the Carlton, two handsome, fully developed examples of Prairie Style architecture that were offered in the 1918 catalog.

Sears's bungalow designs proved to be particularly enduring. With their spacious front porches, leaded glass sash, oak staircases and Craftsman detailing, they were popular in all parts of the country served by the Modern Homes Department. Bungalows were available in a full range of sizes, finishes and styles and dominated the catalogs in the 1920s.

Sears house designs seem to have come from four major sources. First, Sears bought from outside architects designs of houses that had already been constructed and proven successful. This is thought to have occurred throughout the history of the Modern Homes program but was probably most common before 1919. A second source was Sears staff architects, who designed houses specifically for the catalogs. This practice started about 1919, when Sears organized its Architectural Division. A third source was existing popular house designs that Sears staff architects and draftsmen adapted for the Modern Homes program, preparing elevations, floor plans and specifications for the catalogs. This was probably the most common source of designs because Sears was aiming at a popular market with designs of proven public appeal. A final source was house designs purchased from magazines and reproduced exactly in the Sears catalogs. Customers were also able to use plans developed by their own architects and have Sears prepare specifications, supply the materials and supervise the construction.

From 1908 to 1913 the Sears catalog asserted, "Our plans are the work of the best-known licensed architects specially engaged by us for this service," but no names are provided. Sears had an early association with Fred T. Hodgson, author of *Practical Carpentry* and *Builder's Reliable Estimator and Contractor's Guide*, both of which included house plans, and used his books to promote their millwork. However, it does not appear that the Modern Homes designs came directly from that book. As early as 1912, the Sears telephone directory had a listing for "A. J. Caron, Building Plans," although no design has been linked directly to him.

In the spring of 1919, an apparent change occurred in Sears's design process, echoed by the Sears directory, which listed a newly formed Architectural Division. The catalog now read, "Noted architects have contributed their best ideas for our collection of houses. Building experts have worked up on the specifications. . . ." Again, neither the "noted architects" nor the "building experts" are named.

Designs were also derived from other, eclectic sources. The spring 1914 general merchandise catalog displayed the results of a competition for a prize farm residence. According to the advertisement, Sears invited "100 practical farmers" to serve on a building committee and to submit floor plans and ideas for 100 modern farmhouses. The winners were H. R. Selck of Evansville, Wis., and W. L. Richardson of Cambridge, Iowa. First prize was the Hillrose, which appeared in subsequent catalogs until 1922. The source of one early design, Modern Home No. 243 in the 1916 catalog, was taken from the cover of *Bungalow Magazine* of July 1914.

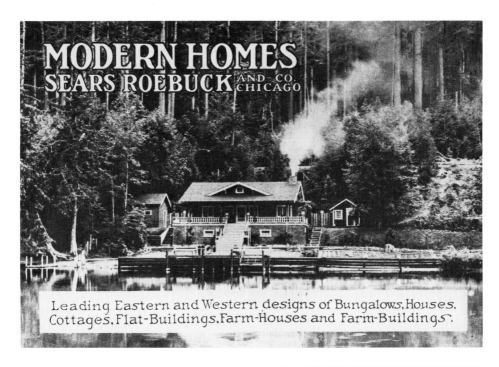

MODERN HOMES
SEARS ROEBUCK AND CO. CHICAGO

Leading Eastern and Western designs of Bungalows, Houses, Cottages, Flat-Buildings, Farm-Houses and Farm-Buildings.

Above and right: Cover of the 1916 catalog, featuring a bungalow-style house adapted from the one appearing on the cover of the July 1914 Bungalow Magazine. *(Library of Congress)*

Left: Page from the fall 1921 Modern Homes catalog showing Sears's architects at their drafting boards, sample blueprints and a three-dimensional floor plan.

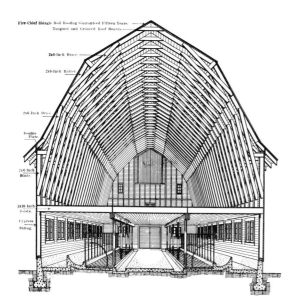

Above and top right: A braced rafter, or balloon roof, barn, from Sears's 1918 Book of Barns. This type of construction was used in several Sears barns at Montpelier, Orange, Va., a property of the National Trust for Historic Preservation. (Russell Wright)

Right and below: Sears's prize-winning plans for model farm buildings—including barns, silos, hen houses, tool sheds, milk houses, corn cribs and hog houses—and a country residence, the Hillrose.

Above and left: Gordon House (1930), a residence, and Gordon Hall (1930), the concert hall, Sears buildings at Music Mountain, Falls Village, Conn. (Courtesy of Nicholas Gordon)

The Architectural Division had a number of chiefs in its years of operation. In 1925 a separate Drafting Division was created; by 1928 each person affiliated with the Modern Homes Department was listed by name in the 1929 catalog. The catalog claimed that "each model is designed and planned by a council of experienced architects, which includes a woman. D[avid] S. Betcone, the Chief Architect, has made Sears, Roebuck and Company the architectural style leader of moderate priced homes in America. All of the planning, designing and arrangement is done under his personal supervision." New up-to-date designs were constantly being developed, and old stand-bys were frequently updated in an effort to provide comfortable homes at a reasonable cost. Designs were seldom featured in the catalogs for more than a few years, with several notable exceptions: The popular Winona appeared from 1916 through 1940, and the Westly debuted in 1912 and ran though 1928.

One interesting example of a community designed by David S. Betcone is Music Mountain in Falls Village, Conn., the home of the Gordon Summer Chamber Music Festival. Jacques Gordon, then concertmaster of the Chicago Symphony Orchestra, presented the idea to Julius Rosenwald, then chairman of Sears. The result was a Sears mortgage and five Sears-designed buildings, four residences and a concert hall, all completed by August 1930. Betcone continued with Sears until at least 1935.

How much design input any of the Sears architects or draftsmen had in the hundreds of stock house designs is a matter of speculation. In several cases, their initials appear on the few surviving blueprints, but it is not possible to assess whether they acted as draftsmen or designers.

A sales kit dating from about 1931 contains photographs of houses constructed by Sears and mentions several architects by name, including B. T. Lourim, Leslie L. Deglow and J. A. Parks. Parks is identified as a registered architect with an office at 1800 E Street, N.W., Washington, D.C.; no address is given for either Lourim or Deglow. Other known architects or designers connected with Sears houses include Randolph Evans, architect, Cranford, N.J.; S. Merrill Clement, Jr., architect, South Norwalk, Conn.; Albert Flegel; and George Biehl, craftsman. A club of women architects in Chicago listed Aileen Anderson as an architect working for Sears in 1937.

INTERIORS AND FURNISHINGS

*S*ears's catalog entries for its houses often included a drawing or photograph of how the house would look furnished. This served a two-fold purpose: first, to show to best advantage the appearance of the interior, and, second, to illustrate furnishings that were also available for sale from the Sears general catalog. Typically, cottage interiors were finished simply, with unadorned plaster walls, plain cased (simply framed) openings and four-panel doors. More elaborate bungalows frequently contained leaded art glass windows, built-in bookcases and mantels in the living room, plate rails and sideboards in the dining room and carved staircases. Larger, more expensive homes featured decorative plasterwork, beamed ceilings and colonnaded openings between rooms.

Sears greatly expanded its offering of home furnishings between 1908 and 1925. Sears furniture, like its houses, ranged from solid Mission-style pieces to more elaborate colonial reproductions, thus fitting a range of budgets. Cottages were shown simply furnished with several tables and chairs; larger homes were illustrated with wallpaper, carpeting and pianos.

What proportion of Sears homeowners also bought Sears furnishings is not known. The 1929 catalog, which lists Sears staff, also includes an "interior design coordinator," a Miss E. L. Mayer. Of her the catalog says: "Every floor plan and interior decorating sketch must bear her approval before it is adopted. She must see that provision is made in the plan for pianos, davenports, radios, beds and dressers and all conveniences appealing to the housewife are not overlooked. She selected kitchen cupboards, the built-in ironing boards, telephone stands and other contrivances so important in home comfort, and assists the Honor Bilt home builder in the selection of draperies, rugs and other furnishings. She also suggests the most effective way of landscaping the various houses to bring out their individual charm and beauty." The catalog continues: "We want to help you furnish that home, when you are ready for new furnishings. We want to sell you the thousands of things that you and your family need from day to day." Sears also opened model homes at fairs and expositions to show off its extensive line of furnishings. Photographs of the bungalow model at the 1910 Illinois state fair show furniture and wallcoverings that were available in the general catalog of the same period.

Porch of the furnished Sears bungalow model at the 1910 Illinois state fair. (Sears, Roebuck and Company)

Left and below: Bedroom and combination living room and dining room of the furnished bungalow model at the 1910 Illinois state fair. (Sears, Roebuck and Company)

Sears apparently was successful in selling houses and furnishings as a single package. "In many instances, homes have been built for customers who bought all of their home equipment and home furnishings at the local Sears retail store," stated the 1939 Sears "News-Graphic." One customer permitted Sears to put his home on public exhibition before he occupied it;12,000 people visited it within 10 days, the local retail store did $20,000 worth of business traceable directly to the exhibit, and the Modern Homes Department sold three more houses as a result.

As Sears modified house styles and designs to keep current with public taste, it also modified illustrations of interior furnishings when it was deemed desirable. The 1926 interior view of the Crescent's living room, for example, was updated for the catalog only two years later. The living and dining room furnishings of the Starlight also were updated in the catalog between 1918 and 1921.

USING THE GUIDE TO IDENTIFY SEARS HOUSES

*B*ecause Sears offered designs in all sizes and styles and used a variety of materials, identifying a Sears house can be difficult. Conventional construction techniques and materials were used for Honor Bilt homes so that Sears houses are, on the surface at least, visually indistinguishable from their neighbors. And some Sears models are similar to those offered by other mail-order companies.

The guide section in this book has been prepared to aid in identifying a Sears house, without having to page through the many Sears home catalogs. The guide is based on the catalogs themselves, the most complete collection of which is located at the Sears archives in Chicago. Arranged by roof shape, number of stories, location of front door and the presence of dormers, the guide illustrates and provides descriptions of nearly every standard residential design manufactured by Sears. Not detailed are garages, outhouses, farm structures and one-of-a-kind house designs Sears custom produced for its customers. House models introduced in those years for which catalogs are missing also are not included. Copies of several catalogs missing from the Sears archives were located in other institutions and private collections. Even so, catalogs for five years are lacking: 1909, 1910, 1915, 1923 and 1930. (A 1920 catalog was purchased by Sears for its collection as this book was in production. Two new house styles that appear only in the 1920 catalog—the Harmony and the Adams—are included in the guide section. For styles repeated from previous years, however, data for 1920 are not included with the entries.) Because most Sears designs were offered for more than one year, however, the guide is as complete as possible and includes 447 models.

The designs in the guide are organized by architectural feature rather than architectural style because there are inherent problems in assigning styles to Sears houses. For example, what Sears refers to, in its catalog, as English style, a historian may label Gothic Revival or Tudor. Even more confusing are those Sears houses—and there are many in this book—that mix architectural motifs with abandon; it is not uncommon to find a bungalow with colonial porch details and Queen Anne windows.

The guide shows and describes what the basic Sears models looked like. In attempting to identify a house, recognize that it is unusual to find a Sears house in its original condition. If a house does not exactly match one of the designs in the guide, it may have been remodeled by past owners—a porch may have been enclosed, a new bathroom added, the kitchen modernized. Or, the original owners may have requested different features or otherwise customized a standard design. Thus, to make a preliminary identification, it will be necessary to disregard later alterations, the location and shape of front porches, window configurations and the exterior cladding materials (clapboards, shingles, brick, stucco and so forth). These details will help you after you have identified the roof type and height. Consider the possibility that your floor plan was reversed, something common for Sears houses. Also, the original exterior cladding materials may have been removed or altered. But if the elevation, configuration and dimensions of the floor plan match the illustrations in the guide, chances are good that the house was manufactured by Sears.

Other clues will aid in identifying Sears houses. Some bathrooms and hardware fixtures made by Sears are so marked. Look for numbered markings on joists and rafters where they are exposed in the attic or cellar. These marks were keyed to the blueprints provided by Sears. It may be possible to remove siding or loose plaster in search of numbered studs.

More details on how to use the guide follow.

Roof Type (all houses). To locate a house in the guide, first determine its basic roof type. Sears houses have six basic roof types: gabled, hipped, hipped gable, gambrel, flat and mansard. A gabled roof forms a vertical triangle at both ends; a hipped roof slopes upward from all four sides of the building; in a hipped-gable roof, the gable rises vertically

Gabled roof, one story, end entrance

 Intersecting gabled roof, one to one and a half stories

 Gabled roof, one and a half to two and a half stories, end entrance

 Intersecting gabled roof, two or more stories

 Gabled roof, one story, corner entrance

 Hipped roof, one to one and a half stories

 Gabled roof, one story, side entrance

 Hipped roof, two or more stories

 Gabled roof, one and a half stories, side entrance, one front dormer

 Hipped-gable roof

 Gabled roof, one and a half stories, side entrance, two or more front dormers

 Gambrel roof

 Gabled roof, one and a half stories, projecting gabled side entrance

 Flat or mansard roof

 Gabled roof, two or more stories, side entrance

These logos represent the 15 house types by which the Sears house styles in this guide are arranged.

about half way to a ridge, resulting in a truncated shape, with the roof inclining backwards from this point; a gambrel roof has two pitches on both sides; a flat roof may have a low parapet; and a mansard roof has two slopes on all four sides, with a much steeper lower slope. Use the accompanying chapter key to identify these roof types. Because gabled roofs are by far the most common, you may need to identify one or more other features or details to locate your house.

Number of Stories (for houses with gabled or hipped roofs only). If you find that your house has a gabled or hipped roof, it will be necessary to identify the number of floors in the house. Do not count the basement or unfinished attic as a floor. A house with one and a half stories has bedrooms on the second floor underneath sloping eaves. A house with two and a half stories has bedrooms on the second floor and an attic above.

Location of Front Door (for houses with gabled roofs only). If you have a house with a gabled roof, determine the location of the front door to aid in identification. An end entrance house is one in which the front door is located on the elevation with the gable above. In a side entrance house, the front door is found away from the gable end, under the roof's slope side. Corner entrances are located on a front corner.

Presence of Dormers (for one-and-a-half-story houses with gabled roofs only). A dormer is a structure projecting from a sloping roof and usually contains a window or louvers. Knowing the number of front dormers your house has will be necessary only if it has a gabled roof and is one and a half stories.

Each entry contains the following information: the model name or number; number of rooms; exterior materials, if other than wood clapboard or shingle; distinguishing details and features on the outside and inside; the years offered and model numbers for each year; the price range over the years; and, where available, sample locations where the

The Arlington, Washington, D.C., one of thousands of Sears houses that survive in large cities and small towns throughout the United States. (Paul Kennedy)

model was built. Designs that are similar, except for slight differences in floor plans, elevations or materials, are noted on the same page. Some designs are identical except for their names, and these also are indicated.

Sears assigned numbers only to house models until 1918, when the models were given names, so some models have only a number rather than a model name. The names and numbers sometimes changed from year to year although the design stayed basically the same. Some designs changed slightly over the years, but the numbers did not. Although Sears provided a wealth of evocative names for its designs, once in a while two or three different models shared a common name (such as the Auburn, Concord and Lorain).

At the beginning of each entry is a brief description of the house, excerpted from the catalog page itself. These colorful promotional descriptions call attention to the building's style, distinguishing features and other selling points. From time to time, they provide clues as to who the prospective buyers might be or possible suitable locations (e.g., farm, suburbs or city). Some catalogs described models more fully than others. More modest models often had only one- or two-sentence descriptions; larger, more pretentious houses would receive two or more pages of advertising copy.

In determining the number of rooms per house, the following spaces were not counted separately: entry, foyer, hall (or reception hall), porch, sleeping porch, breakfast nook, dining alcove, maid's room, closet, wood room or garage. Some models offered a choice of plans, one with more rooms than another. In some cases, attics could be finished as additional bedrooms or a porch enclosed to become a sun room. These models are so noted.

One basic design may have had two or more catalog numbers. In some cases these

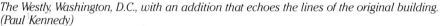

The Westly, Washington, D.C., with an addition that echoes the lines of the original building. (Paul Kennedy)

Top and above: The Alhambra, Washington, D.C., and the Maywood, Washington, D.C., two Sears houses that have been well maintained yet modernized for continued use over the years. (Paul Kennedy)

numbers were used to distinguish Honor Bilt from Standard Built models; in others, to differentiate wood siding from brick or to indicate a subtle variation in floor plan. All known catalog numbers are provided for each entry. The years in which the house was offered are listed with the catalog numbers; if more than one year is listed, the year of the catalog from which the illustration is taken is given in italics. For many years catalogs were issued in both spring and fall, but no distinction is made here.

A range of prices—the lowest and highest—is also given for each model. Even if the model was offered for only one year, two prices may be shown—one for the spring catalog and one for the fall. Costs of materials often fluctuated. Discrepancies in price may be attributed to inflation and also to the fact that one year the model may have been offered as an Honor Bilt house (that is, precut, fitted and more costly) and the next year as a Standard Built house (uncut, unfitted and, thus, cheaper). In some periods—the 1920s, for example—prices for some models actually decreased.

Sears has kept no complete record of where all its houses were built, although individual catalogs frequently listed the towns and cities where examples could be found. Locations are derived from Sears's own listings in the catalogs (any locations that could not be verified have been eliminated) and from our own research. The list is not complete but is intended to give an indication of the range of locations.

Once you have ascertained that your house is, in fact, a Sears design, you may want to find out whether it is eligible for historical recognition by listing in a local, state or national register of historic places. Try to determine whether similar Sears houses survive in the immediate neighborhood or elsewhere in the area. If your house is of an unusual design and is more than 50 years old, historical designation for the house or its neighborhood may be worth pursuing. Contact your local landmarks commission, historical society or state historic preservation office for assistance in learning about designation processes. State preservation offices will also be able to provide information about potential financial and technical assistance for your house.

If you own or contemplate buying a Sears house, you may want to restore the house to its original appearance or rehabilitate it in a manner that preserves its distinguishing qualities while permitting modern amenities such as central air conditioning and a contemporary kitchen. All work should meet the Secretary of the Interior's Standards for Rehabilitation, which are readily available from state preservation offices (addresses are available from any governor's office).

Has your house been added onto in the past? Do the additions or alterations detract from the building's character? If they do not detract, they may be left as evidence of the use and evolution of the house. Restorations should not be attempted without accurate information regarding the original appearance of the property. The elevations and floor plans as they appeared in the catalog are excellent sources of information in planning rehabilitation work. Some interior details and fixtures were illustrated in the Modern Homes catalogs, and a representative sampling of these illustrations is shown here. If your restoration extends to home furnishings, remember that illustrated in the Sears general catalog for each year are furniture, fabric, wallpaper, lighting and plumbing fixtures and hardware. Sears has put all its general catalogs on microfilm and donated these to more than 150 libraries throughout the country; check a nearby library for these. Other sources of information on restoration and rehabilitation are listed in the appendix.

Neither a stylistic nor a technical innovator, Sears nonetheless played an important role during the first three decades of the 20th century in providing affordable housing to American families at every socioeconomic level. Sears simplified the process of selecting, financing and building houses for more than 100,000 families across the country, offering well-conceived floor plans, premium materials and quality construction at reasonable prices, all backed by Sears's reputation for reliability and service. Appreciated then for their practical, economical designs and solid materials, they continue to be appreciated today for the same qualities.

*M*odern Home No. 229 is an attractive and inexpensive bungalow of five rooms with a reception hall, bath and pantry. It has a front porch across the entire house, so arranged that it makes a combination porch and open terrace. We furnish a sufficient quantity of shingle stain, any color, for the sides, front and rear for the price quoted above, but not for the roof. Shingled houses are becoming quite popular and when stained with a suitable color have a very refined and comfortable appearance.

. . . .

Details and features: Five rooms and one bath. Full-width front porch with gabled roof supported by square columns; bay window in dining room; exposed roof rafter tails and knee braces. Corner closet in bedroom.

Years and catalog numbers: *1913* (229); 1916 (229)

Price: $670 to $714

Location: Gary, Ind.

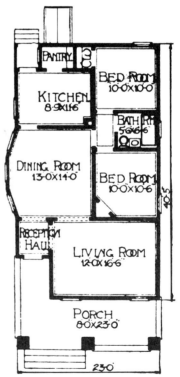

Gabled roof, one story, end entrance

THE ARGYLE

The Argyle is a bungalow whose exterior appearance suggests extra-fine interior arrangement and furnishings. The front elevation, as you glance at it, bespeaks richness and comfort on the inside. The living room and dining room prove this conclusively. Note the bookcase colonnade, the beamed ceiling, the massive brick mantel with the built-in bookcase on the side. Note also the extra depth of the living room and dining room, nearly 30 feet long.

. . . .

Details and features: Five rooms and one bath. Gabled front porch; notched bargeboards; exposed roof rafter tails. Beamed ceiling and fireplace flanked by built-in bookcases with glass doors in living room; paneled dining room.

Years and catalog numbers: 1916 (264P245, 2018); 1917 (C2018, 245); 1918 (2018); 1919 (7018); *1921* (7018); 1922 (17018); 1925 (17018A); 1926 (P17018A)

Price: $827 to $2,150

Locations: Bridgeport, Conn.; Des Plaines and Rantoul, Ill.; Detroit, Mich.; Garvin, Minn.; Niagara Falls, N.Y.; Toledo and Xenia, Ohio; Hellerton, Pa.

Dining room

Living room

THE SOMERSET

The Somerset is an attractive and inexpensive bungalow of five rooms with a vestibule, bath and pantry. It has a front porch across the entire house, so arranged that it makes a combination porch and open terrace. The two front windows are Queen Anne design.

Details and features: Five rooms and one bath. Full-width front porch with gabled roof and square columns; bay window in dining room; exposed roof rafter tails and knee braces; front door with beveled plate glass.

Years and catalog numbers: 1917 (2008, C229A); *1918* (2008); 1919 (2008); 1921 (2008); 1922 (7008); 1925 (7008)

Price: $732 to $1,576

Locations: Chicago, Hillsboro, Oak Park and Park Ridge, Ill.; Elkhart, Gary and Ingalls, Ind.; Moscow, Kans.; Columbus, Minn.; Hannibal, Mo.; Maxwell, Neb.; White Plains, N.Y.; Cincinnati, Cleveland, Hamilton and Junction City, Ohio; Alden, Pa.; Hartford and Kenosha, Wis.

THE SUMNER

*H*ere is a neat-looking bungalow which is a wonder for the price. Note the nice appearance of the cobblestone foundation and porch. The colonial windows bring out the true bungalow effect.

. . . .

Details and features: Four rooms and no bath. Front porch with cobblestone walls and shed roof; exposed roof rafter tails; glazed front door flanked by sidelights.

Years and catalog numbers: 1917 (2027, 027); *1918* (2027, 027); 1919 (2027, 027)

Price: $237 to $853

Locations: Washington, D.C.; Cicero and Morrison, Ill.; Austin and Virginia, Minn.

THE SARANAC

*I*t is no longer necessary to pay an exorbitant price for a small home with a distinctive character. In our Saranac, we offer you a cottage that will look well in almost any community. The blinds secure the popular colonial effect, and the Fire-Chief Shingle Roll Roofing, sea green or dark red in color, which we guarantee for 15 years, looks like wood shingles stained or painted. The trellis gives the finishing artistic touch which will be fully brought out when the vines are in bloom.

. . . .

Details and features: Five rooms and no bath. Front porch with concrete walls and shed roof; shutters on windows; trellis on front wall.

Years and catalog numbers: 1917 (C2030); *1918* (2030, 030); 1919 (2030, 030); 1921 (2030B, 030); 1922 (2030B, 030B)

Price: $248 to $927

Locations: East River, Conn.; Barrington, Ill.; Cannelton, Ind.; Thayer, Kans.; Amelia, Neb.

THE CLYDE

*T*he Clyde has been built in many sections of the country by customers who tell of their satisfaction. Their letters praise our Honor Bilt system, the quality of lumber and millwork. Wood shingle panels and tapered columns, brackets and other little touches make the Clyde an unusually well-balanced and attractive house which will look as well on a narrow lot as on a wide one.

Details and features: Five rooms and one bath. Gabled front porch supported by tapered piers; wide eaves with knee braces; glazed front door. Two floor plans; fireplace flanked by windows in living room.

Years and catalog numbers: *1921* (9030, 7030); 1922 (9030, 7030); 1925 (9030A); 1926 (P9030A); 1928 (C9030A, C9030B); 1929 (P9030A, P9030B)

Price: $1,175 to $1,923

Locations: Wamego, Kans.; Cincinnati and Dayton, Ohio

No. 7030

No. 9030

THE OLIVIA

*Y*ears of study devoted to making the most of every inch of space in a small house have resulted in the Olivia. It is simply astonishing how convenient this house is. Look over the floor plan and judge for yourself. This house can be built with the rooms reversed, as shown in the floor plan.

Details and features: Four rooms and one bath. Front porch with gabled roof supported by tapered concrete piers and wood piers; exposed roof rafter tails.

Years and catalog numbers: *1921* (7028); 1922 (7028); 1925 (7028A); 1926 (P7028); 1928 (C7028); 1929 (P7028)

Price: $1,123 to $1,283

Location: Elkhart, Ind.

Kitchen cabinets

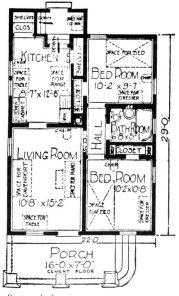

Reversed plan

THE FAIRY

The Fairy is a comfortable bungalow home with shingle siding. It has many features that will appeal to the housewife. There is quality in every foot of material. The porch affords a pleasant place for warm summer evenings. The half-glazed front door enables the housewife to see the caller before opening the door. The combined living room and dining room allow the most economical use of floor space, without sacrifice of appearance. The well-planned kitchen has room to place a cabinet, table, sink and range to make work easy, which reduces the housewife's work and saves many steps each day.

Details and features: Four rooms and one bath. Front porch with flat roof and exposed rafter tails on earlier models; gabled roof with paired columns on later models; glazed front door.

Years and catalog numbers: *1925* (3217); 1926 (P3217); 1928 (C3217); 1929 (P3217); 1932 (3316); 1933 (3316)

Price: $965 to $993

Similar to: The Culver

Differences: Porch and front door off center on right; porch with gabled roof supported by paired pilasters

Year and catalog number: 1933 (3322)

Price: $873

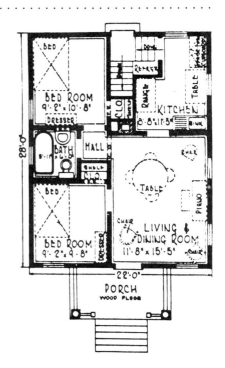

THE WELLINGTON

*H*ere is a masterpiece in a five-room Honor Bilt bungalow. The covered porch with its massive stucco columns and stucco gable, the soft-toned shingle sides and the wood gable siding produce a perfect, harmonious effect. The Wellington has been built in many of the choicest locations and is admired wherever it is built. An artistic touch is added by the flower box beneath the front window and the massive brick chimney on the right elevation.

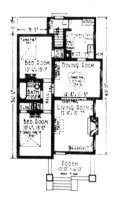

Details and features: Five rooms and one bath. Front porch with square stucco columns and stucco gable. Fireplace in living room; molded paneled walls in dining room.

Years and catalog numbers: 1925 (3223); *1926* (P3223); 1928 (C3223); 1929 (P3223)

Price: $1,760 to $1,998

THE RAMSAY

*T*he Ramsay Standard Built home was designed with the aim of meeting a demand for a modest home at an equally modest price. It has a special appeal to those who live in suburban centers, who have a small family or who want to live modestly in order to save a sum of money for a more elaborate home in the future.

Details and features: Four rooms and one bath. Full-width front porch with gabled roof.

Years and catalog numbers: 1925 (6012); *1926* (P6012); 1928 (C6022)

Price: $654 to $685

THE HUDSON

Ｔhe Hudson Standard Built home is an investment that readily appeals to the thrifty family. Here is everything one expects in a modest and up-to-date house. The exterior presents a neat and becoming appearance.

. . . .

Details and features: Four rooms and one bath. Front porch; exposed roof rafter tails. Two floor plans.

Years and catalog numbers: 1925 (6013, 6013A); *1926* (P6013, 6013A); 1928 (C6023, C6023A)

Price: $495 to $659

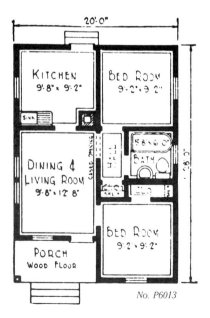

No. P6013

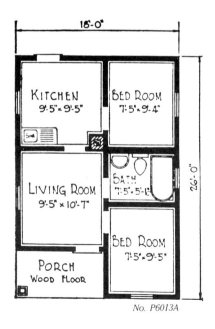

No. P6013A

THE FRANKLIN

The Franklin Standard Built home deserves much praise because it is carefully planned to provide the greatest amount of livable space for its size, it is made of good materials and ready-cut construction, and it gives the utmost value for each dollar invested.

. . . .

Details and features: Four rooms and no bath. Front porch with gabled roof supported by square columns; exposed roof rafter tails.

Year and catalog number: 1925 (6019)

Price: $595

THE SOMERS

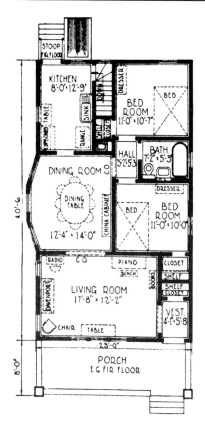

The Somers is an attractive and inexpensive bungalow of five rooms with a vestibule, bath and built-in cupboard. It has a front porch across the entire house, so arranged that it is easily converted to a sun room by glazing the open parts.

. . . .

Details and features: Five rooms and one bath. Full-width front porch supported by square columns; stickwork in gable; bay window in dining room.

Years and catalog numbers: *1926* (P17008); 1928 (P17008); 1929 (P17008)

Price: $1,696 to $1,778

THE MELROSE

*I*f you are looking for something different in a five-room bungalow design, you will find a pleasing exterior and convenient arrangement of rooms in this attractive colonial bungalow. The size of this home will command attention even though built among larger, more expensive homes.

· ·

Details and features: Five rooms and one bath. Lunette window in front gable; six-panel front door with split pediment. Arched opening between living room and hall; stairs off kitchen to basement.

Years and catalog numbers: 1929 (P3286)

Price: $1,698

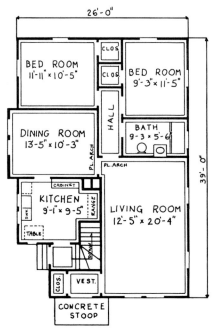

A good, well-built, roomy house. The large parlor connects with the dining room by a large cased opening. Good-sized kitchen and bedroom on first floor. The reception hall connects with the parlor by a sliding door and contains an open stairway of choice grain clear yellow pine.

Details and features: Seven rooms and no bath. Full-width front porch; front door glazed with leaded art glass. Arched opening between dining room and parlor; open stairs.

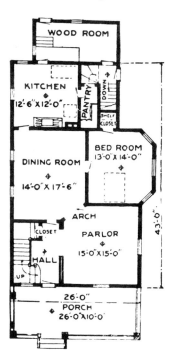

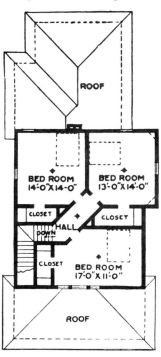

Years and catalog numbers: 1908 (34); *1911* (34); 1912 (34); 1913 (170); 1916 (C170); 1917 (170)

Price: $930 to $1,750

Location: Hillsdale, Mich.

Gabled roof, one and a half to two and a half stories, end entrance

$\mathcal{A}$ large, well-built cottage with all available space made good use of. It has a large living room with a cased opening leading into the hall; there is also a cased opening between the living room and dining room. There is one bedroom on the first floor and two large bedrooms on the second floor.

Details and features: Six rooms and no bath. Front porch with hipped roof; Queen Anne windows on second floor. Open stairs.

Years and catalog numbers: 1908 (36); 1911 (36); 1912 (36); *1913* (100); 1916 (264P100)

Price: $601 to $1,200

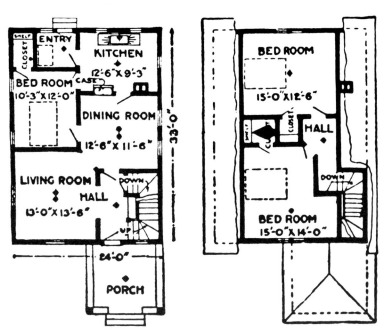

No. 117

*T*his house is handily arranged, all rooms being of good size and so planned that there is hardly a foot of wasted space. A large cased opening between the dining room and parlor makes these two rooms practically into one large room which is frequently used as a parlor and back parlor. The kitchen being so large is often used as a kitchen and dining room, and the sitting room as a bedroom for the first floor.

Details and features: Seven rooms and no bath. Full-width front porch; front door glazed with colored leaded art glass. Pantry off kitchen.

Years and catalog numbers: 1911 (117); 1912 (117); *1913* (117)

Price: $807 to $921

Locations: Hartley, Iowa; Hillsdale and West Branch, Mich.; Culbertson, Mont.; Orangeburg, N.Y.

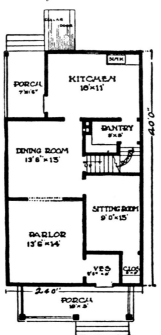

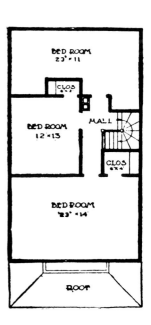

No. 134

This cottage has four rooms and quite a large attic which could very easily be finished into two rooms if desired. It is built on a concrete foundation, has frame construction and is sided with Stonekote.

. . . .

Details and features: Four rooms and one bath. Stucco exterior; full-width front porch; glazed front door. Five-cross panel doors.

Years and catalog numbers: 1911 (134); 1912 (134); *1913* (134)

Price: $459 to $578

No. 141

A four-room cottage with a good-sized front porch, a large pantry, two good-sized closets and a large attic which can be finished into two good-sized rooms at an extra cost of $94 for stairs and other material needed.

. . . .

Details and features: Four rooms and no bath. Front porch with turned columns; glazed front door.

Years and catalog numbers: 1911 (141); 1912 (141); *1913* (141)

Price: $419 to $531

Locations: Wilmington, Del.; Steger and Streator, Ill.; Indianapolis, Ind.; Burlington, Iowa; Hastings, Neb.; Salineville and Cincinnati, Ohio; Central Falls, R.I.; Warrenton, Va.; Milwaukee, Wis.

No. 135

A very compact house with no space that cannot be used to the very best advantage. Extra-large colonnaded openings throw reception hall, living room and dining room into one large room. When you land on the second floor at the head of the stairs, you are within a very few feet of the entrance of all the bedrooms and the bathroom.

· ·

Details and features: Six rooms and one bath. Full-width front porch; leaded crystal windows in living room. Colonnaded opening between hall and living room and between living and dining rooms; open stairs.

Years and catalog numbers: 1911 (135); 1912 (135); *1913* (135)

Price: $733 to $853

Locations: Danbury, Conn.; Chicago and Oak Park, Ill.; Davenport, Iowa; Acushnet, Mass.; St. Louis, Mo.; Oswego, N.Y.; Carnegie and New Park, Pa.; Huntington, W.Va.

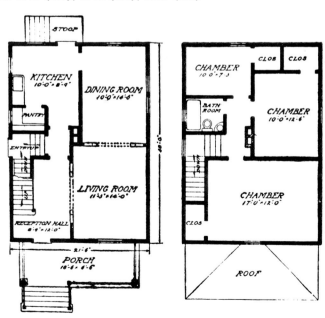

No. 147

*A*n attractive cottage of frame construction and a popular design. The front elevation suggests the bungalow type of architecture. It has a large porch extending across the front of the house which is sheltered by the projection of the upper story and supported with massive built-up square columns. The unique triple window in the attic and fancy leaded art glass windows add much to this pleasing design.

Details and features: Five rooms and one bath. Full-width front porch; triple window in front gable with leaded art glass windows. Nook off living room.

Years and catalog numbers: 1911 (147); 1912 (147); *1913* (147); 1916 (147)

Price: $680 to $872

Locations: Kankakee, Ill.; Great Bend, Kans.; St. Louis, Mo.; Mandan, N.D.; Falls Church, Va.

No. 165

A colonial one-story house particularly planned for southern states. Plenty of room, light and ventilation are its chief characteristics. It has a large front porch with massive colonial columns and a spacious rear porch.

Details and features: Six rooms and one bath. Colonnaded full-width front porch; rear porch. Four corner fireplaces.

Years and catalog numbers: 1911 (165); 1912 (165); *1913* (165)

Price: $1,374 to $1,518

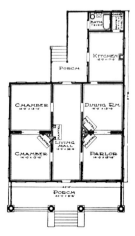

THE NIOTA

*N*ote the square Stonekote columns with panel tops and the Queen Anne windows. The porch with side entrance affords the privacy so much desired by particular people. This is a home good enough for any locality. There is dignity in every line and quality in every piece of material.

Details and features: Seven rooms and one bath. Full-width front porch with square stucco columns; half-timbered front gable. Semiopen stairs.

Years and catalog numbers: 1911 (161); 1912 (161); 1913 (161); 1916 (161); 1917 (C161); *1918* (161)

Price: $788 to $1,585

Locations: Chicago and Elmhurst, Ill.; Indianapolis, Ind.; Westerville, Ohio; Springfield, Mo.

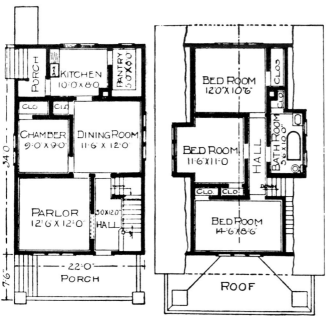

THE MAYTOWN

This is a well-proportioned house which affords a great deal of room at a low cost. It is very popular in all sections of the country.

. . . .

Details and features: Six rooms and one bath. Polygonal turret on front; full-width front porch; front door with beveled plate glass. Semiopen stairs.

Years and catalog numbers: 1911 (167); 1912 (167); 1913 (167); 1916 (264P167, 2017); 1917 (C2017, C167); *1918* (2017); 1921 (7017); 1922 (7017)

Price: $645 to $2,038

Locations: Seymour, Conn.; Bloomington, Ill.; Indianapolis, Ind.; Sioux City, Iowa; Baltimore, Md.; Pittsfield, Mass.; Bay City, Mich.; Garfield, N.J.; Solvay, N.Y.; Struthers, Ohio; Mount Pleasant, Pa.; Galveston, Tex.; Lyndonville, Vt.; Roanoke, Va.; Portage, Wis.

. . . .

Similar to: No. 188

Differences: Wider and longer; floor plans reversed

Years and catalog numbers: 1912 (188); 1913 (188)

Price: $926 to $984

Locations: Windsor, Conn.; Dubuque, Iowa; Auburn, Maine; Steubenville, Ohio; Washington, Pa.

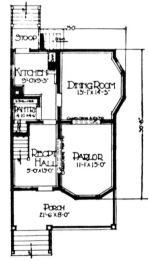

THE MATOKA

*P*leasing but not extreme. A modern type of bungalow sided with the best grade cedar shingles and having an exterior brick chimney. Every owner is well pleased with his investment when he selects this house.

Details and features: Five rooms and one bath. Front porch; stucco front gable; bay window in living and dining rooms. Fireplace flanked by window seats and colored art glass sash in living room.

Years and catalog numbers: 1911 (168); 1912 (168); 1913 (168); 1916 (264P168); 1917 (C168); *1918* (168)

Price: $950 to $1,920

Locations: Lima, Colo.; Westville, Conn.; Chicago, Ill.; Gary, Ind.; Fort Dodge, Iowa; Wrentham, Mass.; Detroit, Mich.; Rochester, Minn.; Shelby, Neb.; Medford, N.J.; Irving, N.Y.; Cincinnati, Ohio; Philadelphia, Pa.; Elk Point, S.D.; Madison, Wis.

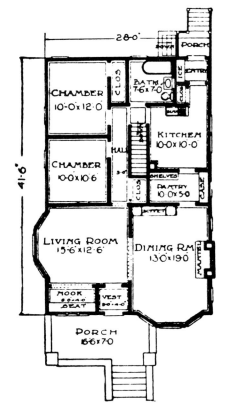

No. 183

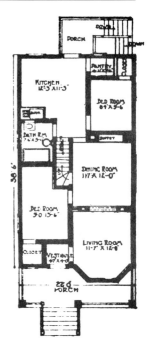

A neat five-room cottage of conventional design. This house can be built on a lot 25 feet wide.

. . . .

Details and features: Five rooms and one bath. Full-width front porch with bay window. Colonnaded opening between living and dining rooms; built-in buffet in dining room.

Years and catalog numbers: 1912 (183); *1913* (183); 1916 (183)

Price: $745 to $908

No. 195

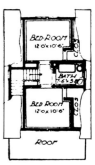

M odern Home No. 195 is a well-built, roomy house of conventional design. Built on a concrete foundation with frame construction of the best quality yellow pine.

. . . .

Details and features: Seven rooms and one bath. Full-width front porch; steeply pitched roof. Open stairs.

Years and catalog numbers: 1912 (195); *1913* (195)

Price: $619 to $670

THE LORAIN

A flat building arranged for one family on the first floor and one on the second floor. Every bit of space is made use of. It is built on very simple and plain lines of architecture, can be constructed at a very low cost and will prove a very good paying investment. Front porch with colonial columns. Arrangement of rooms on each floor almost identical.

Details and features: Ten rooms and two baths. Two-family house. Two-story bay in front; glazed front door.

Years and catalog numbers: 1911 (305); 1912 (305); 1913 (214); 1916 (214); 1917 (C214); *1918* (2040)

Price: $1,030 to $2,558

Locations: Boston, New Bedford and Springfield, Mass.; Olneyville, R.I.; Milwaukee, Wis.

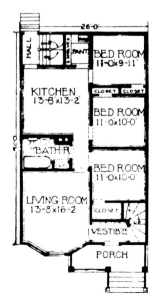

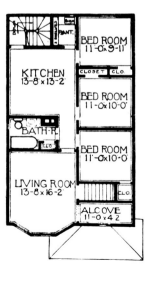

A plain gabled-roof house of good appearance, along plain and simple lines, but with many attractive features. The large front porch can be screened in at a small cost and used as a sleeping porch. The side entrance is a practical feature.

Details and features: Seven rooms and one bath. Full-width front porch supported by square columns; front entrance on side. Fireplace with brick mantel; open stairs.

Years and catalog numbers: 1912 (226); *1913* (226); 1916 (264P226); 1917 (C226); 1918 (226)

Price: $822 to $1,555

Similar to: The Roanoke

Differences: Six rooms and one bath; front entrance; exterior detail modifications

Years and catalog numbers: 1921 (1226); *1922* (1226)

Price: $1,784 to $1,982

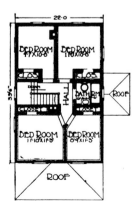

The Roanoke

No. 205

This attractive and solidly constructed cottage represents one of the biggest building bargains in our book. Sided with Oriental Gray Slate Surfaced Siding.

Details and features: Five rooms and one bath. Asphalt shingle exterior; full-width front porch; front door with beveled glass. Built-in buffet in dining room.

Years and catalog numbers: *1913* (205); 1916 (264P205)   **Price:** $707 to $744

No. 264P182

This model is a very well arranged, solidly constructed house with a front porch. Brick foundation is used in contrast with cypress siding for the outside finish.

Details and features: Four rooms and one bath. Full-width front porch; half-timbered front gable with projecting brackets. Fireplace in living room; built-in sideboard with beveled plate mirror in dining room.

Year and catalog number: 1916 (264P182)

Price: $819

Locations: Indianapolis, Ind.; Watervliet, N.Y.; Dallas, Tex.

THE WINONA

The Winona bungalow is a popular American cottage-type home. Broken roof lines, wide overhanging eaves supported with brackets and a full front porch give it a pleasing appearance from either perspective. The outside walls are planned to be covered with beveled siding which we suggest painting white, light gray or ivory.

. . . .

Details and features: Five or six rooms and one bath. Asphalt shingle or wood siding exterior; wide overhanging eaves; full-width front porch. Two floor plans; arched opening between living and dining rooms; built-in sideboard in dining room.

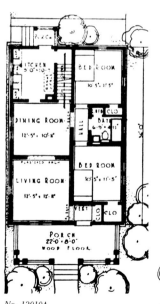

No. 12010A

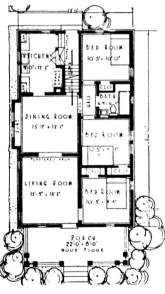

No. 12010B

Years and catalog numbers: 1916 (264P205, 264P205A, 2010); 1917 (C2010, C205, C2042, C205A); 1918 (2010, 2010A); 1919 (2010, 2010A); 1921 (2010, 2010A); 1922 (2010, 2010A); 1925 (2010, 2010A); 1926 (P2010, P2010B); 1928 (C12010, C12010B); 1929 (P2010, P2010B); 1932 (12010A, 12010B); 1933 (12010A, 12010B); *1934* (12010B); 1935 (12010A, 12010B); 1937 (12010A, 12010B); 1939 (12010A, 12010B)

Price: $744 to $1,998

No. 264P207

This house, which has been built in several states at a big saving to each builder, contains eight rooms, all conveniently arranged. It has a large front porch and a balcony on the second floor.

Details and features: Eight rooms and one bath. Full-width front porch supported by square paired columns; balcony on second floor; exposed roof rafter tails and knee braces; front door with beveled plate glass. Open stairs.

Years and catalog numbers: 1916 (264P207); *1917* (C207)

Price: $1,148 to $1,174

No. 264P246

This house can be built on a lot 30 feet wide. The dining room and kitchen are both fair sized, and each of the bedrooms has a large clothes closet.

Details and features: Six rooms and one bath. Full-width front porch; two-story center bay; bracketed eaves. Built-in seat in living room; open stairs.

Years and catalog numbers: 1916 (264P246); *1917* (C246)

Price: $897 to $919

THE ALTON

*A*n attractive home of six rooms and bath. Note the porch roof, with the same effect over the double window on the second floor.

. . . .

Details and features: Six rooms and one bath. Full-width front porch; flower box under second-floor window; notched bargeboards. Built-in buffet in dining room; open stairs.

Years and catalog numbers: 1916 (264P212, 2019); 1917 (C212, C2019); *1918* (2019)

Price: $814 to $1,510

. . . .

Similar to: No. 186

Difference: Stickwork detailing on porch and gable

Years and catalog numbers: 1912 (186); *1913* (186)

Price: $746 to $790

No. 186

THE AVALON

From California comes the idea for this delightful bungalow. Honor Bilt construction makes it cozy and warm enough for any part of the country. The architects of California have studied and experimented until they have built houses of this type which are the most beautiful in the world.

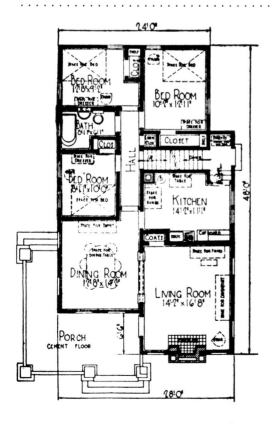

Details and features: Six rooms and one bath. Wraparound front porch with battered piers. Fireplace in living room; built-in bookcases between living and dining rooms.

Years and catalog numbers: 1921 (3048); *1922* (13048); 1925 (13048); 1926 (P13048)

Price: $1,967 to $2,530

Location: St. Bernard, Ohio

Front porch when screened

THE WALTON

This design embodies dignity, strength and gracefulness. It presents a most pleasing appearance and is of a character that will long retain popular favor.

. . . .

Details and features: Six rooms and one bath. Wraparound front porch with wood piers and notched barge-boards. Fireplace in living room; bookcase colonnade between living and dining rooms; cove ceiling in dining room.

Years and catalog numbers: *1921* (3050); 1922 (13050); 1925 (13050X); 1926 (P13050); 1929 (P13050)

Price: $2,225 to $2,489

Location: Tama, Iowa

THE ROCKHURST

The Rockhurst has been designed to meet popular demand for a large, attractive, well-lighted and economically arranged house. This house can be furnished with three exterior designs.

. . . .

Details and features: Six rooms and one bath. Full-width front porch; half-timbered front gable; sleeping porch above rear porch. Fireplace in living room; window seat in dining room; semiopen stairs.

Years and catalog numbers: *1921* (3074); 1922 (3074, 3075, 3076, 3077)

Price: $1,979 to $2,468

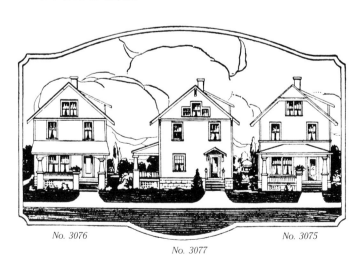

No. 3076   *No. 3075*

No. 3077

THE COLUMBINE

The Columbine, a unique creation in American architecture, has always received praise wherever it has been built. The porch roof and pergolas are supported by six colonial columns. The dentils in the porch gables give it the final touch of elegance and good taste. Don't overlook the triple windows on either side of the porch, the massive brick chimney on the left and the special divided lights in the upper sash of all the windows.

Details and features: Six or eight rooms and one bath. Gabled front porch with pergolas at either side. Optional second floor; fireplace in living room; French doors between living and dining rooms; built-in buffet in dining room.

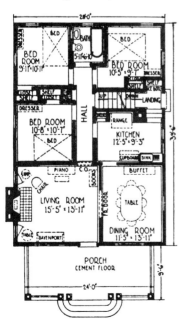

Years and catalog numbers: 1921 (8013); 1922 (8013); 1925 (8013); *1926* (P8013); 1928 (C8013A, C8013B, C8013X); 1929 (P8013A, P8013B)

Price: $1,971 to $2,135

No. P8013B

THE WINDERMERE

*H*ere is a good two-family apartment house with five rooms and bathroom for each family. The exterior is attractive and in good taste. The carefully planned roofs of house and porch, with their enclosed cornices and heavy vergeboards, add to its character and stability. The Windermere, due to unusually good planning, makes a very good paying investment. Arrangement of rooms on each floor almost identical.

Details and features: Ten rooms and two baths. Two-family house. Two-story full-width front porch; glazed front doors. Twin china cases with leaded glass doors and window seats in dining rooms; linen closet off hall.

Years and catalog numbers: *1925* (1208); 1926 (P1208); 1928 (P1208); 1929 (P1208)

Price: $3,410 to $3,534

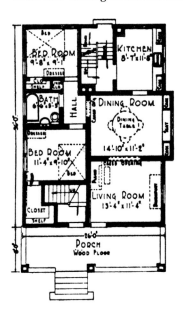

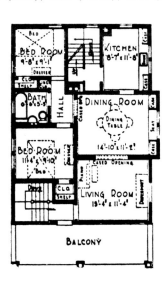

75

THE OAKDALE

One of the most popular types of home is the five-room bungalow. When it is as pretty and homelike as the Oakdale, it commands a good rental or selling price in any neighborhood. And when its rooms are of such comfortable size and arrangment as these, with a convenience in almost every corner, it makes a home to which a family becomes more attached as time passes. It is a masterpiece of one of America's best architects.

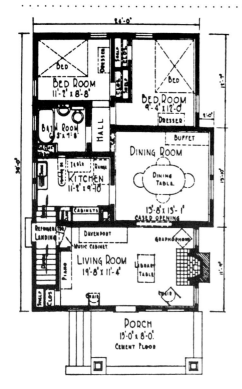

Details and features: Five rooms and one bath. Front porch flanked by paired windows. Fireplace flanked by windows in living room.

Years and catalog numbers: *1925* (3206A); 1926 (P3206A); 1928 (C3206A); 1929 (P3206A); 1932 (3314); 1933 (3314); *1937* (3314)

Price: $1,337 to $1,842

No. 3314

THE HAMPTON

SIX ROOMS AND BATH

*B*ungalow architecture features the Hampton. The interior is designed along practical lines. Full use of space affords a greater amount of room than is usual in a house of this size. The location of each room and its relation to the rest of the house have been planned to promote the comfort of the family.

· ·

Details and features: Six rooms and one bath. Full-width front porch with hipped roof and tapered wood columns; exposed roof rafter tails; glazed front door.

Years and catalog numbers: 1925 (3208); 1926 (P3208); *1928* (C3208); 1929 (P3208)

Price: $1,551 to $1,681

· ·

Similar to: The Grant

Difference: Slightly simpler detailing

Years and catalog numbers: 1925 (6018); *1926* (P6018); 1928 (C6028)

Price: $947 to $999

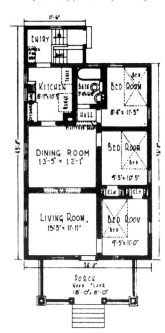

The Grant

THE TARRYTON

EIGHT ROOMS
AND BATH

The Tarryton two-story home is a modernized version of the ever-popular English colonial cottage. Carefully designed as to interior arrangement and exterior decoration, it fulfills every expectation of a good home. A friendly front entrance, good window arrangement and shutters, colonial siding with wide exposure—all add to its permanent attractiveness.

Details and features: Seven rooms and one and a half baths. Portico with trellises; six-panel front door. Fireplace and French doors in living room.

Years and catalog numbers: 1926 (C3247); *1928* (P3247)

Price: $2,967 to $2,998

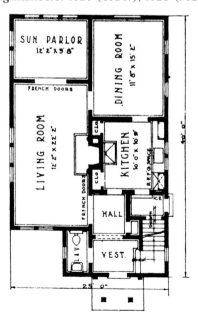

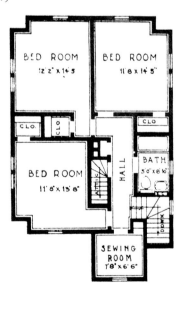

THE CHESTERFIELD

*T*he Chesterfield home has an English ancestry which has stood the test of public favor for many centuries. This particular and interesting design is especially admired for its attractive appearance and splendid interior arrangement. For instance: Consider the informal massing of the walls, the closely clipped gables and the low-swung sloping roof.

. . . .

Details and features: Six rooms and one bath. Vestibule opening onto concrete terrace. French doors between living and dining rooms; breakfast nook off kitchen; semiopen stairs.

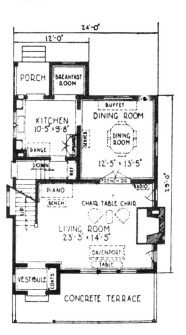

Year and catalog number: 1926 (P3235)

Price: $2,934

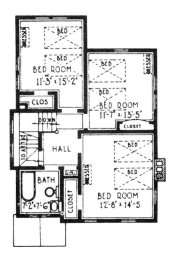

THE CEDARS

*I*t is impossible to add a single feature that will improve the exterior appearance of this beautiful home. While the sloping roof over the porch at the right and over the colonial gate at the left has a tendency to give this house the appearance of being very large, by studying the floor plan you will note it is very compact and will give you a very practical and conveniently arranged home at low cost.

Details and features: Six rooms and one bath. Side porch with paired columns; front entrance with broken pediment. Arched opening between living and dining rooms.

Years and catalog numbers: 1928 (3278); 1929 (P3278); *1931* (3278B)

Price: $2,334

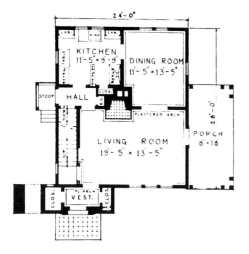

THE CRAFTON

*W*e counted the number of home builders who have been made happy by building one of these attractive low-cost American-type bungalows. When over a thousand vote these plans their choice, there can be only one answer—they meet the requirements where four, five or six rooms are needed at a minimum cost. No "gingerbread"—just attractive, livable space.

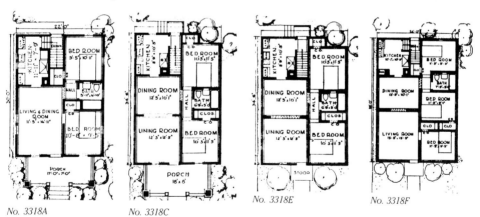

No. 3318A   No. 3318C   No. 3318E   No. 3318F

Details and features: Four, five or six rooms and one bath. Full-width front porch; exposed roof rafter tails; glazed front door. Five floor plans.

Years and catalog numbers: 1932 (3318A, 3318C, 3318D); 1933 (3318A, 3318C, 3318D); *1934* (3318A, 3318C, 3318D, 3318X); *1935* (3318, 3318E, 3318F); 1937 (3318A, 3318C, 3318D, 3318X); 1939 (3318A, 3318C, 3318D)

Price: $916 to $1,399

No. 3318E

LENOX

Once more Sears answers America's demand for *good* low-cost homes. This charming half-timbered English cottage has two bedrooms, a hall, one bath, four closets, a vestibule and a combined living and dining room with a sun room effect.

. . . .

Details and features: Four rooms and one bath. Half-timbered front gable; brick-faced vestibule; glazed front door.

Year and catalog number: 1933 (3395)   **Price:** $1,164

THE DAYTON

The designers of this home kept in mind a plan which would give the maximum livable floor area at the lowest possible cost. It is a typical American home with a semibungalow appearance on account of the wide overhanging eaves—suitable for a narrow city lot or in the country. The exterior is planned to be covered with clear beveled siding with clear cypress exterior trim and moldings.

. . . .

Details and features: Five rooms and one bath. Full-width front porch; glazed front door. Arched opening between living and dining rooms; semiopen stairs.

Year and catalog number: 1937 (3407)

Price: $1,247

No. 139

*A*n attractive little cottage sided with Stonekote. The kitchen, being large, is used as a combination kitchen and dining room. Good-sized pantry. The attic is quite high and could easily be finished off into sleeping rooms if desired.

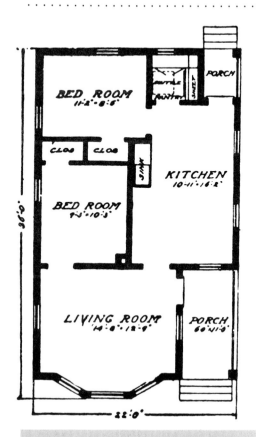

Details and features: Four rooms and no bath. Stucco exterior; front porch; bay window with art glass in living room; glazed front door.

Years and catalog numbers: 1911 (139); 1912 (139); *1913* (139); 1916 (139); 1917 (C139)

Price: $449 to $567

Gabled roof, one story, corner entrance

THE ARCADIA

This inviting little home combines many attractive features with an unusually low price. The arrangement of the porch adds much to the appearance of the house and contributes to the economy in construction.

. . . .

Details and features: Five rooms and no bath. Shed dormer in front; front porch; trellises; glazed front door.

Years and catalog numbers: 1917 (2032); 1918 (2032, 032); 1919 (2032, 032); *1921* (2032B, 032B)

Price: $267 to $946

Locations: Niantic, Conn.; Sheffield, Ill.; Hamlet, Ind.; Cleveland and New Lexington, Ohio; Brownsville, Pa.; Blue Mounds, Wis.

THE ESTES

$\mathcal{T}$he Estes Standard Built bungalow is an inviting little home, priced unusually low. Its front porch is entirely underneath the roof of the house and may be enclosed in glass and used as a sun room.

. . . .

Details and features: Five rooms and no bath. Front porch; glazed front door.

Years and catalog numbers: 1925 (6014); *1926* (P6014); 1928 (C6024)

Price: $617 to $672

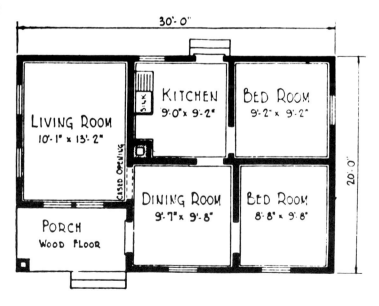

No. 228

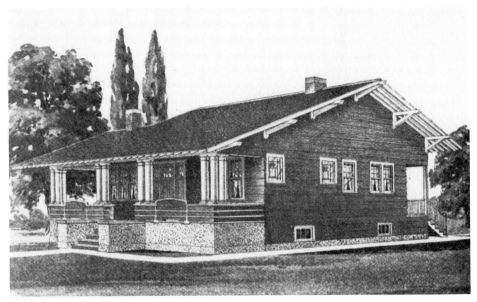

A well-designed bungalow is the most attractive of all styles of houses. With this in mind, our architect has designed what may truly be a perfect bungalow. One is impressed with the exterior appearance, the wide projecting eaves, the low lines suggesting room and comfort.

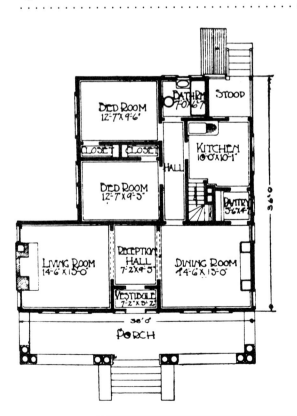

Details and features: Five rooms and one bath. Full-width front porch with paired square piers; exposed roof rafter tails and knee braces. Fireplace flanked by colored art glass windows in living room; built-in buffet flanked by art glass windows in dining room.

Years and catalog numbers: 1912 (228); *1913* (228)

Price: $1,182 to $1,280

Gabled roof, one story, side entrance

No. 241

A 20th-century bungalow. The popularity of cobblestones and boulders for foundations, pillars, chimneys and even for open fireplaces is unquestioned, and the effect obtained here through using cobblestones for a foundation and as porch pillars, in combination with shingles stained a rich brown as a siding, lends to its beauty.

Details and features: Three rooms and one bath. Cobblestone foundation; front porch supported by tapered stone piers; bay window in living room; front door glazed with beveled glass.

Years and catalog numbers: *1912* (241); 1913 (128)   Price: $412 to $429

THE CHICORA

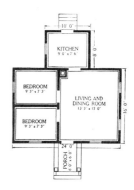

H ere is a home that is solidly constructed and whose appearance alone proves it. Plenty of trellises permit the effective training of vines. The blinds add the popular colonial effect.

Details and features: Four rooms and no bath. Gabled front porch supported by brick walls and tapered wood columns; trellises; notched bargeboards; glazed front door.

Years and catalog numbers: *1917* (C2031, C031); 1918 (2031, 031); 1919 (2031, 031)

Price: $257 to $798

THE ASHMORE

*I*n the original planning of this bungalow, brown was made the predominating color. The treatment of the roof, body finish, floors and walls of the interior, with a careful blending of tone from the darker brown to the light terra cotta and creams, produces a delightful and harmonious contrast. The rugged, massive cobblestone chimney adds the final touch of stability and bungalow character.

Details and features: Six rooms and one bath. Gabled front porch; cobblestone chimney; decorative bargeboards; exposed roof rafter tails; pergola off dining room. Cove ceiling in living room; fireplace nook with built-in bookcases and seats off living room; built-in buffet in dining room; clothes chute in hall.

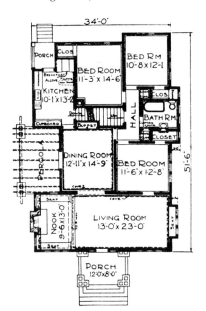

Years and catalog numbers: 1916 (264P250, 2022); 1917 (C250); 1918 (3034); 1921 (3034); *1922* (13034)

Price: $1,608 to $3,632

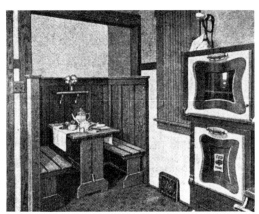

Pullman breakfast alcove

THE ALMO

*T*his house will appeal to the practical man of limited means who is anxious to have an artistic as well as a comfortable home. The interior arrangement is admirable and the exterior leaves nothing to be desired. The kitchen and pantry are decorated with a trellis to balance the trellised side porch. The latter, with vines, will afford a cool and inviting retreat where many pleasant hours can be spent.

Details and features: Four rooms and no bath. Trellised side porch. Pantry off kitchen; some models with stairs off kitchen to basement.

Years and catalog numbers: 1917 (C2033); *1918* (2033); 1919 (2033); 1921 (2033B); 1922 (2033B)

Price: $463 to $1,052   **Locations:** Heyworth, Ill.; Elyria and Minerva, Ohio

THE NATOMA

*T*his up-to-date little Modern Home has three good-sized rooms, is well lighted and can be thoroughly ventilated. No doubt you will be surprised at the idea of getting the material for a house of this kind for such a low price. The picture of the house, however, cannot be expected to show anything of the high quality of the material which we furnish. This is what really sets the standard of value in our houses.

Details and features: Three rooms and no bath. Shed roof porch supported by concrete block and wood piers; trellis around front window; glazed front door.

Years and catalog numbers: 1917 (C2034); *1918* (2034, 034); 1919 (2034, 034)

Price: $191 to $598

Locations: Aurora, Ill.; Winslow, Ind.; Pickney, Mich.; Wayne, Neb.; Hawthorne, N.J.; Chillicothe, Ohio; Monongahela, Pa.

THE BROOKSIDE

The man who builds this bungalow will have made a first-class investment. It is a home that will look well in high-class surroundings. The exposed chimney, shingled gable, solidly constructed and artistic porch and colonial windows all combine in producing a pleasing design at a remarkably low price.

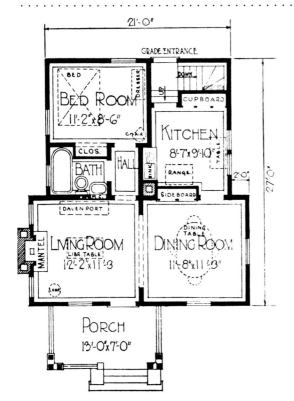

Details and features: Four rooms and one bath. Gabled front porch supported by paired wood piers; notched bargeboards. Fireplace with oak mantel and mirror in living room.

Years and catalog numbers: 1918 (2091); 1919 (2091); *1921* (2091); 1922 (2091)

Price: $1,050 to $1,404

THE ARDARA

The Ardara is a bungalow that will be recognized at once as possessing many unusually attractive features and conveniences. The artistic treatment of the porch and front windows leaves nothing to be desired. The garage attached to the building itself adds to the general pleasing effect.

Details and features: Six rooms and one bath. Attached garage (also available without garage); front porch with curved roof supported by columns; trellises in front; glazed front door with sidelights.

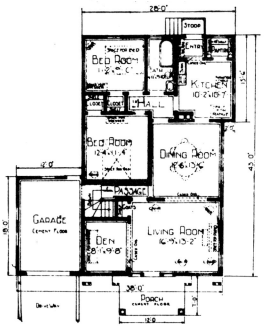

Years and catalog numbers: 1919 (13039); *1921* (3039); 1922 (13039); 1926 (P13039, P13039A); 1928 (C13039, C13039X); 1929 (P13039, P13039X)

Price: $1,773 to $2,483

Location: New York, N.Y.

THE HARMONY

*T*he Harmony meets the demands of those who must have good-sized rooms in a home that is not too big or expensive. The big living room, with windows on two sides and a glazed front door, will always be airy and light.

. . . .

Details and features: Three rooms and one bath. Front porch with gabled roof supported by wood pilasters; exposed roof rafter tails; glazed front door.

Year and catalog numbers: 1920 (3056, 13056)   **Price:** $1,599 to $2,220

THE DUNDEE

*I*n these four good-sized rooms there is real comfort and convenience. Each room has windows on two sides, assuring plenty of light and fresh air. Notice that while the front porch is of good size and is arranged so as to make an outdoor sitting room in hot weather, it does not cut off light from the living room. Long spaces along the walls of the living room provide for furniture. In all rooms, doors and windows are where they are needed, without being in the way of the furniture.

. . . .

Details and features: Four rooms and one or no bath. Front porch with board-and-batten gabled roof supported by brick and wood piers; exposed rafter tails; glazed front door.

Years and catalog numbers: *1921* (3051, 13051); 1922 (3051, 13051); 1925 (3209X); 1926 (P3209); 1928 (P3209); 1929 (P3209)

Price: $733 to $1,405

THE HOMEVILLE

The Homeville suggests home and home comfort in every line. That big exposed chimney, even when covered with vines in summertime, promises security against winter blasts. The French windows and French doors, together with the columned entrance, impart just the right artistic touch. When painted pure white in contrast with red or green roofing, this little home will be rcognized as an architectural gem in any community.

Details and features: Six rooms and one bath. Gabled roof over front door; brick chimney in front. Fireplace with brick mantel in living room; French doors between living and dining rooms.

Years and catalog numbers: *1921* (3072); 1922 (3072)

Price: $1,741 to $1,896

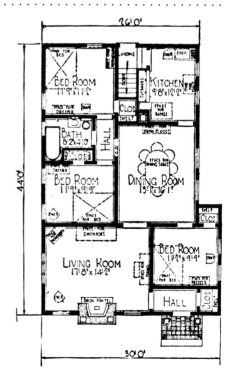

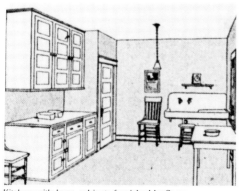

Kitchen with large cabinets furnished by Sears

THE SPRINGWOOD

The Springwood has an attractive exterior with an interior equally inviting and comfortable. The first thing you notice, of course, when you enter the living room is a hospitable mantel, with doors on either side. The kitchen entry makes this home workshop comfortable in winter and cool in summer.

Details and features: Five rooms and one bath. Portico topped with decorative urns and flanked by trellises; side porch off living room. Fireplace flanked by built-in bookcases in living room; built-in buffet in dining room; breakfast nook in kitchen.

Years and catalog numbers: 1921 (3078); *1922* (13078)

Price: $1,797 to $2,089

Location: Long Beach, N.J.

Living room

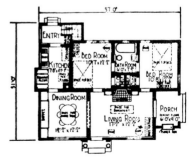

THE CRESCENT

FIVE ROOMS
NEAT PORCH

To the folks who like a touch of individuality with good taste, the Crescent bungalow makes a special appeal. The front door, sidelights and windows have been admirably selected. Seldom, indeed, do you find a more inviting front porch, its hood supported by graceful columns, and entrance than we provide for this house. Your choice of two floor plans as shown.

. . . .

Details and features: Five or seven rooms and one bath. Gabled front porch with arch supported by columns; tripartite windows. Two floor plans; two-story plan has open stairs.

Years and catalog numbers: 1921 (3084, 3086); 1922 (13084, 13086); 1925 (13084, 13086); 1926 (P13086A, 13084A); *1928* (P3258A, P3259A) ; 1929 (P3258A, P3259A); 1932 (3258A, 3259A); 1933 (3258A, 3258B, 3259A, 3259B)

Price: $1,351 to $2,410

Locations: Park Ridge, Ill.; Cincinnati, Ohio; Aldan, Pa.

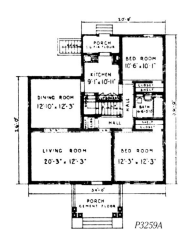

P3259A

Living room

Dining room

THE VALLEY

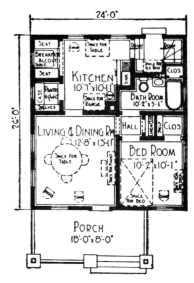

*M*any a city flat dweller has longed for a little home like this. He would have to pay high rent for a flat that was as convenient and embodied as many of the latest ideas, and even then it is unlikely that he could find one with as many windows or with such a nice front porch.

Details and features: Three rooms and one bath. Gabled front porch supported by concrete block and tapered wood piers; exposed roof rafter tails; glazed front door. Breakfast alcove off kitchen.

Years and catalog numbers: *1921* (6000); 1922 (6000)

Price: $904 to $989

THE VINEMONT

*T*he problem of making the outside walls attractive has been successfully solved here by the use of Oriental Slate Surfaced Siding nicely paneled. The solution has been effected with a substantial savings over the cost of wood siding. The three windows in the living room would be enough to assure you of plenty of light and air, but with the entrance being where it is and having a glazed door, you actually have light and air on three sides of this room.

Details and features: Three rooms and no bath. Asphalt shingle exterior; corner front porch supported by concrete block and wood piers; exposed roof rafter tails; decorative bargeboards; glazed front door. Breakfast alcove off kitchen.

Years and catalog numbers: *1921* (6002); 1922 (6002)

Price: $747 to $830

THE ALPHA

A simple house, if it be truly comfortable and substantial, may make a far more happy home than one that is more elaborate than your requirements demand. In this one the rooms are light, the rugs and furniture will fit nicely, and the kitchen is a pleasant place to work in.

Details and features: Four rooms and one bath. Gabled front porch supported by concrete block and tapered wood piers; exposed roof rafter tails.

Years and catalog numbers: *1921* (7031, 17031); 1922 (7031, 17031)

Price: $871 to $1,356

Location: Norwood, Ohio

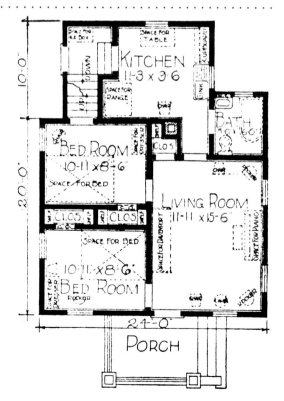

THE PRESCOTT

The Prescott colonial home has a restful and charming appeal. Much has been said and written about its simplicity, modern interior and unusually good construction. The exterior lends itself admirably to the use of wide colonial siding and terraced grade. Painted white or ivory, with green roof, it fully deserves the favorable comment one hears from neighbors and friends.

· ·

Details and features: Five rooms and one bath. Full-width front porch with flat roof topped with decorative balustrade; glazed front door.

Years and catalog numbers: *1926* (P3240); 1928 (P3240); 1929 (P3240)

Price: $1,715 to $1,873

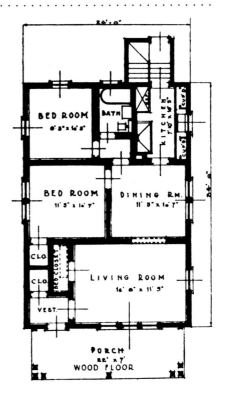

THE SELBY

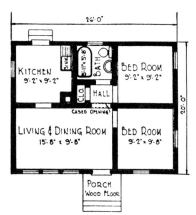

*T*he Selby Standard Built home has been designed with the same care as more expensive houses. Its simple architecture has a universal appeal. Then, again, its four rooms really serve every purpose of five.

Details and features: Four rooms and one bath. Gabled roof over front door supported by brackets; exposed roof rafter tails; glazed front door.

Years and catalog numbers: 1925 (6011); *1926* (P6011); 1928 (C6021)

Price: $590 to $629

THE FERNDALE

*C*onsidering its low cost, this cozy bungalow affords unusual comfort. Privacy given to bedrooms and bath off hall at back. Graceful plastered arch connects the dining room and a living room over 23 feet long with a real fireplace.

Details and features: Five rooms and one bath. Gabled front porch with paired columns. Fireplace in living room; built-in telephone nook in kitchen.

Years and catalog numbers: 1929 (P3284); *1933* (3284)

Price: $1,340 to $1,790

THE KIMBERLY

FOUR ROOMS
AND BATH

The Kimberly bungalow fulfills a popular demand for a combination of English and California architecture. Its interior has an up-to-date floor arrangement, giving the most light, ventilation and easy access between rooms. Important, too, are the sturdy construction and the economy of cost of upkeep which has been planned in every detail by our own staff of architects and engineers. No wonder the Kimberly makes such a desirable investment.

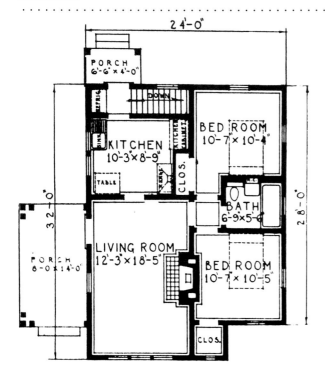

Details and features: Four rooms and one bath. Gabled entrance porch supported by square columns; shutters; small service porch at rear. Fireplace and French doors in living room.

Years and catalog numbers: *1928* (P3261); 1929 (P3261)

Price: $1,442 to $1,815

THE LEWISTON

A home of such outstanding beauty as the Lewiston is a source of pride to the entire family. The first floor forms a complete five-room home, while upstairs two good bedrooms and four closets may be finished whenever desired. Quiet sleeping quarters in back, with cross ventilation, bath, three closets, phone nook and closed stair. Compact kitchen, well equipped and sunny.

Details and features: Five or seven rooms and one bath. Brick chimney in front; crescent window in front gable; round-arched front door. Optional second floor; fireplace in living room; arched opening between dining and living rooms; telephone nook in hall.

Years and catalog numbers: 1929 (P3287); 1932 (3287, 3287A); *1933* (3287, 3287A); 1934 (3287-5, 3287-7); 1935 (3287-5, 3287-7); 1937 (3287, 3287A); 1939 (3287, 3287A)

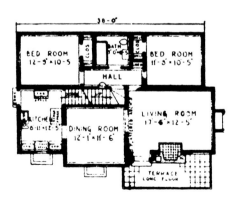

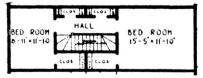

Price: $1,527 to $2,037

Location: Farmington, Mich.

The Colchester

Similar to: The Colchester

Difference: Brick and stone exterior

Years and catalog numbers: 1932 (3292); *1933* (3292, 3292A)

Price: $1,988 to $2,256

THE WEXFORD

*I*f you are looking for something different in a bungalow design, you surely will find a pleasing exterior and convenient arrangement in this colonial home with four or five rooms.

. . . .

Details and features: Four or five rooms and one bath. Side porch with paired columns; small front porch with paired columns and gable with arch. Two floor plans; fireplace in living room.

Years and catalog numbers: *1931* (3337A, 3337B); 1932 (3337A, 3337B); 1933 (337A, 337B)

Price: No price given

. . . .

Identical to: The Bridgeport

Years and catalog numbers: *1933* (13337A, 13337B); 1934 (13337A, 13337B); 1935 (13337A, 13337B); 1937 (13337A, 13337B); 1939 (3416A, 3416B)

Price: $1,128 to $1,555

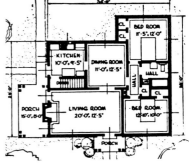

No. 13337B

No. 13337A

THE STANFORD

These small homes rely on simplicity and good taste combined with direct and careful planning to lift them above the ordinary type of home. There is a certain softness and lasting character in this New England type which can be definitely expressed in both large and small homes. White walls and chimney with dark shutters and roof for contrast is the most popular exterior color scheme.

Details and features: Four or five rooms and one bath. Side chimney; six-panel front door with shutters. Two floor plans; fireplace in living room.

Years and catalog numbers: *1931* (3354A, 3354B); 1932 (3354A, 3354B); 1933 (3354A, 3354B)

Price: No price given

Identical to: The Cape Cod

Years and catalog numbers: *1933* (13354A, 13354B); 1934 (13354A, 13354B); 1935 (13354A, 13354B); 1937 (13354A, 13354B)

Price: $908 to $1,163

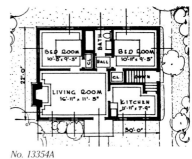

No. 13354A

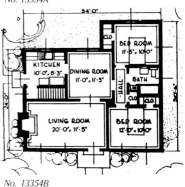

No. 13354B

THE CRESTWOOD

*S*everal different plans are available for the Crestwood, and all are sturdy, well built and most attractive.

. . . .

Details and features: Five or six rooms and one bath. Full-width front porch with gabled-roof. Three floor plans.

Years and catalog numbers: 1932 (3319A, 3319C, 3319D); *1933* (3319A, 3319C, 3319D)

Price: $925 to $1,206

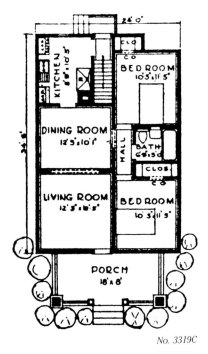

No. 3319C

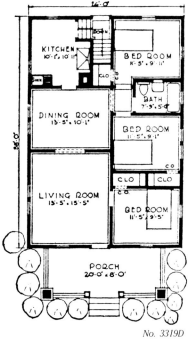

No. 3319D

THE RODESSA

*T*he Rodessa provides real low-cost comfort and a fine appearance. The house is simple and inexpensive to build and requires only a 28-foot lot. The Rodessa has proved to be one of our most popular houses.

. . . .

Details and features: Four rooms and one bath. Gabled front porch supported by paired columns with trellises; glazed front door.

Years and catalog numbers: *1931* (3317); 1932 (3317); 1933 (3317)   **Price: $931**

THE BAYSIDE

*R*arely will you be able to find a home so fully enraptured in solace and restive quietude as this substantial home, a replica of the type to which time-honored fisherfolk of the eastern seaboard were wont to repair after a strenuous day. Properly nestled on a partially wooded lot, this home with its wide shingle siding, picketed gate and sheltered front entrance will prove a source of ever-growing delight.

. . . .

Details and features: Five rooms and one bath. Entrance through picket gate. Full stairs to unfinished attic; sufficient headroom for later installation of one or two rooms.

Year and catalog number: 1938 (3410)

Price: No price given

THE CARVER

*T*his quaint Cape Cod cottage has almost a pioneer charm about its rugged exterior—the lines are simple, yes, but perfectly balanced in every little detail. The Carver is a "find" for young married couples who haven't as yet made their fortunes, because it *is* a money saver in a number of ways.

. . . .

Details and features: Six rooms and one bath. Six-panel front door with shutters. Dining room replaced by smaller dining alcove seating six to eight persons.

Year and catalog number: 1939 (13408)

Price: $1,291

THE FAIRFIELD

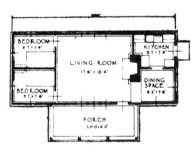

*T*he colonial exterior is very attractive and appropriate for a five-room house like this. Ideal for a summer home because it's designed to catch every breath of breeze. Look at the triple windows on opposite sides of the large living room . . . they're your assurance of an airy, cool house.

. . . .

Details and features: Five rooms and no bath. Front porch supported by four columns. Fireplace in living room.

Year and catalog number: 1939 (no number given)

Price: No price given

THE NIPIGON

he Nipigon has all the rustic backwoods charm you expect in a log cabin. Still, at the end of the summer, you'll say it's just as comfortable as living at home—and a good deal more fun.

Details and features: Five rooms and one bath. Log exterior; gabled porch. Fireplace flanked by open shelves in living room.

Year and catalog number: 1939 (no number given)

Price: No price given

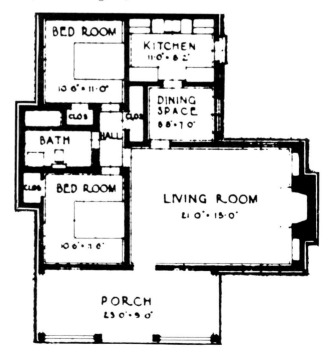

No. 64

𝒜 very substantial house and so designed that it can be constructed at the very lowest possible cost. Six large rooms arranged so that there is practically no wasted space whatever. Inside cellar stairs directly under the stairs leading to the second floor. You will note the convenient arrangement in the floor plan which enables you to go from the kitchen through the bedroom up to the second floor or to the parlor without going through the dining room. The dining room and parlor each have an outside door leading to the front porch.

Details and features: Six rooms and no bath. Concrete block exterior; front porch supported by two columns; shed dormer; glazed front door.

Years and catalog numbers: 1908 (64); *1911* (64); 1912 (64); 1913 (211)

Price: $556 to $1,525

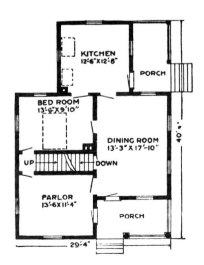
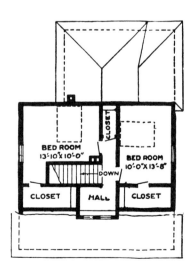

Gabled roof, one and a half stories, side entrance, one front dormer

No. 70

A concrete block house with a good-sized living room and cased opening between the living and dining rooms. The front porch has colonial columns.

Details and features: Six rooms and no bath. Concrete block exterior; front porch; shed dormer; front door glazed with figured glass.

Years and catalog numbers: 1908 (70); *1911* (70); 1912 (70); 1913 (212)

Price: $492 to $1,275

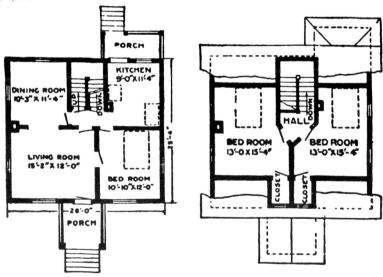

No. 105

A two-story house having three rooms on the first floor with pantry and closet. Inside cellar stairway under the main stairs. Outside cellar entrance in the rear. The bedrooms on the second floor each have two windows, making them well lighted and perfectly ventilated. Front porch is 20 by 5 feet, with colonial columns. Built on a stone foundation.

Details and features: Five rooms and no bath. Full-width front porch; gabled dormer.

Years and catalog numbers: 1908 (105); 1911 (105); 1912 (105); *1913* (105)

Price: $545 to $1,175

No. 140

 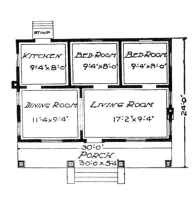

*I*n Modern Home No. 140 we have an attractive cottage or bungalow sided with roughed 10-inch boards. A cobblestone foundation, porch pillars and chimney give this bungalow a rustic beauty seldom seen in buildings at such a low price.

Details and features: Five rooms and no bath. Full-width front porch; cobblestone foundation; shed dormer; front door with beveled plate glass.

Year and catalog number: 1913 (140)

Price: $449

Location: Gary, Ind.

THE ALTONA

This suburban favorite is an attractive six-room cottage for the family of moderate means. It has a good-sized front porch with a cluster of three colonial columns on the outside corner and one column on each end next to the building.

. . . .

Details and features: Six rooms and one bath. Front porch supported by columns; hipped dormer with balcony; front door glazed with leaded art glass. Corner fireplace in parlor; sliding door between dining room and parlor.

Years and catalog numbers: 1911 (121); 1912 (121); *1913* (121); 1916 (121); 1917 (C121); 1918 (121)

Price: $697 to $1,458

Locations: Chicago, Ill.; Davenport, Iowa; Easthampton, Mass.; Waterbury, Neb.; Denville and Somerville, N.J.; Gatesville, N.C.; Almont, N.D.; Oxford, Ohio

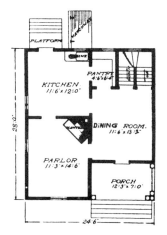

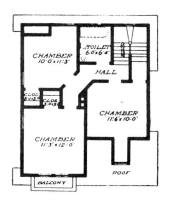

THE GLYNDON

A modern six-room bungalow, built along plain lines of high-grade materials, yet at a price that is within reach of almost every purse. The numerous windows, some of which are double, make every room light and airy.

Details and features: Seven rooms and one bath. Full-width front porch supported by square columns; shed dormer. Sliding door between living and dining rooms; built-in sideboard and plate rails in dining room.

Years and catalog numbers: 1911 (156); 1912 (156); 1913 (156); 1916 (2014, 156); 1917 (C2014, C156); *1918* (2014); 1921 (2014); 1922 (2014)

Price: $595 to $1,990

Locations: Elgin and Peoria, Ill.; Gary, Indianapolis and South Bend, Ind.; Milan, Mich.; Union, N.J.; Schenectady and Webster, N.Y.; Dayton, Gibsonburg, Lima, Marble Cliff and Rocky River, Ohio

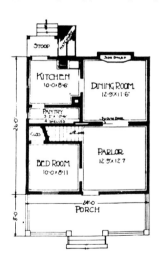

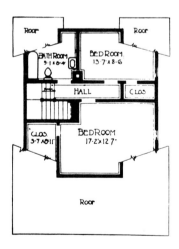

THE HAZELTON

A modern bungalow of frame construction. The extra-wide siding and the visible rafters over porches and eaves give a pleasing rustic effect. The roof is ornamented by an attractive dormer with three sash. The front and side of the bungalow are beautified by triple and double windows, making every room light and airy.

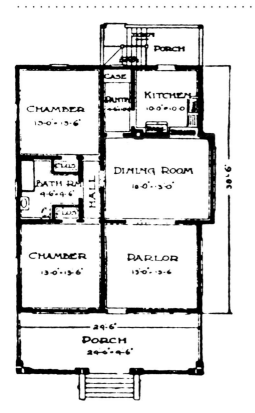

Details and features: Five rooms and one bath. Full-width front porch with paired piers; shed dormer; exposed roof rafter tails. Built-in sideboard in dining room.

Years and catalog numbers: 1911 (172); 1912 (172); 1913 (172); *1916* (264P172); 1917 (C2025, C172); 1918 (C2025, C172); 1921 (2025); 1922 (2025)

Price: $780 to $2,248

Locations: Washington, D.C.; Evanston, Ill.; Gary and Indianapolis, Ind.; New Bedford, Mass.; Port Monmouth, N.J.; Rochester, N.Y.; Salem, Ohio; McKeesport, Pa.; Dallas and Pecos, Tex.; Arlington and Richmond, Va.

THE ELMWOOD

This five-room bungalow of the Craftsman style features an open-air sleeping balcony. The stairs on the second floor are within an arm's reach of either bedrooms or bathroom.

Details and features: Five rooms and one bath. Full-width front porch supported by tapered square columns; open sleeping porch above. Fireplace with oak mantel in living room; built-in sideboard in dining room; open stairs.

Years and catalog numbers: 1911 (162); 1912 (162); 1913 (153, 162); 1916 (264P162, 264P153); 1917 (C162, C153); 1918 (3013, 3014); *1921* (3068, 3069)

Price: $716 to $2,492

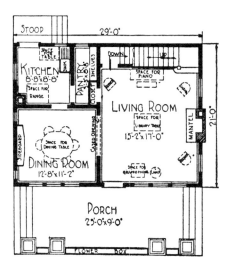

The Elmwood, living room

The Sunbeam, living room

The Elmwood, dining room

The Sunbeam, dining room

Locations: Washington, D.C.; Caldwell, Idaho; Bloomington, Ill.; Gary, Ind.; Calmar, Iowa; Wichita, Kans.; Lockport, La.; Rochester, Minn.; Pass Christian, Miss.; New York, N.Y.; Fargo, N.D.; Cleveland, Ohio; Sioux Falls, S.D.; Huntland, Tenn.; Barboursville, W. Va.; Madison, Wis.

. . . .

Similar to: The Sunbeam

Difference: Sleeping porch screened in

Years and catalog numbers: *1922* (3194); 1925 (3194A); 1926 (P3194A)

Price: $2,425 to $2,707

Location: Pittsburgh, Pa.

The Sunbeam

No. 155

*I*n Modern Home No. 155 we have a two-story house with a bungalow effect. Note the large sloping roof and the spacious screened-in front porch. An abundance of light and ventilation is provided for in this house, as can be seen by the number of windows specified. Ventilation is further provided for by two sleeping balconies on the second floor, one in the front and one in the rear.

Details and features: Six rooms and one bath. Full-width front porch; gabled dormer opening onto balcony; exposed roof rafter tails. French doors between dining and living rooms; built-in buffet in dining room; sleeping porch off rear bedroom.

Years and catalog numbers: *1913* (155); 1916 (264P155); 1917 (C155)

Price: $1,080 to $1,118

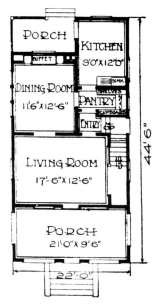

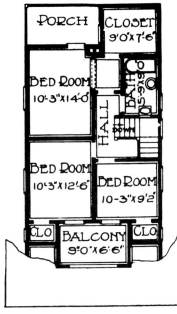

his comfortable little home is pleasing and homelike. It has a large bay window on both the first and second floors. All rooms on the first floor will be perfectly cool on the hottest days, the ventilation being perfect.

Details and features: Six rooms and one bath. Full-width front porch; two-story center polygonal bay; front door glazed with beveled plate glass.

Years and catalog numbers: 1912 (190); *1913* (190)

Price: $828 to $894

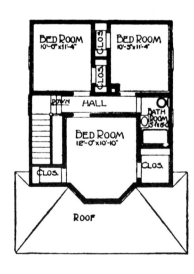

No. 202

*I*f you are looking for a colonial house with 20th-century improvements, our Modern Home No. 202 will be an excellent selection. The combination porch and pergola is a feature that will at once attract your attention. The quadruple colonial windows on the second story afford an abundance of light for the two front bedrooms. The massive colonial columns lend an air of strength and durability to the whole building, while the colonial effect is further strengthened by the use of shingles for siding.

Details and features: Eight rooms and one bath. Combination porch and pergola across front; shed dormer; exposed roof rafter tails. Beamed ceiling in living and dining rooms; built-in seats in dining room and den; open stairs.

Year and catalog number: 1913 (202)   **Price:** $1,389

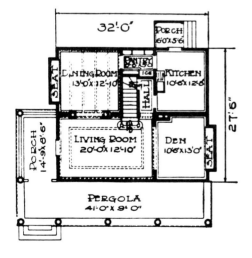
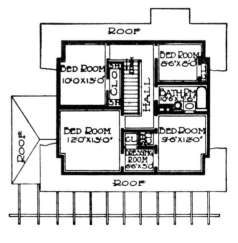

THE ARLINGTON

A colonial house with a bungalow effect. Note the arrangement by which the monotony of the long, sloping roof is broken, permitting four colonial windows, providing the two front bedrooms of the second floor with an abundance of light. The cobblestone outside chimney and the cluster of columns on the front porch with a bay window in the dining room are features that will be sure to please.

. . . .

Details and features: Seven rooms and one bath. Wraparound front porch supported by tapered, paired columns; cobblestone chimney on side. Fireplace with brick mantel in living room; beamed ceiling in dining room; semiopen stairs.

Years and catalog numbers: 1913 (145); 1916 (264P145); 1917 (C145); *1918* (145); 1921 (1145); 1922 (1145)

Price: $1,294 to $2,906

Locations: Manhattan, Kans.; Black Rock, N.Y.

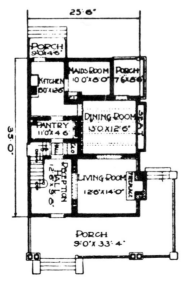

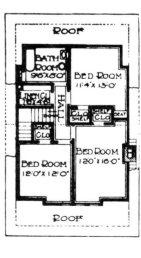

This charming bungalow will appeal to the discriminating home builder. The exterior is very attractive and has many good features. The long sloping roof is relieved by the wide dormer, the grouping of columns at the corners of the porch, the flower boxes and the brick chimneys showing on the outside walls. The wide porch extending entirely across the front of the house, together with the open-air dining room at the back of the house, affords plenty of room for outdoor living.

Details and features: Six rooms and one bath. Full-width front porch supported by paired columns; shed dormer; exposed roof rafter tails. Fireplace with molded brick and beamed ceiling in living room; built-in buffet in dining room; open stairs.

Years and catalog numbers: *1912* (225); 1916 (264P225); 1917 (C225)

Price: $1,381 to $1,465

Locations: Shelton, Conn.; Gary, Ind.; Trenton, Mich.; Dunkirk, N.Y.; Huntington, Pa.

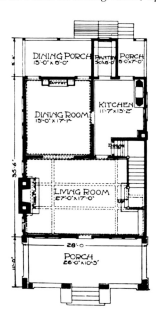

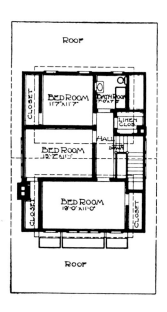

THE SHERBURNE

This house, when built on a lot of proper size and painted in refined contrasting colors, is strikingly attractive. The concrete block foundation and brick chimney, the unique arrangement of the shingles used for siding and the Stonekote panels make this house stand out with an air of distinctiveness. Illustration made from photograph sent us by one of our customers.

Details and features: Six rooms and one bath. Full-width front porch supported by concrete block piers and wood columns; half-timbered gabled dormer; roof brackets. Fireplace flanked by bookcases in living room; built-in buffet in dining room; open stairs.

Years and catalog numbers: 1913 (187); 1916 (264P187); 1917 (C187); *1918* (187); 1921 (187); 1922 (187)

Price: $1,231 to $2,581

Locations: Brooklyn, Ind.; Russell, Iowa; Rudyard, Mich.; Bound Brook, N.J.; Dunkirk, N.Y.; Lehighton, Pa.; Sioux Falls and Vienna, S.D.

Bathroom

THE WAREHAM

*I*n the Wareham Modern Home we have the colonial design prevailing with massiveness and durability. The living room and dining room are always well lighted and ventilated.

. . . .

Details and features: Six rooms and one bath. Full-width front porch supported by tapered cobblestone or square wood columns; shed dormer. Fireplace with brick mantel in living room; cased opening flanked by columns between living and dining rooms.

Years and catalog numbers: 1913 (203); 1916 (264P203); 1917 (S203); *1918* (203); 1921 (203); 1922 (203)

Price: $1,089 to $2,425

Locations: Greenville and Pittsburgh, Pa.; Corpus Christi, Tex.; Madison, W. Va.

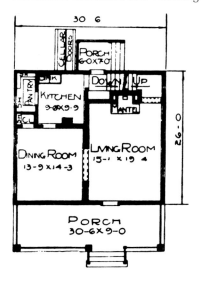

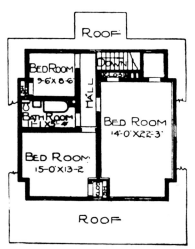

THE WESTLY

This two-story bungalow is built on a concrete block foundation and is sided with narrow beveled clear cypress siding. All rooms on both floors are light and airy.

Details and features: Seven rooms and one bath. Shed dormer opening onto balcony; full-width front porch supported by brick and wood piers; exposed roof rafter tails and knee braces; front door with beveled plate glass. Colonnaded openings off hall; corner fireplace in dining room with oak mantel.

Years and catalog numbers: 1913 (206); 1916 (264P206); 1917 (C206, C2026); *1918* (2026); 1921 (2026, 3085); 1922 (12026, 13085); 1925 (13085); 1926 (P13085); 1928 (P13085); 1929 (P13085)

Price: $926 to $2,543

Locations: Washington, D.C.; Aurora, Ill.; Gary, Ind.; Milford, Iowa; Boston, Mass.; Ord, Neb.; Vineland, N.J.; Fort Covington, N.Y.; Pittsburgh, Pa.; Sioux Falls, S.D.; McLean, Va.; Parkersburg, W.Va.; Kenosha, Wis.

No. 144

Similar to: No. 144

Differences: Dormer and porch design modifications

Years and catalog numbers: 1911 (144); 1912 (144); *1913* (144)

Price: $829 to $926

THE HOLLYWOOD

The charm and homelike aspect of this bungalow will appeal to you. It has received honorable mention in leading architectural magazines. The arrangement of the rooms conforms to the approved bungalow style. Note the large living room with the mantel nook at one end partly separated from the living room by Craftsman colonnades. The main front door is Craftsman design.

Details and features: Five rooms and one bath. Full-width front porch of brick and stucco; gabled dormer; bay window in dining room; exposed roof rafter tails. Fireplace flanked by built-in seats and beamed ceiling in living room; window seat and built-in buffet in dining room.

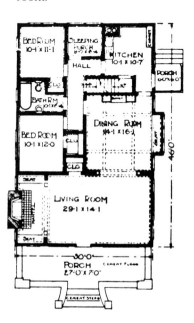

Years and catalog numbers: 1916 (264P234, 2020); 1917 (C234, C2020); *1918* (259); *1921* (259, 2069); 1922 (1259, 12069)

Price: $1,376 to $2,986

Locations: Cairo, Ill.; Urbana, Ohio; Newberry, Pa.; Mukwunago, Wis.

No. 2069

THE CORONA

The Corona gives a true bungalow effect. One of the front bedrooms on the second floor has an alcove which is large enough for a bedroom if desired, or it can be used as a sewing room or a den.

Details and features: Seven rooms and one bath. Wraparound front porch supported by square brick and wood piers; shed dormer; exposed roof rafter tails and knee braces. Fireplace flanked by bookcases in living room; beamed ceiling in living and dining rooms; colonnade between living and dining rooms; built-in buffet in dining room; breakfast nook with built-in seats in kitchen.

Years and catalog numbers: 1916 (264P240); 1917 (C240); *1918* (240); 1921 (1240); 1922 (1240)

Price: $1,537 to $3,364

Locations: Stamford, Conn.; Chicago, Ill.; Arlington Heights, Mass.; Waterford, Mich.

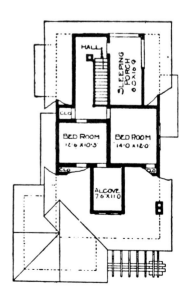

No. 264P243

This pretty bungalow is built on the shore of a beautiful lake in the state of Washington. It is an ideal bungalow for the lakeside or seashore in any part of the country. The big sheltered porch, extending across the house, provides a comfortable retreat. Pergola porches extend back to the rear on both sides. These two pergolas will suggest beautiful vine treatment which, with the cobblestone chimney on the right side, will make a most effective combination. Note the French door and windows and the shingled front. When painted and stained with the proper tones, this bungalow will be an ornament to any neighborhood.

. . . .

Details and features: Four rooms and one bath. Wraparound porch supported by tapered square columns; cobblestone chimney; gabled dormer. Cobblestone fireplace, plate rails and panel strips in living room.

Years and catalog numbers: 1916 (264P243); *1917* (C243)

Price: $1,006 to $1,037

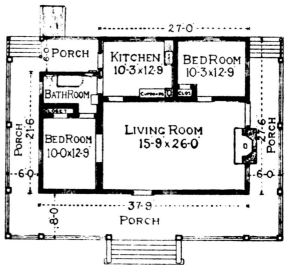

THE SAVOY

This is a California bungalow, a real bungalow in the true sense of the term. It is typically American and commands attention at first sight. It is a bungalow that people will stop to look at and admire.

. . . .

Details and features: Five rooms and one bath. Full-width front porch with flanking pergolas; shed dormer; cobblestone chimney. Beamed ceiling in living and dining rooms; pedestals between living and dining rooms; built-in buffet and sideboard in dining room.

Years and catalog numbers: 1916 (2023); *1918* (2023)

Price: $1,230 to $2,333

. . . .

Similar to: No. 264P233

Differences: Stucco porch columns; fireplace at opposite end of living room

Year and catalog number: 1916 (264P233)

Price: $1,295

No. 264P233

THE ROSEBERRY

*W*e consider this house to be a remarkable bargain for the price. We furnish the material already cut and fitted. It is a house that will look well in any community. The front porch and entire elevation cannot fail to win favorable comment.

. . . .

Details and features: Five rooms and one bath. Full-width front porch supported by tapered wood piers; bracketed gabled dormer. Beamed ceiling in dining room.

Years and catalog numbers: 1917 (2037); *1918* (2037); 1919 (2037); 1921 (2037); 1922 (2037)

Price: $744 to $1,479

Locations: Holder, Ill.; Morocco, Ind.; Dodgeville, N.Y.; Cincinnati, Ohio

No. 2024

*T*his house is quite out of the ordinary in many respects. Note the concrete block posts surmounted by graceful wood columns. The paneled stucco porch gable adds much to the appearance, and the Oriental Red Slate Surfaced Roofing sets off the house to the best advantage.

. . . .

Details and features: Five rooms and one bath. Gabled front porch supported by two tapered piers; shed dormer. Beamed ceiling in dining room.

Years and catalog numbers: 1916 (2024, 264P249); *1917* (C249, C2024)

Price: $624 to $740

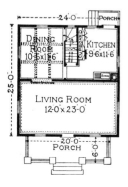

THE MARINA

*T*his house is quite out of the ordinary in many respects. Note the concrete block posts surmounted by graceful wood columns. The paneled stucco porch gable adds much to the appearance, and the Fire-Chief Shingle Roll Roofing sets off the house to the best advantage. You have the choice of two different exterior designs. This house can be built with the rooms reversed.

• •

Details and features: Five rooms and one bath. Full-width front porch supported by concrete and tapered wood piers; gabled or shed dormer with flower box; exposed roof rafter tails. Beamed ceiling in dining room.

Kitchen

Years and catalog numbers: 1918 (2024); 1919 (2024); *1921* (2024, 7024)

Price: $1,289 to $1,632

Locations: Blue Island, Dundee and Oak Glen, Ill.; La Fontaine, Ind.; Hastings, Minn.; Cincinnati, Cleveland and Youngstown, Ohio

No. 2024

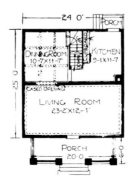

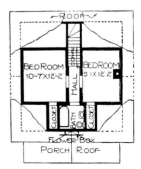

THE CARLIN

The exterior of this house is quite pleasing, and the balcony on the second floor is a much-desired feature. A door can be substituted for one of the second-floor windows leading to the balcony at very little expense.

. . . .

Details and features: Five rooms and one bath. Full-width front porch; shed dormer opening onto balcony; exposed roof rafter tails and knee braces. Semiopen stairs.

Year and catalog number: 1918 (3031)

Price: $1,172

. . . .

Similar to: The Windsor

Differences: Door to kitchen on side; no exposed roof rafter tails

Years and catalog numbers: 1922 (3193); 1925 (3193); 1926 (P3193); 1928 (C3193); 1933 (3193)

Price: $1,216 to $1,605

Location: Washington, D.C.

. . . .

Similar to: The Lebanon

Differences: Shed dormer; no balcony; front porch with gabled roof

Years and catalog numbers: *1918* (3029); 1919 (3029); 1921 (3029); 1922 (3029)

Price: $1,092 to $1,465

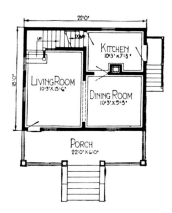

The Lebanon

THE VALLONIA

The Vallonia is a prize bungalow home. It has been built in hundreds of localities. Photographs and many testimonials confirm the splendid features and value. Customers tell of saving as much as $2,500 on their Vallonia and often selling at a big profit. The Vallonia is favored by a sloping, overhanging roof and shingled dormer which has three windows. Roof has a timber cornice effect. Sided with cypress (the wood eternal). Perfect harmony in all details marks the architecture of the Vallonia.

. . . .

Details and features: Eight rooms and one bath. Full-width front porch supported by brick and wood piers; shed dormer.

Years and catalog numbers: 1921 (3049); 1922 (13049); 1925 (13049AX); *1926* (13049A); 1928 (C13049A, C13049B); 1929 (P13049A, P13049B); 1932 (13049A, 13049B); 1933 (13049A, 13049B); 1934 (13049A, 13049B); 1935 (13049A, 13049B); 1937 (13049A, 13049B); 1939 (13049A, 13049B)

Living room

Dining room

Price: $1,465 to $2,479

Locations: Elmhurst and Park Ridge, Ill.; Bowling Green, Ky.; Bridgeton, N.J.; Cincinnati, Ohio; Perrysville, Pittsburgh and Rosalyn, Pa.

Bedroom

THE BANDON

The Bandon is a neat, practical and modern design very much in favor with discriminating builders. From the pleasant shelter of the big front porch one enters the attractive living room. This house can be built with the rooms reversed.

. . . .

Details and features: Six rooms and one bath. Full-width front porch supported by tapered stucco piers; gabled dormer; exposed roof rafter tails and knee braces. Fireplace in living room; French doors between living room and enclosed dining porch; sleeping porch off rear.

Years and catalog numbers: *1921* (3058); 1922 (13058)

Price: $2,499 to $2,794

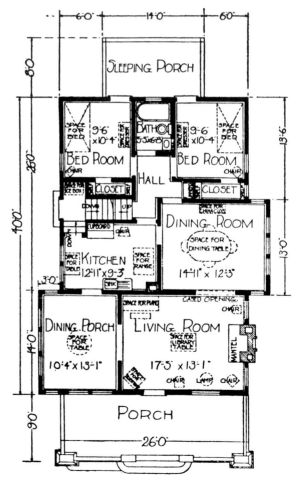

THE VINITA

This house with its stylish entrance and paneled walls will stand favorable comparison with many houses costing nearly twice as much. The size and fine proportions of the living room make it an easy matter to furnish and decorate it attractively. There is a fine sense of balance and good taste about it.

Details and features: Five rooms and one bath. Front porch; shed dormer; exposed roof rafter tails; paneled exterior walls.

Years and catalog numbers: *1921 (6001); 1922 (6001)*

Price: $1,154 to $1,240

THE DELMAR

The Delmar is one of our most popular designs. One looking at the exterior of this house is impressed with its stability. A study of its floor plan reveals the unusual care taken by the architect to give the largest rooms possible. Special attention is drawn to the large living room and large bedroom on the second floor and the well-arranged stairway.

Details and features: Five rooms and one bath. Full-width front porch with gabled dormer above; glazed front door. Fireplace and built-in bookcases in living room; semiopen stairs.

Year and catalog number: 1924 (3210)   Price: $2,220

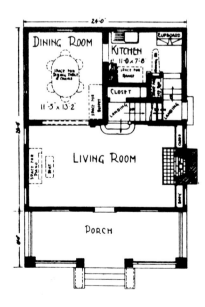

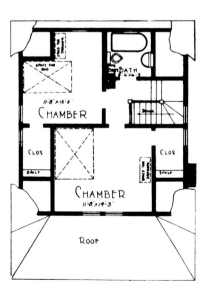

THE AUBURN

*W*hile the Auburn, being only 18 feet wide, is well suited for a narrow lot, it will look very well on a wider lot. The design is suitable for city, suburb or country. The rafter ends around the sun room and the combination of siding and shingles add much to the appearance of the house. In this model you will find a splendid arrangement of the rooms.

. . . .

Details and features: Seven rooms and one bath. Sun room with exposed roof rafter tails; shed dormer. Fireplace flanked by built-in bookcases in living room.

Year and catalog number: 1925 (3199)

Price: $2,116

. . . .

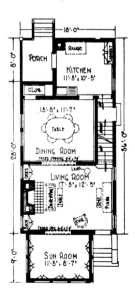

Similar to: The Albany

Differences: Full-width front porch in place of sun room; no fireplace

Year and catalog number: 1926 (P13199)

Price: $2,232

The Albany

THE SHERIDAN

The Sheridan is a popular type of bungalow, planned to give the utmost livable space for its size, 28 by 38 feet. The upkeep cost is very small. All the materials are high grade. The porch extends across the entire front of the bungalow and may be screened or glazed and used as a most desirable room. This house can be built with the rooms reversed.

Details and features: Eight rooms and one bath. Full-width front porch supported by paired square columns; gabled dormer; glazed front door.

Years and catalog numbers: 1925 (3224); *1926* (P3224); 1928 (C3224); 1929 (P3224)

Price: $2,095 to $2,256

THE HOMEWOOD

 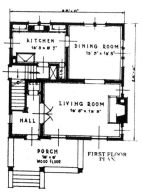

The Homewood has the cozy appearance so much admired in smaller houses, yet skillful planning enables it to retain the good size and decided advantage of large two-story homes. Considerable thought has been given to the design, size, style of the windows, fireplace, chimney, shutters, front porch, trellises and shingles. Moreover, the interior has been planned along modern lines to afford the greatest livable space and convenient arrangement as well as impart an air of quality.

Details and features: Six rooms and one bath. Trellised front porch; shed dormer. French doors between hall and living room; semiopen stairs.

Years and catalog numbers: *1926* (P3238); 1928 (P3238); 1929 (P3238)

Price: $2,610 to $2,809

THE WAYNE

The Wayne is one of our most popular designs. One looking at the exterior of this house is impressed with its stability. A study of its floor plan reveals the unusual care taken by the architect to give the largest rooms possible. Special attention is drawn to the large living room and large bedroom on the second floor and the well-arranged stairway.

. . . .

Details and features: Five rooms and one bath. Full-width front porch supported by square columns; gabled dormer. Swinging door between kitchen and dining room; open stairs.

Years and catalog numbers: 1925 (13210); *1926* (P13210); 1928 (C13210); 1929 (P13210)

Price: $1,994 to $2,121

Living room

Kitchen

Dining room

THE LA SALLE

The La Salle, colonial duplex or "income bungalow," makes a worthwhile and high-grade investment. It provides: (1) a home for the owner; (2) a steady income from rental of the other apartment. In the long run the owner finds such rental actually pays for the investment. That's why the income bungalow is such a decided success.

. . . .

Details and features: Nine rooms and two baths. Two-family house. Front porch supported by paired square columns; shed dormer. French doors between living and dining rooms on first floor; built-in china cabinets between kitchen and dining room on second floor.

Years and catalog numbers: *1926* (P3243); 1928 (C3243); 1929 (P3243); 1932 (3243)

Price: $2,530 to $2,746

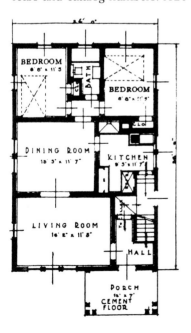

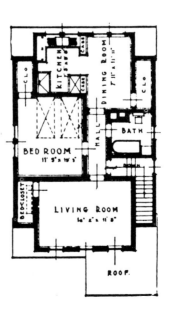

THE BEDFORD

A substantial deservedly popular design, economical because face brick is used for the first story only, the dormer and gables being shingled. Complete five-room home on the first floor, with direct outside access to second floor. Second floor can be left unfinished temporarily or built with choice of two plans as shown.

Details and features: Eight rooms and one or two baths. Brick exterior on first floor; shingled gable; full-width front porch with brick piers; gabled dormer. Optional second floor, with two floor plans; fireplace in living room.

Years and catalog numbers: 1926 (P3249); 1928 (C3249A, C3249B); 1929 (P3249A, P3249B); *1933* (3249A, 3249B)

Price: $2,242 to $2,673

THE PITTSBURGH

T he Pittsburgh is a two-story house, designed to reflect the pleasing exterior lines of a modern bungalow and the interior efficiency of a high-grade apartment. Every detail is of Honor Bilt quality and construction, thereby establishing a high value. Our very attractive direct-from-factory price makes the Pittsburgh a money-saving opportunity.

Details and features: Five rooms and one bath. Brick veneer on first floor exterior; full-width front porch supported by three brick piers; shed dormer; bay window in dining room. Open stairs.

Years and catalog numbers: *1928* (C3252); 1929 (P3252)

Price: $1,827 to $1,838

THE ASHLAND

SIX ROOMS
BATH AND
BIG PORCH

he Ashland, a two-story home of Dutch colonial adaptation, is one of our most distinctive designs. It is the kind of a home that is always popular, has the most livable space for its size, is economical to erect and maintain, because it is square, and has a ready and profitable resale value. Typical of Dutch colonial architecture are the beautiful downward sweep of the roof, the dormer windows with their green shutters, the sheltered porch and snow-white columns, terraced front lawn, etc. Each architectural feature has its own historical or modernized background, even to the wood shingled roof, red brick chimney, cypress siding and divided light windows.

Details and features: Six rooms and one bath. Full-width front porch; shed dormer. Fireplace with built-in bookcase in living room; semiopen stairs.

Years and catalog numbers: 1927 (C5253); *1928* (C5253)

Price: $2,847 to $2,998

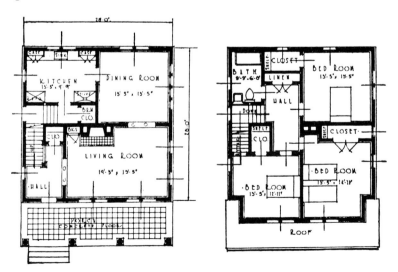

$\mathcal{E}$ nglish colonial architecture is expressed in this home, which was designed for a narrow city lot. It possesses a degree of character and distinction seldom found in a home of this size. The large front porch will be appreciated and enjoyed by all members of the household.

Details and features: Five rooms and one bath. Full-width front porch with square columns; 15-light front door. Arched opening between living and dining rooms.

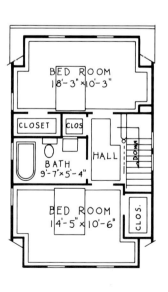

Year and catalog number: 1929 (P3275)

Price: $1,912

THE LORAIN

$\mathcal{A}$ t first glance, few would suppose that this charming colonial house contains six large, well-balanced rooms. You usually view the front entrance first and last, and your impression of this should be good as it is well balanced with the rest of the exterior features. From the modern woman's point of view, it is almost impossible to overemphasize the importance and convenience of having a first-floor bedroom. It not only comes in handy for guests but can be furnished to also act as a den or library.

Details and features: Six rooms and one bath. Portico with paired columns and arched gable; arched dormer. Arched opening between living and dining rooms.

Years and catalog numbers: 1929 (P3281); 1933 (3281); *1934* (3281); 1935 (3281); 1937 (3281); 1939 (3281)

Price: $1,287 to $1,845

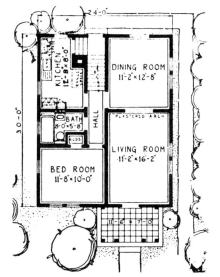

THE KENFIELD

$\mathcal{F}$rom every viewpoint, the Kenfield reveals the charm of those lovely old Maryland homes which seem literally tied to the ground by ramblers and hollyhocks. Large sunny rooms and numerous conveniences fulfill all the fair promises of the exterior.

. . . .

Details and features: Seven rooms and one and a half baths. One-story wing with gabled roof in front; two-story porch in rear. Fireplace in living room; built-in china cabinet in dining room; built-in window seat in upstairs bedroom.

Years and catalog numbers: *1931* (3343); 1932 (3343); 1933 (3343)

Price: No price given

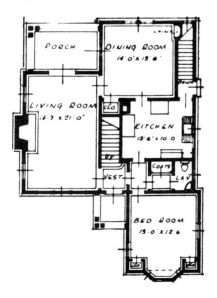

THE MILLERTON

This new type of American design home is meeting with considerable popularity on account of the compact, efficient room arrangement but gives a very serviceable arrangement at a minimum cost. The exterior is planned to be covered with brick, which we suggest finishing with whitewash, leaving the quoins at the corners with a red colored brick exposed.

. . . .

Details and features: Six rooms and one and a half baths. Brick exterior; one-story entrance; corner quoins; hipped dormer. Fireplace in living room.

Years and catalog numbers: *1931* (3358); 1932 (3358); 1933 (3358)

Price: No price given

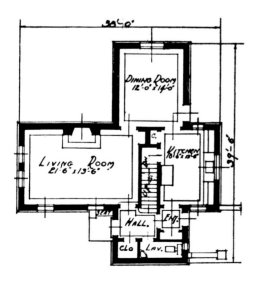

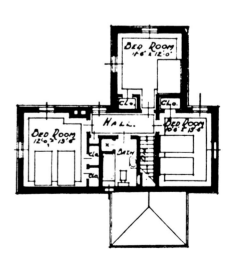

THE HAWTHORNE

The Hawthorne fits modern conditions by turning the living and dining rooms toward the garden and building a garden porch under the main roof. The side entrance prevents tradesmen from intruding. With the kitchen in front, the housewife can keep an eye on things and reach either front or back door in a few steps. A compact, comfortable and up-to-date colonial home at a real saving.

· ·

Details and features: Six rooms and one bath. Enclosed vestibule; shed dormer. Arched opening between living room and dining room and rear porch off living room.

Years and catalog numbers: *1931* (3311); 1932 (3311); 1933 (3311)

Price: No price given

THE LAKECREST

This story-and-a-half bungalow-type design contains everything to be desired in a small home. Exterior attractiveness and practical interior arrangement at a very low cost. Note the graceful way the main roof curves down over the large front porch. At a small additional cost, the porch can be screened in for summer.

· ·

Details and features: Five rooms and one bath. Full-width front porch supported by tapered piers; gabled dormer. Fireplace in living room; semiopen stairs.

Years and catalog numbers: *1931* (3333); 1932 (3333); 1933 (3333)

Price: No price given

· ·

Identical to: The Marion

Years and catalog numbers:
1933 (13333); 1934 (13333);
1935 (13333); 1937 (13333);
1939 (3415)

Price: $1,330 to $1,537

THE HONOR

The Honor is a home that not only looks well at a distance but makes a still more favorable impression upon closer investigation. You will recognize in this house some of the features that have made the historical colonial homes of America admired for years, together with many modern touches that add to its attractiveness. Notice the thatched effect of the roof, the inviting front entrance, the big handsome windows and the decorative trellis.

. . . .

Details and features: Eight rooms and one bath. Rounded roof edges; trellises on front wall; three eyebrow dormers; sleeping porch on second floor. Breakfast alcove off kitchen; semiopen stairs.

Years and catalog numbers: 1921 (3071); *1926* (P13071)

Price: $2,747 to $3,278

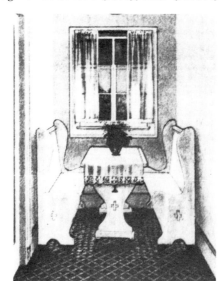

Breakfast alcove

Gabled roof, one and a half stories, side entrance, two or more front dormers

THE WINTHROP

FIVE ROOMS AND BATH

The Winthrop presents a modernized edition of early American architecture, when simplicity and perfect balance featured that period. Examples of this really fine type are found in many sections originally settled by our ancestors. Yet, in spite of the changing times, this style of architecture is still considered one of the best. A visit to some of the better suburban communities of our largest cities reveals the fact that handsome profits are made when houses of this style are on the market. The exterior expresses good taste. Interior planning is admittedly practical and modern.

. . . .

Details and features: Five rooms and one bath. Hooded gabled front entry supported by six columns; batten shutters. Fireplace with colonial mantel in living room; arched opening between living and dining rooms.

Year and catalog number: 1928 (P3264)

Price: $1,921

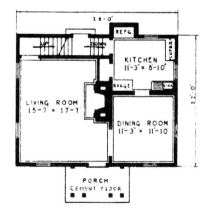

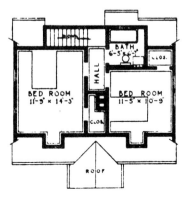

THE TRENTON

*I*n the Trenton a graceful roof line over a trim exterior tells its own tale of quiet good taste and pleasant living. Spacious, airy, well-arranged rooms with unusual built-in features afford utmost comfort. Living, dining and breakfast rooms face the garden, likewise all three upstairs bedrooms. Service entrance connects with garage or any part of house.

. . . .

Details and features: Eight rooms and three baths. Attached garage; two chimneys; four gabled dormers; six-panel front door. Fireplace flanked by bookcases in living room; concave china closet in dining room; dining alcove off kitchen; maid's room; open stairs.

Years and catalog numbers: *1932* (3351); 1933 (3351)

Price: No price given

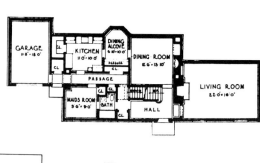

THE GORDON

The simple dignity and beauty of colonial architecture found many expressions, one of the most interesting being the Cape Cod colonial, exemplified in the Gordon. Many of these sturdy houses still standing in New England are objects of pilgrimage to those who appreciate and love beautiful homes. Although face brick is often used for the chimney, good effect is obtained by using common brick whitewashed.

Details and features: Five or seven rooms and two baths. Side brick chimney; pilasters flanking front door; three gabled dormers. Optional second floor; fireplace in living room.

Years and catalog numbers: *1931* (3356); 1932 (3356); 1933 (3356)

Price: No price given

THE ATTLEBORO

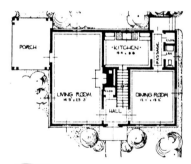

This type of Cape Cod home is one of the first designs built by the early New England settlers. Homes built over a hundred years ago grow old gracefully and still retain a certain warmth and beauty. It seems to have many friends in both urban and suburban areas. The Attleboro achieves distinction with its fine doorway, dormers, shuttered windows and correct architectural details. No "gingerbread" to get out of date. Outside walls are shown of cedar shingles but will look equally attractive with siding.

Details and features: Six rooms and one and a half baths. Side porch with paired columns; six-panel front door with transoms. Fireplace in living room; semiopen stairs.

Years and catalog numbers: 1933 (3384); 1934 (3384); 1935 (3384); *1937* (3384); 1939 (13384)

Price: $1,810 to $2,197

THE MILFORD

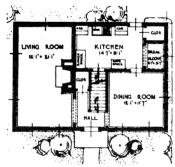

*T*he Milford is another true example of the Cape Cod New England home, more popular today than ever. Men are judged largely by the home they live in. A home like the Milford is a credit to you, your family and every neighborhood. This home expresses good taste on account of its carefully planned architectural details.

Details and features: Five rooms and one bath. Slat-type shutters; six-panel front door with transom. Fireplace in living room; semiopen stairs.

Years and catalog numbers: 1933 (3385); *1934* (3385); 1935 (3385); 1937 (3385, 3385A); 1939 (3385)

Price: $1,359 to $1,671

THE COLEBROOK

A small home but there is space on the second floor for a future bedroom, when your family and your pocketbook grow into it. The Colebrook has a quiet charm all its own. Two very nice features are the built-in window seat in the living room and the side porch off the living room. The dining nook, one of those step-saving, time-saving arrangements typical of small homes, is just large enough for your needs. A compact little house, you'll say, with one eye to the future and one to your budget.

Details and features: Four or five rooms and one bath. Fieldstone front wall; side porch with paired columns; two gabled dormers. Optional second floor; built-in window seat in living room; dining nook off kitchen.

Year and catalog numbers: 1939 (13707, 13707A)   Price: $1,608 to $1,728

THE WARREN

*I*t's just like meeting an old friend when you see the Warren—that same feeling of complete ease and satisfaction comes over you. The Warren is a restful home—a haven for you to shut out the rest of the world. The lines are typically Cape Cod—trim and neat as a pin, broken only by the two dormer windows. It's so simply arranged that you can easily build it on as small as a 35-foot lot.

Details and features: Five rooms and one bath. Two gabled dormers; dentil cornice; six-panel front door.

Year and catalog number: 1939 (13703)

Price: $1,506

THE BRANFORD

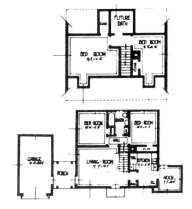

A gracious, seven-room house with a thought to the future—you may add a second-floor bath whenever you feel you can afford it. The porch off this living room serves as a shelter for you to reach the garage in bad weather. (It's an efficient, time-saving idea to connect the garage to the house. You'll appreciate it.) The elongated plan balances itself on the opposite side by an extended, very compact kitchen.

Details and features: Seven rooms and one or two baths. Detached garage connected by breezeway; two gabled dormers. Six-panel front door with shutters; semiopen stairs.

Year and catalog number: 1939 (13712)

Price: $2,010

THE MALDEN

*T*he Malden is the kind of house that puts a lift in your soul—good looks galore, yet full of practical, pet economies. The garage is conveniently attached to the house, and there is a lavatory on the first floor. We like to call it "common-sense planning." The living room is a dream—large, roomy, with a fireplace . . . the kitchen, a homemaker's paradise-on-earth.

Details and features: Six rooms and one and a half baths. Attached garage; side porch with paired columns; two gabled dormers; six-panel front door with sidelights. Fireplace in living room; open stairs.

Year and catalog number: 1939 (3721)   **Price:** $2,641

THE NANTUCKET

*T*he Cape Cod cottage design is the backbone of the Nantucket. It gives the house character and a type of beauty and balance that cannot be achieved by any other kind of design. The Nantucket has one of those pleasant, unmistakable New England personalities. It impresses you definitely from the first moment you see it. The Nantucket can be as large or as small as you want. You may finish only the first-floor rooms and still have comfortable living quarters. You can finish the second floor any time in the future.

Details and features: Four or six rooms and one bath. Two gabled dormers; dentil cornice; six-panel front door. Optional second floor.

Year and catalog numbers: 1939 (13719A, 13719B)

Price: $1,360 to $1,536

THE MEDFORD

$\mathcal{M}$ ove into the Medford— bag and baggage—and rub elbows with prim Cape Cod charm and New England traditions. You'll like the Medford for all its little conveniences that make a home comfortable. For instance, the cheery fireplace in the living room and the portico which leads from the attached garage to the front door.

· · · · · · · · · · · · · · · · · · · ·

Details and features: Six rooms and one bath. Attached garage; three gabled dormers; six-panel front door. Fireplace in living room; semiopen stairs.

Year and catalog numbers: 1939 (13720A, 13720B)

Price: $1,715 to $2,068

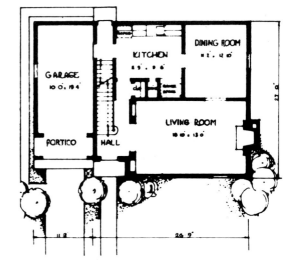

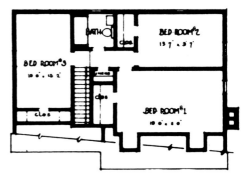

THE BARRINGTON

The Barrington retains the dignity of an old English home and has the practical interior of modern American architecture. Whether you consider economy, beauty or convenience as of first importance, the Barrington assuredly meets these and every point of merit with satisfaction. Exterior features at once stamp the mark of quality. The well-balanced projection at the front forms the entrance; leading to it is a tapestry brick terrace, guarded by a decorative iron railing. Sided with wide shingles and exposed fireplace chimney.

. . . .

Details and features: Six rooms and one bath. Glazed front door off open terrace with iron railing. Fireplace flanked by high casement windows in living room; breakfast nook off kitchen.

Years and catalog numbers: *1926* (P3241); 1928 (C3260); 1929 (P3260)

Price: $2,329 to $2,606

. . . .

Similar to: The Cambridge

Differences: Brick exterior; half-timbered and stucco gables; batten door with wrought iron hinges; diamond-paned casement windows

Year and catalog number: 1931 (3289)

Price: No price given

The Cambridge

Gabled roof, one and a half stories, projecting gabled side entrance

THE WILLARD

The Willard is a two-story English cottage type of home and is a remarkable value due to careful planning and saving created by our Honor Bilt system of construction. The projection at the front, which forms the vestibule and closet, is very graceful in appearance. The exterior walls are covered with clear red cedar shingles, a very popular wall covering for this type of home. The front door is made of clear white pine of V-shape batten design and is decorated with a set of ornamental wrought iron hinges. The lantern over the front door is of English design. Batten-type shutters to match the front door design are used with the double windows in the front of the dining room on the first floor.

. . . .

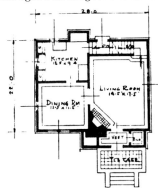

Details and features: Five rooms and one bath. Brick chimney in front; front terrace; arched front door with strap hinges. Corner fireplace with colonial mantel in living room.

Years and catalog numbers: 1928 (C3265); 1929 (P3265); 1932 (P3265); 1933 (3265); *1937* (3265)

Price: $1,477 to $1,997

. . . .

Similar to: The Randolph

Difference: Stucco and brick exterior

Year and catalog number: 1932 (3297)

Price: No price given

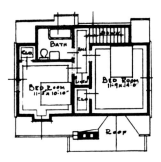

THE CLAREMONT

*A*mericanized English style of architecture is expressed in the lines of this six-room bungalow. The front entrance is unusual in design and forms a convenient vestibule and clothes closet.

Details and features: Six rooms and one bath. Arched front door.

Years and catalog numbers: 1929 (P3273); *1931* (3273); 1932 (3273); 1933 (3273)

Price: $1,437

THE ROCHELLE

*B*y careful planning, it is possible to obtain an efficient, practical arrangement in a small design. Americanized English architecture has been expressed in the lines of this home. Good window arrangement, with batten-type shutters, solid white pine batten front door and wood shingles for siding—all a few of the noticeable exterior details.

Details and features: Four rooms and one bath. Batten shutters; arched front door with strap hinges.

Years and catalog numbers: 1929 (P3282); *1931* (3282); 1932 (3282); 1933 (3282)

Price: $1,170

Similar to: The Fair Oaks

Difference: Front gable reversed

Year and catalog number: 1933 (13282)

Price: $972

THE BELLEWOOD

The Bellewood is another happy combination of a well laid out floor plan with a modern attractive exterior. The design is an adaptation of a small English cottage. Exterior walls are planned to be covered with gray prestained clear red cedar shingles. The graceful manner in which the front gabled roof curves over the vestibule gives this home an unusually inviting entrance. Careful grouping of the windows and batten-type shutters also add to the exterior.

. . . .

Details and features: Five rooms and one bath. Shingled exterior; arched front door with strap hinges. Arched opening between vestibule and living room.

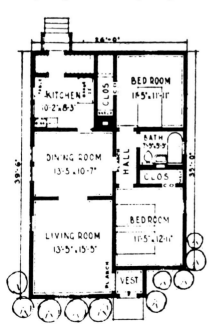

Years and catalog numbers: *1931* (3304); 1932 (3304); 1933 (3304)

Price: No price given

. . . .

Similar to: The Pembrook

Difference: Shingled exterior

Year and catalog number: 1933 (3325)

Price: $1,259

THE BROOKWOOD

*E*nglish lines in this exterior harmonize well with the excellent window arrangement and the entrance detail. Six large rooms of real comfort at a low cost.

. . . .

Details and features: Six rooms and one bath. Vestibule with steeply pitched roof; shutters; glazed front door.

Years and catalog numbers: 1932 (3033); *1933* (3033)   Price: $1,328

THE MAPLEWOOD

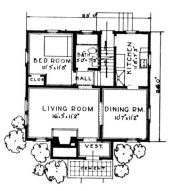

*T*he Maplewood is a story-and-a-half English type in which the front gable projection and fireplace chimney form an important part. The exterior walls are planned to be covered with gray prestained wood shingles laid with a wide exposure to form a pleasing background for the dark colored shutters, roof and chimney. A batten-type front door with ornamental iron strap hinges and English lantern above add considerably to the front elevation.

. . . .

Details and features: Six rooms and one bath. Brick chimney in front; batten shutters; arched front door with strap hinges. Fireplace in living room.

Years and catalog numbers: *1932* (3302); 1933 (3302)

Price: No price given

THE STRATHMORE

The lure of Old World charm and the luxury of New World comfort are incorporated in this beautiful six-room bungalow. Equal to the skill with which stucco, stone, brick and wide shingles are used in the English exterior are the elegance and completeness of the interior appointments. Colors which will emphasize the protecting sweep of the roof as it shelters the entrance and enhance the contrast which makes the exterior effective would be as follows: buff stucco, cream stone, dark red and brown brick and gray wood shingles.

. . . .

Details and features: Six rooms and one and a half baths. Stucco and shingled front wall; front terrace; pointed arched front door with strap hinges. Fireplace flanked by built-in window seat and cove ceiling in living room; arched opening between living and dining rooms.

Years and catalog numbers: 1932 (3306); 1933 (3306); *1934* (3306); 1935 (3306); 1937 (3306)

Price: $1,627 to $1,757

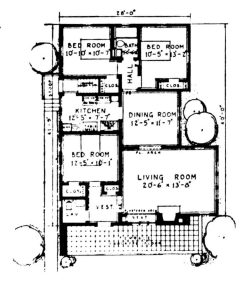

THE CLIFTON

*T*he Clifton's first floor is a complete bungalow in itself. If the second floor is finished, the front bedroom on the first floor can be converted into a cheerful nursery, sewing room or library.

. . . .

Details and features: Five or seven rooms and one bath. Arched front door. Optional second floor; twin closets flanking front entrance; arched opening between living and dining rooms.

Years and catalog numbers: 1932 (3305); *1933* (3305)

Price: $1,660

THE HILLSBORO

*T*he exterior walls of this most attractive home are planned to be finished with old English or tavern face brick. We suggest colors ranging from light reds and browns to dark blues and a few blacks. Lots of color and a little careless touch to the stonework, shutters and wrought iron rail will give the right feeling. Warm shades of cream and brown in the stone will be helpful.

. . . .

Details and features: Six rooms and one and a half baths. Brick and stone exterior; attached garage; front terrace; arched front door with strap hinges. Fireplace flanked by built-in window seats in living room; semiopen stairs.

Years and catalog numbers: 1932 (3308); 1933 (3308); *1934* (3308); 1935 (3308); 1937 (3308)

Price: $2,215 to $2,803

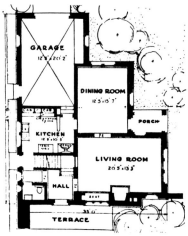

THE LYNNHAVEN

*E*nglish influence is seen in this cheerful, well-proportioned residence with deep-set door and flower boxes. Fitted within the steep front gable are a vestibule, closet, lavatory and upstairs bath. Cross ventilation throughout. The china closet in the breakfast room simplifies entertaining and saves steps.

. . . .

Details and features: Six rooms and one and a half baths. Shed dormer on front; front door recessed behind arch. Breakfast alcove off kitchen; semiopen stairs.

Years and catalog numbers: 1932 (3309); *1933* (3309); 1934 (3309); 1935 (3309); 1937 (3309)

The Belmont

Price: $2,227 to $2,393

Location: Waukesha, Wis.

. . . .

Similar to: The Belmont

Differences: Brick exterior; floor plan reversed

Years and catalog numbers: 1932 (3345); *1933* (3345)

Price: $2,600

No. 3309

No. 3309

THE HARTFORD

The Hartford's large combination living room and dining room opens from the front vestibule. The kitchen provides ample space for all necessary equipment. The exterior walls are planned to be covered with 24-inch red cedar stained shingles. Note the large, well-arranged windows and graceful roof lines.

Details and features: Four or five rooms and one bath. Front door with strap hinges. Two floor plans; front vestibule closet with window.

Years and catalog numbers: *1932* (3352A, 3352B); 1933 (3352A, 3352B)

Price: No price given

Identical to: The Aurora

Year and catalog numbers: 1933 (13352A, 13352B)

Price: $989 to $1,110

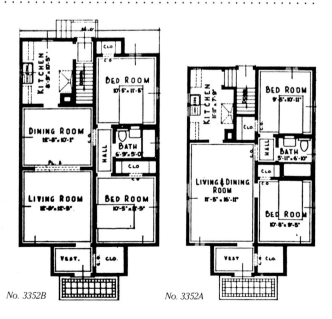

No. 3352B　　　　　No. 3352A

THE RIVERSIDE

*T*he distinctive entrance of this pleasant English cottage provides a vestibule and closet. Note the soft-toned walls of cedar shingles.

. . . .

Details and features: Six rooms and one bath. Arched front door.

Years and catalog numbers: *1933* (3324); 1937 (3324)

Price: $1,200 to $1,257

. . . .

Similar to: The Kendale

Difference: Brick and stucco exterior

Years and catalog numbers: 1932 (3298); *1933* (3298)

Price: $1,358

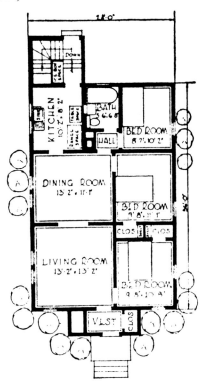

The Kendale

THE WILMORE

A five-room bungalow-type design, probably the most popular of all American homes. Harmonious gables, batten shutters, circle-head door and attractive grouping of windows show English influence, but the interior is typically modern American. The vestibule opens into a large, pleasant living room, with windows on two sides and good wall space.

. . . .

Details and features: Five rooms and one bath. Front terrace; batten shutters; arched front door. Arched opening between living and dining rooms.

Years and catalog numbers: *1933* (3327); 1934 (3327); 1935 (3327); 1937 (3327); 1939 (3327)

Price: $1,191 to $1,414

. . . .

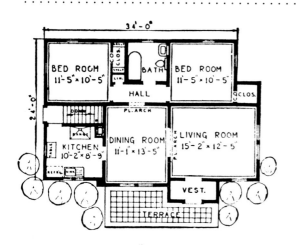

Identical to: The Jewel

Year and catalog number: 1932 (3310)

Price: No price given

. . . .

Similar to: The Roxbury

Difference: Brick exterior

Years and catalog numbers: 1932 (3340); 1933 (3340)

Price: $1,459

THE RIDGELAND

he Ridgeland is a story-and-a-half English-type home in which the details of the front gable projection and a fireplace chimney play an important part in the exterior appearance. The outside walls are planned to be covered with 24-inch clear red cedar shingles laid with a wide exposure and, when stained a light gray or painted white, form a pleasing background with the dark colors on the shutters, roof and chimney. The shutters are the batten type to match the circle-head front door, which is made more interesting by the use of ornamental iron hinges. The first-floor bedroom, if not needed, can be converted into a library, den or sun parlor.

. . . .

Details and features: Six rooms and one bath. Brick chimney in front; arched front door with strap hinges. Fireplace in living room.

Years and catalog numbers: 1933 (13302); *1934* (13302); 1935 (13302); 1937 (13302); 1939 (13302)

Price: $1,293 to $1,496

THE CROYDON

he Croydon will give you and your family a spanking new outlook—fresh and inspiring as the spring of the year. It will prove to you that you can have a small house, absolutely modern, without a single trace of faddishness—and that it can be really impressive, too.

. . . .

Details and features: Five rooms and one bath. Brick exterior; side porch with paired columns.

Year and catalog number: 1939 (13718)

Price: $1,407

No. 124

*T*his two-story bungalow is fast becoming a great favorite in the central eastern and western states. Everyone who has built it is pleased with the fine quality of the materials furnished and the big savings made on the order. It will be seen that this bungalow is so arranged that the large reception hall, dining room and extra-large living room practically make one big room extending the entire length of the house. This bungalow can be finished with Craftsman hardwood trim at a small advance in price.

· ·

Details and features: Eight rooms and one bath. Full-width front porch with shed roof; bay window in dining room; front door glazed with leaded glass. Fireplace with brick mantel in living room; open stairs.

Years and catalog numbers: 1911 (124); 1912 (124); *1913* (124); 1916 (124); 1917 (C124)

Price: $899 to $1,292

Locations: Texarkana, Ark.; Washington, D.C.; Clayton, Ga.; Lombard and Taylorville, Ill.; Grand Rapids, Mich.; Montvale, N.J.; Akin, Brooklyn, Dunkirk and New York, N.Y.; DuBois, Pa.

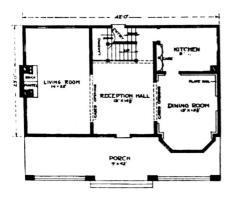

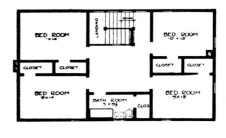

Gabled roof, two or more stories, side entrance

THE SPRINGFIELD

A simple house, Honor Bilt according to our plans and with our material. It will prove a very good paying investment, as it affords a great deal of room for a small amount of money.

Details and features: Seven rooms and one bath. Side and end entrances; gabled end porch; leaded crystal window in living room. Corner fireplace in living room; semiopen stairs.

Years and catalog numbers: 1911 (133); 1912 (133); 1913 (133); 1916 (133); *1918* (133)

Price: $660 to $1,516

Locations: Bloomington, Barrington and Sherman, Ill.; Gary, Ind.; Des Moines, Iowa; Big Timber, Mont.; Orange and Plainfield, N.J.; Fishkill on the Hudson, Oneida and Mount Kisko, N.Y.; Cincinnati, Toledo and Youngstown, Ohio; Philadelphia, Pa.

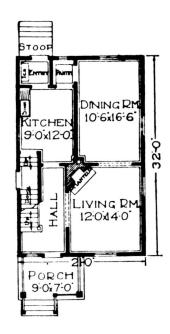

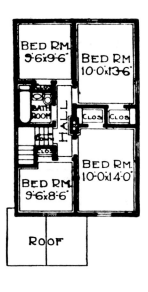

No. 166

A colonial Stonekote house with brick veneered corners, veneered brick base, a
large exterior brick chimney, Queen Anne windows
and French front doors. Hall doors are of Craftsman
design and glazed with leaded art glass.

· ·

Details and features: Six rooms and one bath. Stucco
exterior with brick veneered corners; wraparound
front porch. Rustic fireplace in living room; colored
leaded art glass in dining room; pocket doors between
dining room and hall; open stairs.

Years and catalog numbers: 1911 (166); *1912* (166)

Price: $1,001 to $1,095

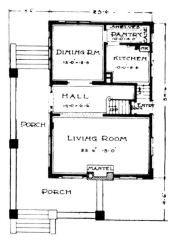

Living room

A Craftsman-style two-story house with a bungalow-style roof. Top lights of windows are divided into square designs to harmonize with this style of architecture. The arches between the porch columns are raised high enough to give good light in the rooms on the second floor.

Details and features: Seven rooms and one bath. Two-story front porch supported by square tapered columns. Beamed ceiling in living and dining rooms; built-in seats, bookcases and buffet in dining room; semiopen stairs.

Years and catalog numbers: 1911 (178); 1912 (178); *1913* (178)

Price: $1,250 to $1,611

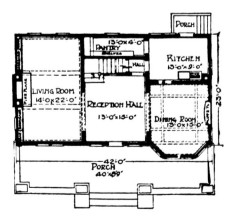

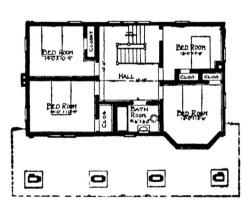

THE IVANHOE

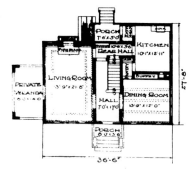

T his modern home was designed by one of Chicago's leading architects. It is up to date, attractive and well arranged for good ventilation and convenience. It contains many features found only in the more expensive houses, and, considering the low cost at which this house can be built, it makes a fine investment as well as a desirable home.

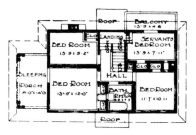

· ·

Details and features: Seven rooms and one bath. Two-story porch on side; shed roof over front entrance. Fireplace flanked by built-in bookcases and art glass windows in living room; French doors opening into living and dining rooms; paneled dining room with built-in buffet and beamed ceiling; open stairs.

Years and catalog numbers: 1912 (230); 1913 (230); *1916* (264P230, 264P200); 1917 (C230); 1918 (230)

Price: $1,663 to $2,618

Locations: Oak Park, Ill.; Ames, Iowa; Ann Arbor, Mich.

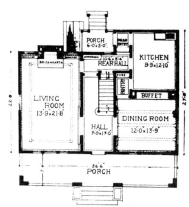

No. 200

· ·

Similar to: No. 200

Difference: Full-width one-story front porch

Years and catalog numbers: *1913* (200); 1916 (200)

Price: $1,528 to $1,663

No. 200

No. 200

No. 204

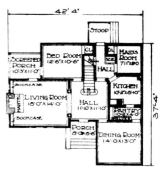

here is an individuality about this house that will please the man who is looking for something really different from the general run of buildings in any vicinity. Two unique features are apparent on the first glance at the illustration, namely, the wing for the dining room affording light from three sides and the screened sleeping porch on the second floor.

. . . .

Details and features: Seven rooms and one bath. Screened sleeping porch on second floor. Fireplace flanked by bookcases in living room; semiopen stairs.

Year and catalog number: 1913 (204)

Price: $1,318

THE MILTON

A colonial-style house with a wide overhanging roof. The center portion of the porch is two stories high with a gabled roof. On both ends there is a large open terrace with a pergola roof.

. . . .

Details and features: Seven rooms and one bath. Two-story gabled porch over entrance supported by square tapered columns; bay window in dining room; front door with beveled plate glass. Built-in bookcases and seats in living room; built-in buffet in dining room.

Years and catalog numbers: 1913 (210); 1916 (264P210); 1917 (C210); *1918* (210)

Price: $1,520 to $2,491

Locations: Norfolk, Neb.; Somerville, N.J.; New York, N.Y.; Fayette, Ohio

No. 264P202

*I*f you are looking for a house with 20th-century improvements, our Modern Home No. 264P202 will be an excellent selection. The massive brick columns lend an air of strength and durability to the whole building.

Details and features: Eight rooms and one bath. Porte-cochere with shed roof supported by brick columns; sleeping porch above front door; projecting eaves with triangular supports; bay window in den. Colonnaded opening between living and dining rooms; open stairs.

Year and catalog number: 1916 (264P202)   **Price:** $1,164

THE SEAGROVE

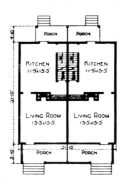 

*T*he Seagrove is a plain design relieved by a wide front porch. The arrangement of the rooms on both floors utilizes every inch of space. Built to accommodate two families, each family having a living room and kitchen on the first floor and two bedrooms with closets on the second floor. Separate doors from each porch to each living room.

Details and features: Eight rooms and no bath. Two-family house. Full-width front porch with hipped roof. Fireplace in living rooms.

Year and catalog number: 1918 (2048)   **Price:** $1,854

THE PALOMA

*F*or the man who is looking for a good-sized, two-story, six-room house, with bath, our Paloma will certainly make a profitable investment. Note the treatment of the front porch and how the square columns and exposed rafter ends contribute in making an unusual but impressive and dignified appearance. This house, painted white and with a red or sea green Fire-Chief Shingle Roll roof, which we furnish, will command the attention of those who see it.

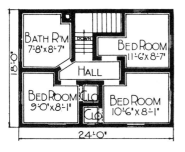

Details and features: Six rooms and one bath. Gabled porch over front door supported by paired square columns. Semiopen stairs.

Years and catalog numbers: 1917 (C2035); *1918* (2035); 1919 (2035)

Price: $688 to $1,418

Locations: Maitland, Fla.; Rochester, Minn.; Lincoln, Neb.; Manon and London, Ohio; Grove City, Pa.

THE PRESTON

A real Dutch colonial home, set off to its best advantage in pure white amidst luxurious foliage. The living room will satisfy the most exacting, and the paneled walls of the dining room reflect the most modern taste in interior decoration. Wall safe included at no extra cost.

. . . .

Details and features: Seven rooms and one bath. Sleeping porch on second floor; window boxes and shutters on second floor; recessed front door behind arch. Fireplace with rustic mantel and bookcases in living room; paneled dining and living rooms; kitchen with breakfast nook; open stairs.

Years and catalog numbers: *1918* (2092); 1921 (2092)

Price: $2,978 to $3,766

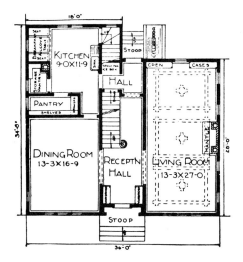

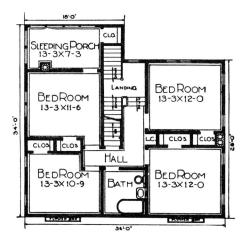

Living room

Dining room

Sleeping porch

Reception hall

Breakfast alcove in kitchen

Colonial stairway in reception hall

THE NORWOOD

*F*or thrifty builders this house can be built on a lot 20 feet wide. The second floor of the Norwood has two good-sized bedrooms and a bathroom.

Details and features: Five rooms and one bath. Side and end entrances; gabled end porch.

Years and catalog numbers: *1918* (2095); 1919 (2095); 1921 (2095); 1922 (2095); 1925 (2095); 1926 (P2095); 1928 (C2095)

Price: $948 to $1,667

Location: Cincinnati, Ohio

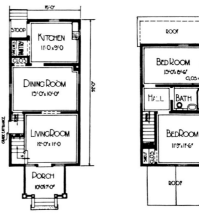

THE MORLEY

*T*his house was designed as a bargain in price, with special attention to an attractive exterior and an economical arrangement of floor plan. The shingles on the second story, laid alternately six and two inches to the weather, together with the colonial windows, produce a pleasing effect seldom found in a house priced so low.

Details and features: Four rooms and one bath. Side and end entrances; end porch with shed roof. Open stairs.

Year and catalog number: 1918 (2097)

Price: $837

THE BEAUMONT

$\mathcal{W}$e show in the illustration above a good view of the left elevation of our Beaumont Modern Home. This is done to secure your attention to the garage, which is part of the building, with the very popular private porch and the comfortable balcony on the second floor. This house can be built with the rooms reversed or without the garage.

Details and features: Six rooms and one bath. Attached garage; side porch with roof deck above; shed roof over front door supported by brackets. Window seat in dining room; semiopen stairs.

Year and catalog number: 1921 (3037)

Price: $2,136 to $2,374

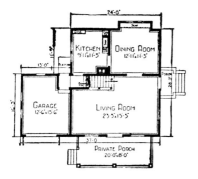

THE WARRENTON

$\mathcal{T}$his house has been selected by one of the largest corporations in the country for its better-class employees. The solidly constructed porch, the wood shingles on the second story and the Fire-Chief Shingle Roll Roofing give it a substantial and attractive appearance.

Details and features: Six rooms and one bath. Gabled porch over front door.

Year and catalog number: 1918 (3030)

Price: $1,288

THE LEXINGTON

*W*here can you find a more imposing and dignified study in modern colonial architecture? The wide entrance of pure white, contrasted with the green shutters, red brick chimney and green roof, surely will appeal even to the most aesthetic. Observe the stately pilasters at the corners, the dentils beneath the eaves and in the gables, the balance of design afforded by the sun parlor at the left and the dining porch on the right. Observe the stately colonial porch, in harmony with the rest. This house can be built with the rooms reversed.

Details and features: Seven or nine rooms and one and a half baths. Gabled porch over front door; roof deck over sun room. Fireplace with brick mantel in living room; French doors throughout ground floor; open stairs. Floor plan and exterior details change slightly in years 1928-33.

Years and catalog numbers: 1921 (3045); 1925 (13045); *1926* (P13045); *1928* (C3255); 1929 (P3255); 1932 (3255); 1933 (3255)

Price: $2,958 to $4,365

No. 13045

No. P3255

No. 13045

No. C3255

THE DURHAM

*W*hen you have admired the illustration of this house and glanced over the floor plans, you will agree that it is a model country house with the appearance of a city or suburban residence. The library is large enough to be used for a dining room if this arrangement suits the family better.

Details and features: Eight rooms and one bath. Gabled entrance porch; shed dormer above. Semiopen stairs.

Years and catalog numbers: *1921* (8040); 1922 (8040)

Price: $2,498 to $2,775

THE PRINCETON

*T*he Princeton possesses the dignity and charm of a high-class colonial home, combined with the most modern conveniences of the present day. The beautiful colonial porch with a modern or colonial entrance with sidelights—the pure white siding contrasted with green shutters, colonial brick chimneys and red or green roof—will appeal to the most discriminating.

Details and features: Six rooms and one bath. Front arch with gabled roof; shutters on front windows; front door with sidelights. Fireplace and built-in bookcases in living room; open stairs.

Year and catalog number: 1924 (3204)

Price: $3,073

THE MONTROSE

The Montrose is justly considered a beautiful home in any community, no matter how exclusive. Assuredly handsome and substantial, it is a rare tribute to the best of English colonial architecture. It is conveniently appointed, well planned and economical of upkeep. The exterior is adorned by a long projection around the middle of the house, varied only by the unusually lovely and hooded vestibule entrance. There are the red brick fireplace chimney, colonial windows with green shutters, except for the sun room, flower boxes on dining room and front living room windows, wide colonial siding and brick porch.

Details and features: Seven rooms and one bath. Entrance with hooded gable. Fireplace in living room; French doors between living and dining rooms.

Years and catalog numbers: *1926* (P3239); 1928 (C3239); 1929 (P3239)

Price: $2,923 to $3,324

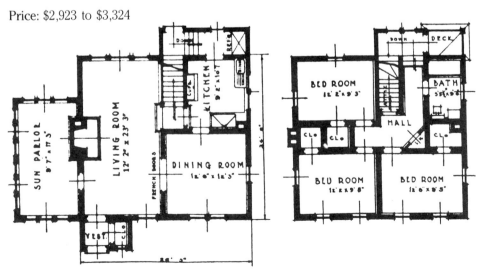

THE SPAULDING

SIX ROOMS, BATH AND BIG PORCH

The Spaulding combines a well-balanced exterior with an inviting and roomy interior. The Spaulding should bring a good return if rented out, a profit if sold or a heaping measure of satisfaction if the owner lives in it himself. Passersby look approvingly upon this house. The exterior includes a sheltered front porch supported, as it is, by two columns and a balustered railing with latticework beneath. The body of the house is sided with cypress beveled siding and roofed with wood shingles.

. . . .

Details and features: Six rooms and one bath. Full-width front porch with gabled roof. Corner fireplace in living room.

Year and catalog number: 1928 (P3257)

Price: $2,281

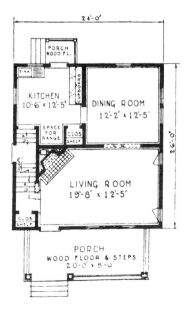

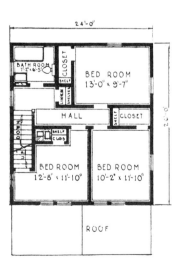

THE NEWARK

*A*rchitecturally correct in every detail, this splendid home has simple dignity and an unusually desirable floor plan, with center halls.

Details and features: Six rooms and one bath. Red cedar shingle exterior; projecting front entrance. Fireplace and nook in living room.

Years and catalog numbers: 1929 (P3285); *1933* (3285)

Price: $2,048 to $2,678

Similar to: The Worchester

Difference: Brick exterior

Years and catalog numbers: 1932 (3291); *1933* (3291)

Price: $2,315

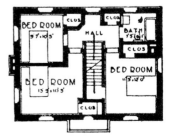

The Worchester

THE NEW HAVEN

This attractive colonial home speaks for itself. It is that type that is always admired, and its beauty lasts for years to come on account of its simplicity. That extra living room downstairs so often needed for library or den also opens off the main hall. Note the step-saving features of being able to go from the rear hall to the kitchen, rear porch or front entrance.

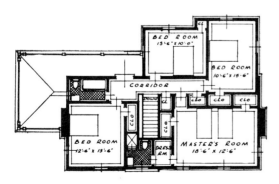

Details and features: Eight rooms and two and a half baths. Side porch with paired columns and roof deck above; pedimented front door. Fireplace in living room and library; open stairs.

Years and catalog numbers: *1931* (3338); 1932 (3338)

Price: No price given

THE JEFFERSON

The Jefferson is designed along the same lines as historic Mount Vernon and is a true example of southern colonial architecture—the same type that has endured in many instances for generation after generation. Exterior walls of white painted brick provide a substantial appearance and form a pleasing background for the dark green shutters and roof.

. . . .

Details and features: Eight rooms and two and a half baths. Brick exterior; two-story colonnaded porch. Fireplace in living room; open stairs.

Years and catalog numbers: 1932 (3349); 1933 (3349); *1937* (3349)

Price: $3,350

THE NORWICH

This attractive home is the answer to many requests for a compact colonial type with attached garage. This picturesque home makes an instant appeal to all who see it. The architect has ingeniously utilized every bit of available space and at low cost. The exterior walls are planned to be covered with wide siding, which when painted white or ivory forms a pleasing background for dark colored shutters and roof.

. . . .

Details and features: Seven rooms and one and a half baths. Attached double garage; front porch off living room; hooded gable over front door. Fireplace in living room; semiopen stairs.

Years and catalog numbers: 1932 (3342); 1933 (3342); *1937* (3342)

Price: $2,952

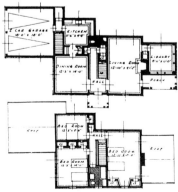

THE CARRINGTON

The Carrington derives its individuality and charm from the colonial houses of Salem, having an overhung second story. The stone finish of the first-story front wall adds strength and color and ties in nicely with the stone chimney and siding. A large dining room bay and wide terrace in back make the garden but an outdoor room. Notice the large size of the rooms and the step-saving position of the kitchen with its side entrance.

Details and features: Seven rooms and two and a half baths. Stone walls on ground floor; terrace off dining room; second-floor overhang. Built-in bookcases and fireplace in living room; open stairs.

Years and catalog numbers: *1931* (3353); 1932 (3353); 1933 (3353)

Price: No price given

THE HAMPSHIRE

Though recalling the historic Paul Revere House, with its overhung second story, shuttered windows and quaint individuality, the Hampshire within is a most modern home. For instance, the up-to-date house turns its back on an endless procession of autos and faces the living and dining rooms toward the garden. Service entrance with refrigerator alcove is at the side, convenient to driveway, and those who approach can be seen from the kitchen.

Details and features: Six rooms and two baths. Stone exterior on ground floor; second-floor overhang; bay window in living room. Fireplace in living room; open stairs.

Year and catalog number: 1933 (3364)

Price: No price given

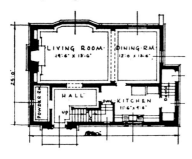

THE RICHMOND

*A*n American colonial home of exceptional beauty. Stately, with an air of real hospitality, this six-room Sears home is far lower in cost than its beautiful appearance suggests. The living room is 18 feet long, the dining room has a delightful bay window, and the kitchen is really modern.

Details and features: Six rooms and one bath. Side and end entrances; wood siding exterior; side porch with paired columns; bay window in dining room.

Years and catalog numbers: 1932 (3360); *1933* (3360)

Price: $1,692

The Berkshire

Similar to: The Berkshire

Difference: Brick exterior

Year and catalog number: 1933 (3374)   **Price:** $1,564

THE ALDEN

The designer who originated this center-entrance type of colonial home certainly anticipated the exact needs and tastes of many American families. As in the famous Paul Revere House, a second-story overhang gives unique character and affords more space upstairs.

Details and features: Six rooms and two and a half baths. Stone exterior on ground floor; second-floor overhang; steel casement windows. Fireplace in living room; sewing room off master bedroom; semiopen stairs.

Years and catalog numbers: *1933* (3366); 1934 (3366)

Price: $2,418 to $2,571

Similar to: The Haverhill

Differences: Brick exterior; five rather than three bays wide; pedimented front door

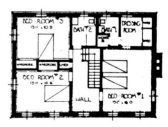

Years and catalog numbers: 1933 (3368); 1934 (3368); 1935 (3368); *1937* (3368); 1939 (3368)

Price: $2,276 to $2,585

The Haverhill

THE WEBSTER

*T*he newest homes, designed to meet today's needs, are frequently faced away from monotonous passing traffic, with living and dining rooms toward the garden. Thus the yard space is not cluttered by a drive to the back and by long walks for tradespeople. Front or back can be answered with few steps. From the kitchen an eye can be kept on both approaches. All parts of the house, including the lavatory, are reached from the garage, unseen from the living room. The large porch may be enjoyed without the family being on public view.

Details and features: Seven rooms and two and a half baths. Brick exterior on first floor; attached garage; second-floor overhang; six-panel door with sidelight. Built-in bookcases and fireplace in living room; open stairs.

Year and catalog number: 1933 (3369)

Price: $3,204

THE DARTMOUTH

*T*he striking beauty and convenience of this fine six-room colonial reflects real architectural skill and painstaking attention to detail. Instead of a center hall, the living room with fireplace occupies the front with a reception hall and well-lighted stair along the wall. Dining room, kitchen and delightful breakfast room overlook the garden.

Details and features: Six rooms and two and a half baths. Stone exterior on ground floor; second-floor overhang; bay window in dining room. Fireplace in living room; breakfast nook off kitchen; open stairs.

Years and catalog numbers: *1933* (3372); 1934 (3372)

Price: $2,648 to $2,864

THE BRISTOL

*A*rchitectural beauty and distinction mark this fine home. The low sweeping roof, broken by prim dormers, provides for the built-in garage, large entry and coat closet. The contrasting texture of stonework, brick and wide siding, the overhung second story, perfect proportion and sturdy construction promise long-lasting satisfaction.

. . . .

Details and features: Seven rooms and two and a half baths. Stone exterior on ground floor; attached garage; second-floor overhang; bay window in dining room. Fireplace in living room; "diner" off kitchen with built-in cupboards.

Year and catalog number: 1933 (3370)

Price: $2,958

. . . .

Similar to: The Schuyler

Differences: One additional room (a study above front entrance); gable over garage

Year and catalog number: 1933 (3371)

Price: $2,974

The Schuyler

THE GLEN VIEW

*W*ho would not take pride in being pointed out as the owner of this beautiful colonial home? There is a deep satisfaction in the possession of a home which truly expresses the good taste and the hospitality of the family and a keen enjoyment in pleasant, well-proportioned rooms arrayed for gracious living. The exterior is true colonial and is finished with clear beveled siding, painted white, with slat-type window shutters painted a contrasting dark color.

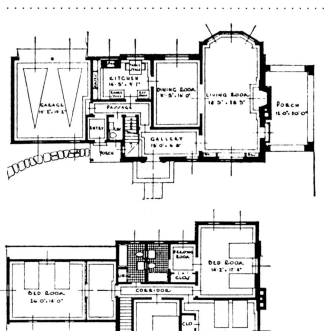

Details and features: Seven rooms and two and a half baths. Stone exterior on ground floor; attached double garage; second-floor overhang; side porch. Fireplace and built-in bookcases in living room; semiopen stairs.

Years and catalog numbers: 1933 (3381); *1937* (3381)

Price: $3,375 to $3,718

THE AMHERST

*W*ith its colonial front doorway, iron-railed stoop and varied wall covering, this home is an attractive realization of the factors which are favored in better suburban and city home developments today. Some home builders prefer these homes of brick, others of siding. The Amherst is a good example of satisfactory results by using both materials. The brickwork at the corners of the front wall is built out to form pilasters against which the frame projection of the second story finishes. The rear wall is treated full height with brick, while both gables have wide beveled siding.

Details and features: Seven rooms and one and a half baths. Brick and wood exterior; six-panel front door. Fireplace in living room; built-in bookcases in library.

Years and catalog numbers: 1933 (3388); *1934* (3388); 1935 (3388); 1937 (3388); 1939 (3388)

Price: $1,608 to $1,917

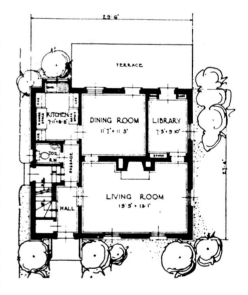

THE BELFAST

The Belfast, reminiscent of the beautiful colonial architecture so popular among the home builders of the early United States, reflects that good cheer and gracious dignity which made their hospitality famous. The colonial front entrance is a replica of the design which stands so invitingly on the entrance to the Perkins House, built at Castine, Maine, in 1769.

. . . .

Details and features: Six rooms and one and a half baths. Side and end entrances; side porch; pedimented end entrance.

Years and catalog numbers: *1934* (3367A); 1935 (3367A); 1937 (3367A)

Price: $1,604 to $1,698

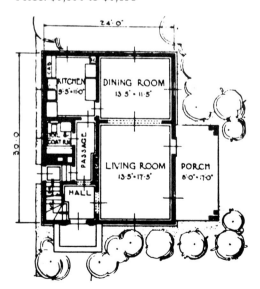
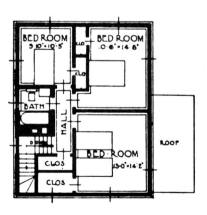

THE BERKLEY

The Berkley, with its plan A and its grown-up companion, plan B, has been created to illustrate that it is possible to plan and start your home in a small way and add "as you need." It has individuality and character, largely achieved by those touches of personality which lift it out of the commonplace. The exterior walls are planned to be covered with a clear grade of siding.

. . . .

Details and features: Five or seven rooms and one bath. Latticed columns supporting front porch. Two floor plans; fireplace in living room; semiopen stairs.

Years and catalog numbers: 1934 (3401A, 3401B); 1935 (3401A, 3401B); *1937* (3401A, 3401B)

Price: $1,110 to $1,435

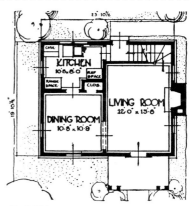

No. 3401A

No. 3401B

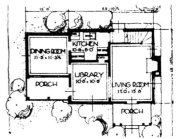

No. 3401B

THE NEWCASTLE

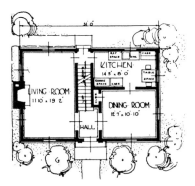

Standing four square to cheerful sunshine and admitting plenty of light in every room on cloudy days, this plan employs every inch of floor space advantageously. Here is a design of perfect symmetry in the disposition of windows and front doorway. You will be proud to know that this type of front entrance graced the homes of some of our famous early settlers. The original Richards House, built at Litchfield, Conn., in 1730 (over 200 years ago and still standing), has details almost identical to ones shown on the Newcastle.

Details and features: Six rooms and one bath. Second-floor portion of front wall has flush pattern boards; six-panel front door. Fireplace in living room.

Years and catalog numbers: 1934 (3402); *1935* (3402); 1937 (3402); 1939 (3402)

Price: $1,576 to $1,813

THE FULTON

The Fulton is a thoroughbred—a regular blue-blood of American colonial design. Every detail is completely, all-the-way correct. But still, it's not the least bit stiff or grim looking. (See how the high-rising roof breaks what would otherwise be square, solid lines!)

Details and features: Six rooms and one bath. Front entrance flanked by paired pilasters. Fireplace in living room.

Year and catalog number: 1939 (13702)

Price: $1,667

No. 59

A cozy cottage with three good-sized rooms, built of cement blocks. It has both a front porch and a rear porch.

Details and features: Three rooms and no bath. Concrete block exterior; front porch with shed roof; exterior doors glazed with lace design glass.

Years and catalog numbers: 1908 (59); *1911* (59)

Price: $163 to $765

No. 104

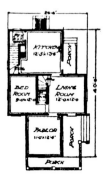

A seven-room house built on a stone foundation. It is sided with narrow beveled-edge cypress siding and has a cedar shingle roof.

Details and features: Seven rooms and no bath. Wraparound front porch supported by wood columns; glazed front door.

Years and catalog numbers: 1908 (104); 1911 (104); 1912 (104); *1913* (104)

Price: $580 to $1,425

Intersecting gabled roof, one to one and a half stories

*T*his cottage has three good-sized rooms with a pantry and closet. This is just the type of cottage that is being put up in large numbers by factory or mine owners who furnish their employees with cottages. It is sometimes built on a frame foundation instead of stone.

Details and features: Three rooms and no bath. Front porch with turned columns; decorated bargeboards; leaded glass window in living room; glazed front door.

Years and catalog numbers: 1908 (107); 1911 (107); 1912 (107); *1913* (107)

Price: $107 to $650

No. 116

A very good, substantial house, suitable for town, suburban or country home. All rooms are of good size and well arranged for convenience. Large cased opening between the sitting room and dining room, which practically makes these two rooms into one large room. Has an open stairway in the sitting room which faces directly toward the entrance of the parlor.

Details and features: Eight rooms and one bath. Corner front porch; gingerbread barge-boards. Built-in china closet in dining room; semiopen stairs.

Years and catalog numbers: 1908 (116); 1911 (116); 1912 (116); *1913* (116)

Price: $790 to $1,700

Locations: Gary, Hammond and Mishawaka, Ind.; Fenton, Iowa; Aurora, Neb.; Ithaca, N.Y.; Dresden, Ohio; Fairmont, W.Va.

THE AVOCA

A good substantial house with all rooms arranged to make the best possible use of all the space. The living room has three windows forming a bay, the center one having crystal leaded glass. A large kitchen with a good-sized pantry adjoining is entered through a door leading from the hall, thus enabling one to go to the kitchen without passing through the other rooms.

· ·

Details and features: Six rooms and no bath. Front porch; leaded glass window in front bay; front door glazed with beveled plate glass. Built-in china closet in dining room; open stairs.

Years and catalog numbers: 1908 (109); 1911 (109); 1912 (109); 1913 (109); 1916 (264P109); 1917 (C109); *1918* (109); 1919 (109)

Price: $590 to $1,754

Locations: East Hampton, Conn.; Belleville, Freeport and Oak Lawn, Ill.; Manly and Muscatine, Iowa; Bazine, Kans.; Mount Rainier, Md.; Greenfield, Mass.; Hart and Pearl, Mich.; Minnesota City, Minn.; Johnson and Ossining, N.Y.; Wheatland, Pa.; West Point, Va.

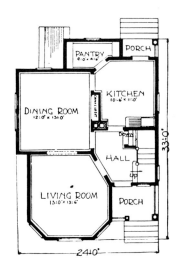

No. 136

A five-room house built of frame construction on a concrete block foundation. Sided with narrow beveled-edge cypress siding; gables and roof are shingled with cedar shingles.

. . . .

Details and features: Five rooms and one bath. Full-width front porch; front door glazed with leaded art glass. Sliding door between hall and parlor; open stairs.

Years and catalog numbers: 1911 (136); *1913* (136)

Price: $628 to $767

THE CRANMORE

*I*n the Cranmore we have a cottage of low cost, suitable for a 30-foot lot, and particularly adapted for a large family of moderate means. There is a large porch extending almost across the front of the house. Either of the two bedrooms on the first floor or kitchen may be entered from the living room.

. . . .

Details and features: Seven rooms and no bath. Front porch with hipped roof; glazed front door.

Years and catalog numbers: 1912 (185); 1913 (185); 1916 (185); 1917 (C185); *1918* (185)

Price: $637 to $1,283

Locations: Baileyville and Joliet, Ill.; Spencer, Iowa; Burr and Grand Meadow, Minn.; Stotzer, Wis.

*E*ight large and well-arranged rooms, with a vestibule and pantry on the first floor. A great deal of room for a small amount of money.

· ·

Details and features: Eight rooms and one bath. Front porch with shed roof supported by columns; double-hung sash with diamond panes in upper sash. Fireplace in parlor; sliding doors between living and dining rooms.

Years and catalog numbers: 1908 (1232); 1911 (1232); 1912 (1232); *1913* (175)

Price: $815 to $1,732

Locations: Brush, Colo.; Plainville, Conn.; Springerton, Ill.; Peabody, Kans.; Milford, Ky.; Edmore, Mich.; Manitowoc, Wis.

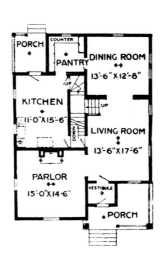

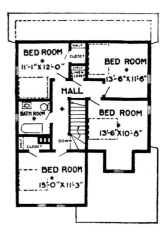

THE ROSSVILLE

*I*n the Rossville we have a neat-appearing cottage at a low cost compared with the average house of this size. It is so arranged that the ventilation is perfect throughout, and yet so compact that it may be heated at a very low cost.

Details and features: Six rooms and no bath. Wraparound front porch supported by wood columns; glazed front door. Semiopen stairs.

Years and catalog numbers: 1911 (171); 1912 (171); 1913 (171); 1916 (264P171); 1917 (C171); *1918* (171)

Price: $452 to $1,096

Locations: Windsor, Conn.; Freeport and Lansing, Ill.; LaPorte, Ind.; Sanborn, Iowa; Louisville, Ky.; Wrentham, Mass.; Virginia, Minn.; Sterling, Neb.; Franklin and Long Branch, N.J.; Poughkeepsie, N.Y.; Middlefield and Painesville, Ohio

Similar to: The Greenview

Difference: Turned porch columns; slightly different plan for second floor

Years and catalog numbers: 1911 (115); 1912 (115); 1913 (115); 1916 (264P136, 2015); 1917 (C2015, C136); 1918 (2015); 1921 (2015); 1922 (2015)

Price: $443 to $1,462

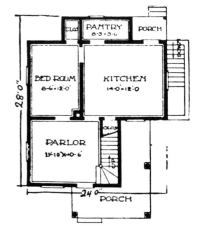

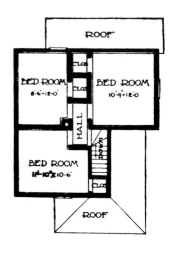

This bungalow is of the California type and has many points to recommend it to the builder who desires a real home. It is sided with roof boards up to the height of nine feet from the ground. Stonekote or stucco under the wide overhanging eaves. There are two entrances from the front porch, one being a French door which opens into the dining room and the other a Craftsman door which opens into the living room. A glance at the floor plan will show that this bungalow is admirably laid out.

Details and features: Five rooms and one bath. Half-timbered and stucco gables; overhanging eaves; exposed roof rafter tails. Beamed ceiling and fireplace in living room; built-in buffet in dining room.

Years and catalog numbers: 1912 (191); *1913* (191); 1916 (264P191)

Price: $892 to $966

Location: Springfield, Mass.; North Braddock, Pa.

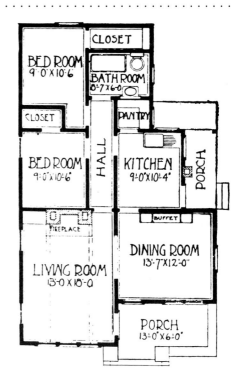

No. 199

A nicely arranged home of five rooms and bath. This cottage can be built at a low cost and will go nicely on a 25-foot lot. The front door opens into the living room. A large cased opening between the living room and dining room practically makes one large room of these two rooms.

. . . .

Details and features: Five rooms and one bath. Front porch with flat roof and square wood columns; exposed roof rafter tails. Pantry off kitchen.

Years and catalog numbers: *1912* (199); 1913 (199)

Price: $558 to $572

No. 264P105

A two-story inexpensive five-room frame house, suitable for any section of the country. It is just the kind of house for a family of moderate size. The large front porch with colonial columns adds greatly to its appearance.

. . . .

Details and features: Five rooms and no bath. Full-width front porch with hipped roof; stickwork in gables; overhanging eaves.

Years and catalog numbers: *1916* (264P105); 1917 (2012)   **Price:** $630 to $686

THE OSBORN

*B*ungalow authorities agree that this type of architecture has come to stay. They claim that as the years go by the bungalow will be even in more demand than at the present time, and should one wish to sell he will have little difficulty in finding a buyer. While the Osborn is neither extreme nor extravagant, it has all the earmarks of a cozy, well-planned, artistic home. The stuccowork of the porches, with red brick coping, the gables and chimneys at once draw the attention of the passerby. Then, again, the Craftsman front door and colonial windows still further enhance the bungalow effect.

Details and features: Five rooms and one bath. Stucco exterior; full-width front porch with gabled roof supported by stucco and wood piers; overhanging eaves, exposed roof rafter tails and bargeboards. Fireplace flanked by built-in bookcases in living room; beamed ceiling, plate rail and built-in buffet in dining room.

Years and catalog numbers: 1916 (264P144); 1917 (C244); *1918* (2050); 1919 (2050); 1921 (2050); 1922 (12050); 1925 (1205A); 1926 (P12050A); 1928 (C12050A); 1929 (P12050A)

Price: $1,163 to $2,753

Locations: Chicago and Joliet, Ill.; Dearborn, Mich.; Bay Village, Ohio; Brightwood, Morton and New Cumberland, Pa.

Sleeping porch

THE EDGEMERE

A nicely arranged home of five rooms and bath. Front door opens into the living room. A large cased opening between the living room and dining room practically makes one large room of these two rooms. Kitchen has a good-sized pantry with pantry case.

. . . .

Details and features: Five rooms and one bath. Corner porch; exposed roof rafter tails and knee braces; window boxes; glazed front door. Pantry off kitchen.

Years and catalog numbers: 1916 (264P199); 1917 (C199); *1918* (199)

Price: $647 to $1,124

Locations: LaPorte and Osgood, Ind.; Northwood, Iowa; Ann Arbor, Mich.; Massillon, Ohio

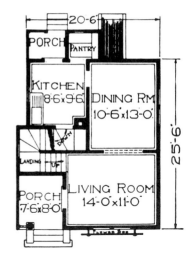

THE BELMONT

*I*n the Belmont bungalow we have one of those practical designs so much in favor along the Pacific coast. Built in the proper surroundings and given the proper color treatment, a bungalow of this kind will be an ornament to any community and a constant source of pleasure to the owner. A good color scheme is golden brown for the body of the house, which is sided with shingles, with white trim and green for the roof.

Details and features: Five rooms and one bath. Gabled front porch supported by tapered brick and wood piers; exposed roof rafter tails and knee braces. Fireplace with brick mantel in living room; bracketed opening between living and dining rooms; beamed ceiling in dining room.

Years and catalog numbers: 1916 (264P237); 1917 (C237); *1918* (237); 1921 (1237)

Price: $1,204 to $2,558

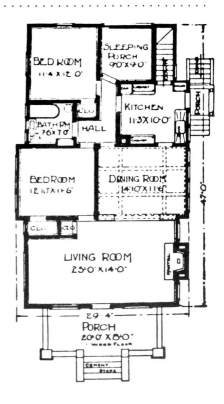

THE STONE RIDGE

*H*ere is a large comfortable house that will identify its owner as a person of good taste and judgment. It is of a type that will conform to the architecture of the best neighborhood and will be a place of distinction anywhere. "There is no place more delightful than one's own fireside," wrote Cicero, and here is a fireplace that will indeed be a delight, being so situated that it adds much to the exterior and lends its cheer to the whole living room.

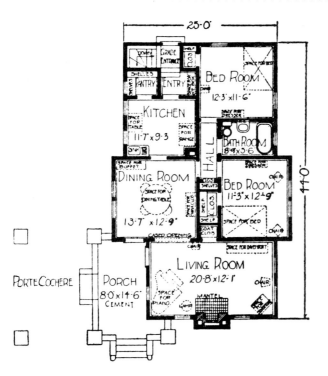

Details and features: Five rooms and one bath. Gabled front porch supported by tapered stone and wood piers; exposed roof rafter tails; cobblestone chimney; glazed front door. Fireplace in living room.

Year and catalog number: 1921 (3044)

Price: $1,995 to $2,229

THE URIEL

A neat home with five comfortable rooms and bath, conservative and economical. The wonder of the house is how exactly right all the little points are. It has a grade entrance and space for an ice box on the same level as the kitchen floor. The front bedroom and kitchen have cross ventilation. The bathroom is entered from a little hallway and not directly from the living room and is unusually well arranged. There are three big closets, and all rooms are well planned to accommodate furniture.

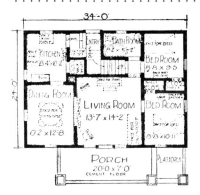

Details and features: Five or seven rooms and one bath. Gabled front porch supported by brick and wood piers; exposed roof rafter tails; glazed front door flanked by windows. Optional second floor.

Years and catalog numbers: *1921* (3052); 1922 (3052X); 1925 (3052X)

Price: $1,374 to $1,527

Location: Cleveland, Ohio

Similar to: The Conway

Differences: Concrete block porch piers; no half-timbering in porch gable

Years and catalog numbers: *1926* (P3052, P13052); 1928 (P13052); 1929 (P3052, P13052A, P13052B); 1933 (13052A, 13052B)

Price: $1,310 to $2,099

Location: Washington, D.C.

The Conway

THE LORNE

*I*n the Lorne the living room also serves as a dining room, an economy in space and money that has come into vogue very much in recent years. The house consists of four large rooms and a bath. There is a front porch and a modern grade entrance. Basement, attic, closets—every convenience, and every nook and corner a pleasure to those who appreciate a well-planned home.

. . . .

Details and features: Four or eight rooms and one bath. Front porch with half-timbered gable; exposed roof rafter tails. Optional second floor.

Years and catalog numbers: *1921* (3053, 13053); 1922 (3063, 13063)

Price: $1,286 to $2,002

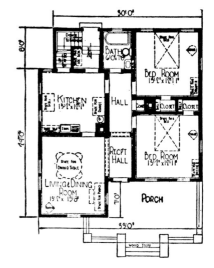

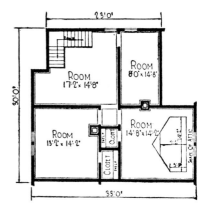

THE DEL REY

*W*ith its Roma-Tile roof, handsome entrance and French front door and windows, the Del Ray spells "Welcome" as plainly as modern architecture can make it. The Del Rey bungalow was first built in Pasadena, Calif., where it was admired by travelers from all parts of the world. Among its many unique features is the wide overhanging roof that shelters the windows and side walls from rain and sun and affords special protection to the three long French windows at the front, reflecting a touch of Italian and Spanish architecture.

. . . .

Details and features: Five rooms and one bath. Front porch with gabled canopy over front door; overhanging eaves and exposed roof rafter tails; casement windows. Fireplace flanked by built-in bookcases with glazed doors in living room; French doors between living and dining rooms.

Years and catalog numbers: *1921* (3065); 1922 (13065); 1925 (P13065); *1926* (P13065)

Price: $1,978 to $2,557

Locations: Pasadena, Calif.; Olmstead Falls, Ohio

No. P13065

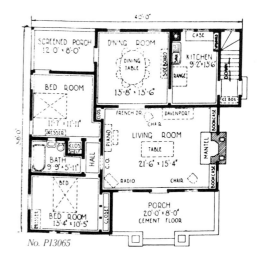

No. P13065

THE SUNNYDELL

This design, originally planned for a farmhouse, will look well in a suburban setting. On the second floor are located three good-sized bedrooms with a clothes closet and linen closet.

. . . .

Details and features: Six rooms and one bath. Asphalt shingle and half-timbered exterior; wrap-around front porch; gabled dormer in front. Semiopen stairs.

Year and catalog numbers: 1921 (3079, 3979)   **Price:** $1,571 to $1,746

THE VERNDALE

In this attractive home there are not many rooms, but they are really worthwhile in size and convenience. The exterior is pleasing in every detail. When extra sleeping room is needed, there is the big attic.

. . . .

Details and features: Three or five rooms and one bath. Asphalt shingle exterior; shed front porch supported by wood piers; exposed roof rafter tails; glazed front door. Optional second floor; breakfast alcove off kitchen.

Years and catalog numbers: *1921* (6003); 1922 (6003)

Price: $900 to $1,130

THE KILBOURNE

A customer who built the Kilbourne bungalow recently wrote to us as follows: "Our house has been the object of much admiration, not only from our friends but strangers, who in passing by will stop to look at the artistic front." The Kilbourne bungalow satisfies every family that has built it. Judge for yourself! The photograph and floor plan show the reason why the Kilbourne is such an outstanding value. See its sloping roof, the dormer, the overhanging eaves, the fireplace chimney, the large porch and the massive porch pillars!

. . . .

Details and features: Five or eight rooms and one bath. Front porch with steeply pitched gabled roof supported by tapered piers; exposed roof rafter tails. Optional second floor; fireplace flanked by windows in living room; French door between living and dining rooms.

Years and catalog numbers: 1921 (7013); 1925 (17013); *1926* (P17013); 1928 (P17013); 1929 (P17013)

Price: $2,500 to $2,780

Location: St. Matthews, Ky.

THE MITCHELL

FIVE ROOMS
AND BATH

he Mitchell follows the latest idea in English architecture with a touch of the popular California studio type. Two gables, one higher than the other, bring out the beauty of the shingled sidewall and high roof. The higher gable is right over the French doors, and it has a louver near the peak. A picturesque stone and brick chimney rises at the left of the door between the gables. At its base, on the terrace, is a decorative colonial bench. Strap iron hinges on the sturdy arched front door and a quaint English lamp hanging above bespeak the hospitality and happiness that dwell within.

. . . .

Details and features: Five rooms and one bath. Shingled exterior; steeply pitched roof; brick and stone chimney; arched front door with strap hinges. Fireplace and built-in bookcases in living room; telephone nook in hall.

Years and catalog numbers: *1928* (P3263); 1929 (P3263); 1932 (3263); 1933 (3263); 1937 (3263); 1939 (3263)

Price: $1,493 to $2,143

. . . .

Similar to: The Stratford

Difference: Brick exterior

Years and catalog numbers: 1932 (3290); 1933 (3290)

Price: $2,122

THE SHEFFIELD

FIVE ROOMS
AND BATH

The Sheffield reflects the latest plan in bungalow architecture. It is another good example of combining beautiful English lines with just a touch of the famous California studio type. The high shingled roof, sloping down from the pointed gables, is an outstanding feature. The front gable has rough cypress siding at the peak and an attractive louver in the center. Observe the smart effect of the brick chimney, topped with three pots, and its pleasing lines carried down to the ground.

Details and features: Five rooms and one bath. Front porch; steeply pitched sloping gables. Fireplace flanked by windows in living room; arched opening between living and dining rooms. Slight differences between 1928 and 1929 models.

Years and catalog numbers: *1928* (P3266); 1929 (P3266)

Price: $2,033 to $2,098

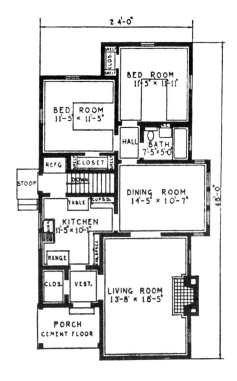

THE SAN JOSE

FIVE-ROOM
SPANISH
BUNGALOW

The San Jose bungalow architecture is derived from the time when old Spain ruled our southern Pacific coast. It is another example of combining the beautiful Spanish mission lines with the latest idea in a splendid floor plan. Adaptable to any section of the country, it offers every modern comfort possible in a design of this kind.

Details and features: Five rooms and one bath. Stucco exterior; tower entrance with pyramidal roof and windows with grilles; arched gate to side entry. Fireplace with built-in bookcases in living room; arched opening between living and dining rooms.

Years and catalog numbers: *1928* (P3268); 1929 (P3268)

Price: $2,026 to $2,138

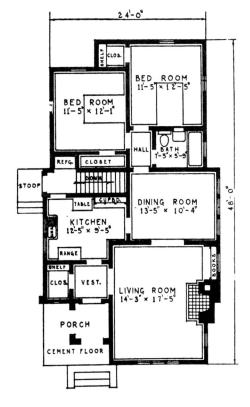

THE BERWYN

lower box, batten-type shutters and cozy arched entrance make this a friendly home, simple in outline and inexpensive to build the Sears way. Five bright sunny rooms are the most approved bungalow arrangement, bath and bedrooms opening off hall, basement stair under the main roof. The exterior looks equally attractive when finished with beveled siding or wide stained shingles.

. . . .

Details and features: Five rooms and one bath. Wood siding or shingle exterior; batten shutters; arched entrance.

Years and catalog numbers: 1929 (P3274); *1931* (3274); 1932 (3274); 1933 (3274)

Price: $1,249

. . . .

Identical to: The Mayfield

Years and catalog numbers: 1933 (3326); 1937 (3326); 1939 (3326)

Price: $1,082 to $1,189

. . . .

Similar to: The Galewood

Difference: Brick exterior

Years and catalog numbers: 1932 (3294); 1933 (3294)

Price: $1,252

THE JEANETTE

This attractive little home is available in two floor plans. Although classed as a four-room home, it has five-room efficiency. The front of the plan contains a large living room, dining alcove, kitchen and rear hall containing refrigerator platform and cellar stairs. A small hall opening out of the living room gives the two bedrooms and bath the necessary privacy.

. . . .

Details and features: Four rooms and one bath. Batten shutters; arched front door with strap hinges; available with projecting vestibule. Arched opening between living room and hall; dining alcove off kitchen.

Years and catalog numbers: 1929 (P3283); *1931* (3283, 3283A); 1932 (13283, 13283A); 1933 (3283, 3283A)

Price: $1,661

. . . .

Identical to: The Parkside

Years and catalog numbers: 1933 (13283A); 1934 (13283A); 1935 (13283A); 1937 (13283A); 1939 (13283A)

Price: $1,231 to $1,372

No. 3283A (with vestibule)

THE WHEATON

*I*nteresting roof lines are the order of the day from skyscrapers to cozy bungalows like the Wheaton, the interior arrangement of which is as well planned as the exterior. Opening off the center hall are a model kitchen, a bath with clothes chute and medicine case, a linen closet and four comfortable corner rooms with cross ventilation. Front and back entrances are protected by vestibules, and the amount of closet space is remarkable.

Details and features: Five rooms and one bath. Paired windows in front with shutters; segmental-arched front door surrounded by trellis.

Years and catalog numbers: *1931* (3312); 1932 (3312); 1933 (3312)

Price: $1,235

THE ELMHURST

*I*n presenting the Elmhurst design we do not hesitate in advising our prospective builders that this home contains convenient interior arrangement and exterior attractiveness, both of which can be secured at a minimum cost due to our time- and labor-saving ready-cut method of construction. The main walls of the exterior are planned to be covered with face brick, while the gables are given an added touch of individuality by the use of half timber and stucco.

Details and features: Six rooms and one and a half baths. Brick exterior; steeply pitched roof with half-timbered and stucco gable. Fireplace in living room; semiopen stairs.

Years and catalog numbers: *1931* (3300); 1932 (3300); 1933 (3300)

Price: No price given

THE DETROIT

A livable home with all rooms of the original plan on one floor—yet designed so that additional rooms can be added on the second floor. The combination of face brick and siding used for exterior walls is especially pleasing. From the vestibule entry, which has a closet for outer wraps, you step into the living room—a beautiful room size with a lot of light. The dining room is also a cheerful spot with four large windows and good wall space. The kitchen is ideal in size and arrangement—just right for the housewife who appreciates a step-saving plan.

. . . .

Details and features: Five rooms and one bath. Brick exterior; clapboard gables; projecting front vestibule; front door with strap hinges. Optional second floor.

Years and catalog numbers: *1931* (3336); 1932 (3336); 1933 (3336)

Price: $1,431

THE HAMMOND

*I*n the Hammond, we present the always popular five-room bungalow in a new guise, up to date outside and in, with beauty and distinction seldom found in houses of this size and remarkably low cost. In sturdy Honor Bilt construction, with high-quality guaranteed materials, it will make the finest kind of investment. The main walls are to be covered with brick and the gables with wide siding. Dark face brick with stained siding would be attractive, but common brick whitewashed and white painted gables would be just as beautiful.

. . . .

Details and features: Five rooms and one bath. Brick with clapboard gables; tripartite casement sash with transoms. Fireplace in living room.

Years and catalog numbers: 1932 (3347); 1933 (3347); *1934* (3347); 1935 (3347); 1937 (3347); 1939 (3347)

Price: $1,253 to $1,408

THE ELLSWORTH

$\mathcal{A}$ few years ago, a number of property owners called at one of our Modern Homes offices, explaining they owned some beautiful wooded lots adjoining a golf club in their city. They wanted to build small, inexpensive homes but were afraid they could not get permits and would be criticized by adjoining home owners who had lived up to the $12,000 restrictions. The designs shown here were among the many offered for their consideration. Now that they are built, they are the pride of the owners and surrounding community. A more compact arrangement of four well-proportioned rooms and bath would be hard to work out in such a limited floor area.

Details and features: Four rooms and one bath. Side porch; lunette window in gable. Fireplace in combination living and dining room; breakfast nook in kitchen.

Years and catalog numbers: 1932 (3341); 1933 (3341); *1934* (3341); 1935 (3341); 1937 (3341)

Price: $1,178 to $1,236

Similar to: The Sunbury

Differences: A small vestibule instead of an open porch; No. 3350B has a hipped roof

Years and catalog numbers: 1932 (3350A, 3350B); 1933 (3350A, 3350B); *1934* (3350A, 3350B); 1935 (3350A, 3350B); 1937 (3350A, 3350B)

Price: $1,141 to $1,237

The Sunbury, No. 3350B

THE CORNING

The Corning, with dormers cut into the eaves, interesting door detail and a dozen delightful points of departure from other colonial styles, suggests old-time Maryland. But it is a far cry from the rambling houses of those leisurely times to the Corning's efficient floor plan. Tucked in with the seven rooms are two complete baths, a toilet with shower and an extra first-floor toilet. Add 12 closets, a breakfast room, halls, vestibules, four entrances, front and back stairs and an attached double garage, and it is seen that the Corning is very modern indeed.

. . . .

Details and features: Seven rooms and three and a half baths. Attached garage; side porch; freestanding chimney in front; six-panel front door with transom above. Fireplace in living room; breakfast alcove; front and back stairs.

Years and catalog numbers: *1932* (3357); 1933 (3357)

Price: No price given

THE ELLISON

The Ellison is a popular flexible bungalow-type design which gives the prospective home builder the option of having five complete rooms and bath on the first floor and two additional rooms and the second bath which can be finished on the second floor when more space is needed. The use of stained shingles, siding and brick seems to be equally popular with home builders.

. . . .

Details and features: Five or seven rooms and one or two baths. Optional brick veneer exterior; front porch; two recessed dormers. Optional second floor; one-and-a-half-story living room with fireplace and beamed ceiling.

Years and catalog numbers: 1932 (3359); 1933 (3359, 3359A); *1934* (3359, 3359A); 1935 (3359); 1937 (3359, 3359A); 1939 (3359, 3359X)

Price: $2,185 to $2,845

THE CONCORD

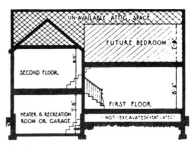

The Concord, section

The Concord is a true American Cape Cod home. Its beautiful exterior and practical floor plan have won it the reputation of "America's most popular low-priced home." We are very proud to present this home, employing a new principle in construction which is a big money saver. The plan has four floor levels. The recreation room can be converted into a motor room, where an attached garage is wanted. This house is a good example of careful planning and how you can secure seven-room efficiency in the same space ordinarily devoted to five rooms.

Details and features: Five, six or seven rooms and one bath. Side porch; gabled dormer over glazed front door; projecting vestibule. Split-level plan; open stairs.

Years and catalog numbers: 1933 (3379); 1934 (3379); *1935* (3379); 1937 (3379); 1939 (13379)

Price: $1,334 to $1,676

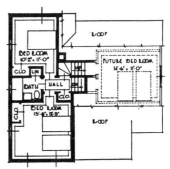

No. 3376

Similar to: The Homestead

Differences: Front porch; garage in place of the recreation room

Years and catalog numbers: 1933 (3376); *1934* (3376); 1935 (3376); 1937 (3376); 1939 (3376)

Price: $1,319 to $1,566

Similar to: The Oldtown

Differences: Front porch; reversed floor plan

Year and catalog number: 1933 (3383)

Price: $1,322

The Homestead

The Oldtown

THE AUBURN

The Auburn is another good example of what proper design will accomplish in the way of large convenient rooms in a small area. It has four floor levels. The exterior walls are treated with a number of different finishes. The front wall under the overhanging gable has perpendicular siding, the vestibule has stucco and half-timber, and the balance of the house has 24-inch shingles.

Details and features: Six or seven rooms and one bath. Projecting front vestibule in stucco and half-timbering; front door with strap hinges. Split-level plan.

Years and catalog numbers: 1933 (3382); 1934 (3382); *1935* (3382); 1937 (3382)

Price: $1,402 to $1,473

Similar to: The Chester

Difference: Garage in place of the recreation room

Years and catalog numbers: *1933* (3380); 1934 (3380); 1935 (3380); 1937 (3380)

Price: $1,443 to $1,535

The Chester

THE GAINSBORO

*M*uch can be said about both the exterior and interior of this attractive home. The construction of common brick painted white and siding exterior walls is inviting and ties in with the English lines. The plan lends itself to the "house that grows" idea, as you have complete living on the first floor, consisting of living room, dining room, bedroom, kitchen and bath. Most families need a first-floor bedroom or find it will come in handy as a library or den. The second floor, which contains two large bedrooms (one with three exposures) and four closets, can be finished as a part of your original building program or at some future date.

Details and features: Six rooms and one bath. Front gable faced with brick; segmental-arched front door with strap hinges; batten shutters. Fireplace in living room.

Years and catalog numbers: 1933 (3387); *1934* (3387); 1935 (3387); 1937 (3387)

Price: $1,475 to $1,548

THE GATESHEAD

*T*he Gateshead is an Americanized English type, particularly adaptable to narrow city lots. The exterior is of clear beveled siding with half-timber and stucco on the front gable. The main roof sweeps gracefully over the front vestibule, and the front gabled roof is treated in the same way. If your requirements can be filled with a compact five-room plan, it will be hard to improve on the arrangement shown by the floor plans.

Details and features: Five rooms and one bath. Side porch; steeply pitched roof; half-timbered and stucco front gable; segmental-arched front door. Corner fireplace in living room.

Years and catalog numbers: 1933 (3386); *1934* (3386); 1935 (3386)

Price: $1,345 to $1,392

THE NORMANDY

This attractive French- or Normandy-type house is another good example of a flexible plan, giving the maximum livable area at the lowest cost consistent with good construction. Distinguished by a beautifully designed turret, capped with antique weathervane and supported by a half-timber and stucco pediment, forming an interesting circular-shaped vestibule. The exterior walls, as shown in the photograph, are planned for brick (not included in base price). We recommend using common brick painted white for best appearance. Stained shingles or wood siding can be used with equally pleasing results and at considerable saving in cost.

Details and features: Five, six or seven rooms and one bath. Conical turret above entrance; bay window on front. Split-level plan; French doors in dining room opening onto terrace.

Years and catalog numbers: 1933 (3390); *1934* (3390); 1935 (3390)

Price: $1,598 to $1,867

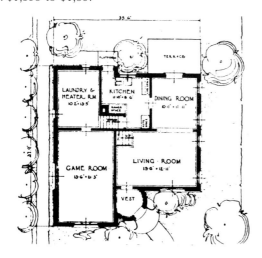

THE SALEM

*H*igh rents and the additional cost of living in the city have created a desire on the part of many American families to own a small home in some attractive suburban area. Many people have requested an inexpensive home, yet one which would be livable with comfortable-sized rooms and modern equipment and architecturally correct. This attractive four-room colonial home, the Salem, received immediate consideration from many prospective home builders. We know it will be a credit to your family and neighborhood.

. . . .

Details and features: Four rooms and one bath. Front porch with shed roof supported by trellised columns.

Years and catalog numbers: 1933 (13377X); 1934 (13377X); 1935 (13377X); *1937* (13377X); 1939 (13377X)

Price: $908 to $971

THE HOMECREST

*T*he exterior is true colonial and is finished with clear beveled siding, painted white, with slat-type window shutters painted a contrasting dark color. Each perspective is equally attractive on account of the broken lines of the main building, garage unit and porch, as well as the well-balanced window arrangement.

. . . .

Details and features: Seven rooms and one bath. Attached garage; side porch with square columns; six-panel front door. Split-level plan.

Years and catalog numbers: *1934* (3398); 1935 (3398); 1937 (3398)

Price: $2,010 to $2,017

THE OXFORD

$\mathcal{F}$or many years the bungalow-type home has been popular in all parts of this country. Successful designs with colonial, English or Spanish character are to be found in the most restricted area. The Oxford house is a modern adaptation of English architecture and is meeting with success among home builders where convenience and beauty are wanted at a low cost. The exterior walls are planned to be covered in cedar shingles. The treatment of the front gable with half-timber and stucco relieves any suggestion of plainness.

. . . .

Details and features: Four rooms and one bath. Half-timbered and stucco gable. Available with reversed floor plan.

Years and catalog numbers: 1933 (13393A, 13393B); *1934* (13393C); 1935 (13393C); 1937 (13393C)

Price: $808 to $999

. . . .

Similar to: The Brentwood

Differences: Clapboard or shingle siding; no half-timbering in front gable

Years and catalog numbers: 1933 (13394A, 13394B); *1934* (13394A, 13394C, 13394D); 1935 (13394A, 13394C, 13394D); 1937 (13394C, 13394D)

Price: $774 to $969

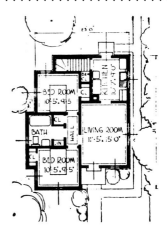

The Brentwood, No. 13394D

THE FRANKLIN

The Franklin is one of our newest suggestions, and its immediate acceptance by home builders indicates that it will be one of our most popular designs. The recreation room located under the bedroom portion can be converted into a third bedroom or motor room.

. . . .

Details and features: Five rooms and no bath. Front porch with shed roof; glazed front door. Split-level plan.

Years and catalog numbers: *1934* (3405); 1935 (3405); 1937 (3405)

Price: $1,118 to $1,119

THE PORTSMOUTH

There is a dignity and grace exemplified in a low, rambling home which would be difficult to achieve in the design of other types. The gracious exterior of this Cape Cod home with its wide open porch, two outstanding bays, wide shingle siding and shuttered front entrance is rivaled only by its elegant interior.

. . . .

Details and features: Six rooms and one and a half baths. Two bay windows in front; side porch; six-panel front door with shutters. Fireplace in living room; dressing room off master bedroom.

Year and catalog number: 1938 (3413)

Price: No price given

THE YATES

A mellow house, pleasantly flavored with English-cottage characteristics. It's a warm, friendly kind of house with its prominent chimney as the focal point on the exterior. You can finish only the downstairs and still have a complete home (four rooms plus a bath and a cunning little breakfast nook). Then, when your family and income get larger, you can finish the second floor into three nice bedrooms and a conveniently located bath.

Details and features: Four or seven rooms and one or two baths. Freestanding chimney in front; front door with strap hinges. Optional second floor; fireplace in living room; breakfast nook between kitchen and dining room.

Year and catalog numbers: 1939 (3711, 3711A)

Price: $1,812 to $2,058

THE LYNN

M ore than often simplicity means good taste. Always in building a house, simplicity means economy, because it lessens the amount of labor required. The Lynn, with its simple, symmetrical lines, is a reserved, practical, yet pleasing style that has inherited that marvelous New England sense of thrift. Shuttered front windows are the only dress-up, formal touch on the neat-as-a-pin colonial exterior.

Details and features: Five rooms and one bath. Front porch; six-panel front door with shutters.

Year and catalog number: 1939 (13716)

Price: $1,342

No. 24

This house makes a very comfortable country or suburban home, having a large parlor, living room, kitchen and bedroom on the first floor, two large and one small bedrooms on the second floor. While this house can be built for a very small cost, it is well arranged to accommodate a large family. The building of this house at this low cost is made possible by our furnishing you a high grade of material at low prices.

. . . .

Details and features: Seven rooms and one bath. Front porch supported by wood columns; decorative bargeboards. Combination dining room and kitchen.

Years and catalog numbers: 1908 (24); *1911* (24); 1912 (24); 1913 (169); 1916 (264P169); 1917 (C169)

Price: $704 to $1,400

Locations: Ellington, Conn.; Peru, Ind.; Modoc, Kans.; Maple Grove, Ky.; Fulda, Minn.; Pleasanton, Neb.; Port Jefferson, N.Y.; Morrisville and Wade, Pa.; Aurora, S.D.; Boscobel and Janesville, Wis.

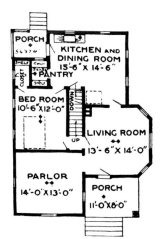
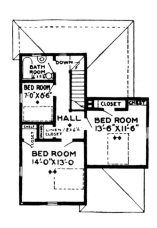

Intersecting gabled roof, two or more stories

THE SARATOGA

*O*ne of our finest. Note the extra-large living room with paneled oak beamed ceiling and rustic brick fireplace. The doors are veneered oak of the latest Craftsman design with oak trim to match. Like the rest of the plan, every foot of space on the second floor is utilized to the very best advantage.

Details and features: Seven rooms and one bath. Full-width front porch with stucco columns; Palladian windows in attic gables; bay window in living room. Fireplace and window seat in living room; built-in buffet and seats in dining room; beamed ceiling in living and dining rooms; semiopen stairs.

Years and catalog numbers: 1908 (108); 1911 (146, 108); 1912 (146, 108); 1913 (146, 108); 1916 (264P108); 1917 (C108); *1918* (2087); 1921 (2087); 1922 (12087)

Price: $1,468 to $3,506

Locations: Chicago, Gladstone and West Union, Ill.; Sioux City, Iowa; Duluth, Minn.; Lancaster, New Rochelle and New York, N.Y.; Dayton and Macedonia, Ohio; Horsham, Pittsburgh and Reading, Pa.; Bennington, Vt.

Living room

THE SILVERDALE

A comfortable home, suitable for a suburban or country residence. It has a large front porch with colonial columns and a rear porch. At the price it is a very desirable investment.

. . . .

Details and features: Seven rooms and one bath. Wraparound front porch with angled front steps; glazed front door. Bath off kitchen.

Years and catalog numbers: 1908 (110); 1911 (110); 1913 (110); 1916 (264P110, 2011); 1917 (C2011, C110); *1918* (2011); 1921 (2011); 1922 (2011)

Price: $1,623

Locations: Ordway, Colo.; Challis, Idaho; Eureka, Lansing, Rock Falls and Warrensburg, Ill.; Gary and Seafield, Ind.; Lawrence, Kans.; Boston, Mass.; Lansing and Royal Oak, Mich.; Pine Island, Minn.; Nelson, Neb.; Albany and Hamburg, N.Y.; Bethel and Mount Vernon, Ohio; Gillett, Pa.; Thunder Hawk, S.D.; Beaver Dam and Milwaukee, Wis.

No. 119

This is a good substantial design, constructed with a view to economy and affording a great deal of room. It has a large front porch with a balcony over part of it. It is built on a concrete block foundation, sided with narrow beveled-edge cypress siding and has a cedar shingle roof.

Details and features: Nine rooms and one bath. Full-width front porch with partial balcony above; paired columns; bay window in sitting room; front door with leaded art glass. Corner fireplace in parlor; open stairs.

Years and catalog numbers: 1911 (119); 1912 (119); *1913* (119); 1916 (119); 1917 (C119)

Price: $1,518 to $1,731

Location: Hereford, Tex.

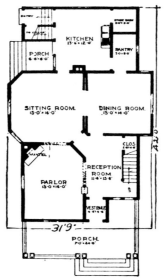

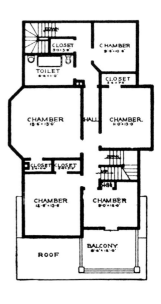

No. 159

This house is well arranged, having no wasted space. Has six good-sized rooms, well lighted and ventilated with large windows. Suitable for a suburban or country home and has been frequently built in large numbers, proving to be a very good investment. It rents well, as it is practically two full stories high and of good appearance. It has a large front porch with colonial columns.

. . . .

Details and features: Six rooms and no bath. Wraparound front porch; overhanging eaves. Open stairs.

Years and catalog numbers: 1911 (159); 1912 (159); *1913* (159); 1916 (264P159B); 1917 (C159B)

Price: $548 to $762

Locations: Aurora, Ill.; LaPorte, Ind.; Perryville, Md.; Boston, Mass.; Ely, Minn.; Fulton, Mo.; Patterson, N.J.; Bay Shore, N.Y.; Canton and Dorset, Ohio; Waynesboro, Pa.; Mount Pleasant, Tenn.; Brydon, W.Va.

No. C2001

This house is well arranged, having no wasted space. Has six good-sized rooms, well lighted and ventilated with large windows. Suitable for a suburban or country home and has been frequently built in large numbers, proving to be a very good investment. It rents well, as it is practically two full stories high and of good appearance. It has a large front porch with colonial columns.

. . . .

Details and features: Six rooms and one bath. Wraparound porch with tapered wood piers; decorative bargeboards; brackets; shed roof over second-floor front window; front door with beveled glass.

Year and catalog number: 1917 (C2001)

Price: $899

No. 301

$\mathcal{M}$ odern Home No. 301 is an imposing brick residence, having a large veranda of solid concrete with a concrete floor. On the second floor is a large balcony of the same size as the porch. The reception hall, parlor and dining room are finished in clear red oak, having six-cross panel veneered oak doors for the interior. The open stairway to the second floor is of clear red oak, having two landings. The feature of this stairway is a door off the second landing leading down to the bathroom, which is on the first floor. This enables one to go from the second floor to the bathroom on the first floor without going through any of the rooms on the first floor.

. . . .

Details and features: Seven rooms and one bath. Brick exterior; curved wraparound porch with balustraded balcony above; front door with beveled plate glass window. Sliding doors between parlor and dining room; open stairs.

Year and catalog number: 1911 (301)

Price: $1,261

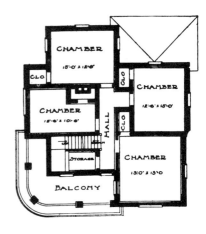

THE HOPELAND

The Hopeland is a popular farm residence with many modern conveniences. Note the colonial windows on both floors. Back of the kitchen is a washroom with sink, which is entered from the rear screened porch. This makes it possible for workmen to wash up at mealtime before entering the kitchen. The rear porch makes a comfortable retreat in hot weather. This house can be built with the rooms reversed.

. . . .

Details and features: Eight rooms and one bath. Front porch with hipped roof supported by wood columns; overhanging eaves; glazed rear porch. Built-in sideboard in dining room.

Years and catalog numbers: *1921* (3036); 1922 (3036)

Price: $2,622 to $2,914

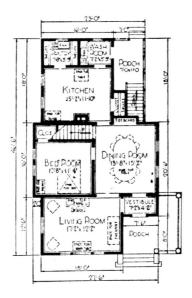

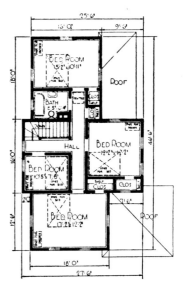

THE SHERWOOD

A type of home desired most by the American builder of today is one which carries the touch of English architecture and which can be built of standardized materials at a minimum cost. The Sherwood not only has an attractive exterior but also a very efficient, economical interior.

. . . .

Details and features: Six rooms and one and a half baths. Steeply sloped gables; shutters on front windows; circle-head batten front door with ornamental wrought-iron hinges. Fireplace in living room; arched opening between living and dining rooms; open stairs.

Year and catalog number: 1929 (P3279)   **Price:** $2,445

THE PENNSGROVE

P leasing proportions, picturesque detail, contrasting surfaces and softly blended colors give the Pennsgrove that rare charm characteristic of the countrysides of Kent and Surrey across the sea. The interior has similar distinction, with the comfort that only American homes achieve. Rooms center around a wide central hall with a handsome railed stairway. The long living

room, opening on a terrace toward a garden, is one and a half stories high.

. . . .

Details and features: Seven rooms and two baths. Stone, brick and stucco exterior; attached garage; projecting half-timbered and brick gable; freestanding chimney. Fireplace, paneled side walls and beamed ceiling in living room; open stairs.

Year and catalog number: 1931 (3348)

Price: No price given

THE TORRINGTON

*M*en are concerned with ruggedness of construction—with quality of material and an economical plan to finance the home—and women are, too. But women are interested in other things as well—with beauty and with style. They are concerned with convenience in room arrangement; with features that add to the appearance of interior and exterior; with the many modern-day improvements that help to lighten the task of housekeeping. This beautiful colonial design is planned with outside walls of siding and brick. The gabled ends and front and back walls of the wings are of face brick while the center portion is of siding. Not only has careful thought been given to the front entrance, dining room bay, well-balanced dormer and other exterior details, but the floor plans are ideal for a home of this size.

Details and features: Seven rooms and two and a half baths. Brick and wood exterior; attached garage; side porch; bay window in front; pedimented entry. Fireplace in living room; semi-open stairs.

Years and catalog numbers: 1932 (3355); 1933 (3355); *1934* (3355)

Price: $3,189

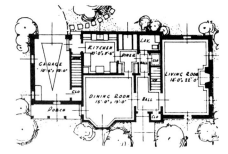

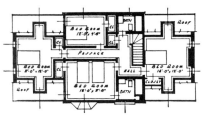

THE CONCORD

This modern type of residence can be built at a surprisingly low cost. A high-class house in every sense of the word. It has a large front porch 26 feet long. The combination of hipped and gabled roof and colonial porch columns gives it a massive, refined appearance.

Details and features: Eight rooms and one bath. Full-width front porch with hipped roof; two gabled dormers in front; glazed front door. Sliding doors between living and dining rooms.

Years and catalog numbers: 1911 (114); 1912 (114); 1913 (114); 1916 (114); 1917 (C2021, C114); *1918* (2021); 1921 (2021); 1922 (2021)

Price: $815 to $2,546

Locations: Colorado City, Colo.; Norwalk, Conn.; Joliet, Lincoln, Mount Pulaski and Ohio, Ill.; Bedford, Iowa; Coldwater, Kans.; Maple City and Marshall, Mich.; Sweet Springs, Mo.; Elizabeth, N.J.; Addison, N.Y.; Alliance, Hoytville, Marion, Sandusky and Wooster, Ohio; Halifax and Monongahela, Pa.; Bennington, Vt.; Racine, Wis.

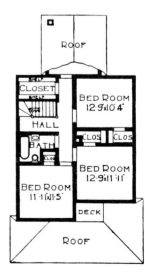

Hipped roof, one to one and a half stories

No. 106

A one-story cottage with attic finished into one large room. This home has two good-sized windows in each room on the first floor and four sash in the room in the attic. Outside cellar entrance.

Details and features: Five rooms and no bath. Front porch with hipped roof; hipped dormer in front.

Years and catalog numbers: 1908 (106); 1911 (106); 1912 (106); *1913* (106)

Price: $498 to $1,190

No. 125

A n ideal cottage for a summer home or water's edge resort. You will notice the large living room with rustic mantel and fireplace and doors leading to four of the six bedrooms and to the kitchen.

Details and features: Eight rooms and no bath. Full-width front porch supported by four wood columns; shed dormer in front with vent; front door glazed with leaded glass. Fireplace in living room; beaded wood partitions between bedrooms.

Years and catalog numbers: 1911 (125); 1912 (125); *1913* (125); 1916 (125); 1917 (125)

Price: $587 to $844

A popular, inexpensive and graceful bungalow, well lighted and ventilated. The large overhanging roof serves for the porch roof also and is supported by beams, requiring no porch columns.

. . . .

Details and features: Four rooms and one bath. Overhanging eaves; front terrace; windows flanking glazed front entry. Fireplace in living room.

Years and catalog numbers: 1911 (126); 1912 (126); *1913* (126)

Price: $675 to $814

Locations: Aurora and Chicago, Ill.; LaPorte, Ind.; Des Moines, Iowa; Glencoe, Ky.; Adrian, Mich.; Omaha, Neb.; Merchantville, N.J.; Maysville, Okla.; Houston, Tex.

. . . .

Similar to: No. 208

Differences: Gabled porch; porch piers with wood rails

Year and catalog number: 1913 (208)

Price: $814

No. 208

THE CANTON

$\mathcal{P}$ eople who like a cement block house will find this one entirely satisfactory. It has been carefully designed and presents an inviting appearance. Many of our customers make their own blocks and in this way effect a wonderful saving.

. . . .

Details and features: Eight rooms and no bath. Cement block exterior; full-width front porch with hipped roof. Open stairs; pantry off kitchen.

Years and catalog numbers: 1911 (152); 1913 (152); 1916 (264P152); 1917 (C152); *1918* (152)

Price: $251 to $750

Locations: Aurora and Freeport, Ill.; Holland, Minn.; Barberton, Ohio; Augusta and Horicon, Wis.

No. 142

$\mathcal{A}$ good and well-built cottage with four rooms, two closets and pantry. We furnish the same high-standard quality of material for this cottage as we do for the higher-priced houses shown in this book.

. . . .

Details and features: Four rooms and no bath. Shed dormer in front. Pantry off kitchen.

Years and catalog numbers: 1911 (142); *1912* (142); 1913 (142)

Price: $153 to $298

THE AVONDALE

A fine example of a modern bungalow, conveniently arranged, perfectly lighted and ventilated with a great many large windows. Pronounced a success by practical builders. The colonial columns and balustrade work are up-to-date features which are being used only in high-priced houses.

Details and features: Front porch with hipped roof and tapered columns; front door glazed with beveled plate glass. Fireplace flanked by window seats and colored leaded art glass in living room; beamed ceiling in living and dining rooms; built-in buffet and mirror in dining room.

Years and catalog numbers: 1911 (151); 1912 (151); 1913 (151); 1916 (264P151, 2006); 1917 (C2006, C151); *1918* (2006); 1921 (7006); 1922 (17006)

Price: $1,198 to $2,657

Locations: Greeley, Colo.; Shelton, Conn.; Des Plaines, Ill.; Culver, Ind.; Ames, Iowa; Wichita, Kans.; Mexico, Ky.; Boston, Mass.; Breckenridge, Mich.; Marks, Miss.; Lewiston, Mo.; Alliance, Neb.; Ithaca, N.Y.; Coats, N.C.; Dayton, Ohio; Ridgway, Pa.; Elroy, Wis.

Living room

THE PRINCEVILLE

This dandy home contains three well-lighted, thoroughly ventilated bedrooms, all of which have good-sized closets. Interior doors are five-cross panel, with trim and flooring to match, all yellow pine, in beautiful grain and color.

Details and features: Six rooms and one bath. Wood siding or stucco exterior; full-width front porch supported by three piers; hipped dormers on front and sides; bay window in stairwell; glazed front door. Colonnaded opening between living and dining rooms; built-in window seat in stairwell.

Years and catalog numbers: 1911 (173); 1912 (173); 1913 (173); 1916 (173); 1917 (C173); *1918* (257)

Price: $810 to $1,794

Locations: Chicago and St. Charles, Ill.; Blue Hill, Neb.; Dover, Ohio

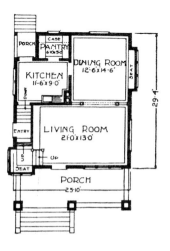

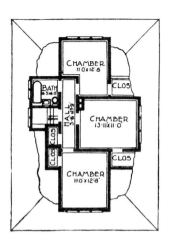

No. 198

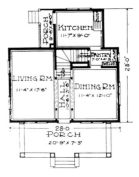

This attractive little home of five rooms and bath is well arranged. The exterior presents a neat and well-balanced appearance and at the same time shows originality.

. . . .

Details and features: Five rooms and one bath. Full-width front porch with hipped roof; shed dormers. Square columns and balustrades in hall; semiopen stairs.

Year and catalog number: 1912 (198)   **Price:** $834

No. 182

Modern Home No. 182 is a very well-arranged, solidly constructed house with a private front porch, the main entrance being on the right. Stonekote and chimney brick are used in pleasing contrast with cypress siding for the outside finish. Colonial windows are specified for this house to match the French doors and windows in the living room.

. . . .

Details and features: Five rooms and one bath. Full-width front porch; overhanging eaves; front door on side. Fireplace and French doors in living room; built-in buffet and mirror in dining room.

Year and catalog number: 1913 (182)   **Price:** $902

On the first floor the living room is connected with the hall and dining room by large cased openings. On the second floor there are two bedrooms and a bathroom; each bedroom has a good-sized clothes closet. Inside doors have four panels, made of best-quality yellow pine.

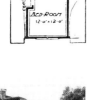

Details and features: Five rooms and one bath. Front porch with square columns; gabled dormer; exposed roof rafter tails; glazed front door. Open stairs with built-in seat.

Years and catalog numbers: 1912 (196); *1913* (196)

Price: $599 to $656

Similar to: No. 193

Differences: Six rooms and one bath; gambrel roof; hipped-gable dormer; applied gable over porch

Years and catalog numbers: 1912 (193); *1913* (193)

Price: $599 to $656

Similar to: No. 194

Differences: Six rooms and one bath; hipped-gable roof with half-timbering in front gable; hipped-gable dormer

Years and catalog numbers: 1912 (194); *1913* (194)

Price: $599 to $656

No. 193

No. 194

THE HAWTHORNE

A house of sunshine. This is a splendid type of modern bungalow, conveniently arranged and perfectly lighted and ventilated. Note the extra-large living room and dining room. The second floor is reached by an open stairway in the dining room and has one large room and a den which may be used as a library or sewing room.

. . . .

Details and features: Eight rooms and one bath. Front porch with hipped roof; bay window in dining room; exposed roof rafter tails; front door glazed with beveled plate glass. Fireplace flanked by built-in seats and leaded art window in living room; beamed ceiling in living and dining rooms; arched opening between living and dining rooms supported by four columns.

Years and catalog numbers: 1913 (201); 1916 (264P201); 1917 (C210); *1918* (2053)

Price: $1,488 to $2,792

Locations: McHenry and Orion, Ill.; Beatrice, Neb.; Columbus and Prospect, Ohio

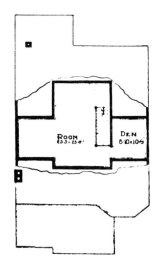

No. 216

*I*n bungalow No. 216 we offer a house at a low price with an absolute guarantee as to the quality of the materials we furnish. Built on a concrete foundation, not excavated. Frame construction and sided with narrow beveled clear cypress siding.

. . . .

Details and features: Four rooms and no bath. Full-width front porch with low hipped roof; small hipped dormer in front; exposed roof rafter tails; glazed front door.

Year and catalog number: 1913 (216)

Price: $402

THE KISMET

*T*his four-room bungalow is suitable for almost any location. We furnish a double floor, also good wood sheathing and plenty of building paper so that the house will be perfectly comfortable in the coldest weather. As this house can be built on a lot 25 feet wide, it is suitable for town or country. For a farm house, for a small family, it represents a splendid investment. It is gracefully proportioned and when nicely painted will look well in any community.

. . . .

Details and features: Four rooms and one bath. Front porch with shed roof supported by tapered wood columns; glazed front door. Changes in number of porch columns between 1916 and 1925 models.

Years and catalog numbers: *1916* (216A, 2002); 1917 (C216A, C2002); 1918 (2002); 1919 (2002); 1921 (7002); 1922 (7002); *1925* (17002X); 1926 (P17002)

Price: $428 to $1,148

Locations: Aurora and Havana, Ill.; Culver, Elkhart and Hamilton, Ind.; Highlands, N.J.; Cleveland, Ohio

No. 216A

THE STARLIGHT

This tasty design of a bungalow is a winner for the price which we ask for all the materials required in its construction. Nearly 200 of these houses have been built. As will be seen by the floor plan, the porch extends across the entire front of the house. Five rooms, also a pantry and bathroom, all of good size, make this house quite convenient for the average family desiring to own a home at small cost.

Details and features: Five rooms and one or no bath. Full-width front porch supported by wood columns; shed or hipped-gable dormer in front; glazed front door. Two floor plans.

Years and catalog number: 1913 (217); 1916 (264P217, 2009); 1917 (C217, 2009, 2038); 1918 (2009); 1919 (2009); *1921* (7009); 1922 (7009); 1925 (3202, 7009); 1926 (P3202, P7009); 1928 (C3269); 1929 (P3269); 1932 (3007); 1933 (3007)

Dining room

Living room

Price: $543 to $1,645

Locations: Delman, Del.; Bloomington, Joliet and Peoria, Ill.; Franklin, Gary and LaPorte, Ind.; Albert City, Iowa; Havre de Grace, Md.; Jackson, Mich.; Newark, N.J.; Albany, N.Y.; Zanesville, Ohio; Belle Vernon, Pa.; Sioux Falls, S.D.; La Follette, Tenn.; Alton, Tex.; Thaxton, Va.

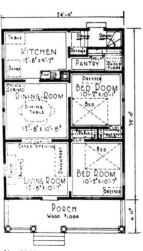

No. 3202

No. 7009

THE WABASH

*U*ncle Sam's idea. This is a house planned and designed by United States government architects after extensive investigation and at considerable cost. We have added an additional door with porch on the front, the gable being sided with cedar shingles.

. . . .

Details and features: Four rooms and no bath. Gabled front porch supported by concrete and wood piers; screened front porch. Fireplace in living room.

Years and catalog numbers: 1916 (248, 2003); 1917 (C2003, C248); *1918* (2003); 1919 (2003); 1921 (2003); 1922 (2003)

Price: $507 to $1,217

Locations: Atlanta, Cerro Gordo, Farmer City and Williamsfield, Ill.; Hoover and Indianapolis, Ind.; Hamlet, Ohio

Living room

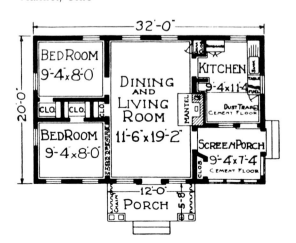

Kitchen

THE ALBERTA

For industrial communities, mining towns or for farmers locating in new sections or on claims, our Alberta is especially suitable. This house has been built by a number of our customers with perfect satisfaction. It has a double floor, the walls are solidly sheathed and sided with good-quality limber and lined with building paper so as to assure perfect protection against cold. A number of houses built according to this design should sell quickly.

Details and features: Four rooms and no bath. Front porch with shed roof supported by brackets; gabled dormer in front; glazed front door. Pantry off kitchen.

Years and catalog numbers: 1916 (264P107); 1917 (C107); *1918* (107)

Price: $330 to $596

Locations: Rockford and St. Ann, Ill.; Cedar Lake and Fort Wayne, Ind.; Sperry, Iowa; Stoutsville and Wickliffe, Ohio

Similar to: The Wayside

Difference: Porch supported by square wood columns

Years and catalog numbers: 1916 (107B, 2004); 1917 (107B, 2004); *1918* (2004); 1919 (2004)

Price: $372 to $945

Locations: Downer's Grove, Flossmore and Shirley, Ill.; Kendallville and Paoli, Ind.; Seaman, Stockport and Toledo, Ohio

The Wayside

THE ELSMORE

The Elsmore is a popular, inexpensive and graceful bungalow, well lighted and ventilated. Large porch, with bungalow columns and porch rail. Note the beautiful Craftsman front door glazed with square lights of glass to match the windows.

. . . .

Details and features: Five rooms and one bath. Front porch with stucco and wood gable; overhanging eaves; brackets; glazed front door flanked by windows. Two floor plans; fireplace in living room.

Years and catalog numbers: 1916 (2013, 208); 1917 (C2013, C208); 1918 (2013); 1919 (2013); *1921* (2013, 3192); 1922 (12013, 13192); 1925 (13192); 1926 (P13192)

Price: $858 to $2,391

Locations: Brookfield, Chicago, Logan, Park Ridge and Rockford, Ill.; Clinton and LaPorte, Ind.; Des Moines and Farnhamville, Iowa; Cohasset, Mass.; Crystal Falls, Mich.; Bertrand, Mo.; Albany, N.Y.; New Philadelphia, Ohio; Glenshaw, Pa.; Fox Lake, Wis.

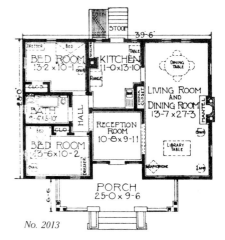

No. 2013

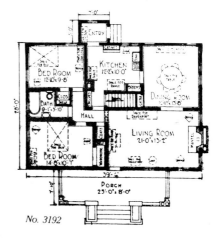

No. 3192

No. C2009

This tasty design of a bungalow is a winner for the price which we ask for all the materials required in its construction. Over 100 of these houses have been built. As will be seen by the floor plan, this house is quite convenient for the average family desiring to own a home for the smallest possible cost.

· ·

Details and features: Five rooms and one or no bath. Full-width front porch; exposed roof rafter tails; shed dormer in front; glazed front door. Two floor plans; cased opening between living and dining rooms.

Year and catalog numbers: 1917 (C2009, C2038, C217, C217A)

Price: $599 to $635

No. C217

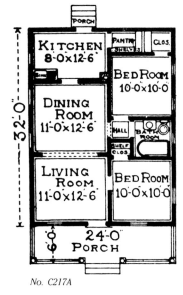

No. C217A

THE KATONAH

*L*overs of the bungalow type of architecture who have been prevented from owning a home of this kind because of the high cost will marvel at our price. When built in the ordinary way, a bungalow like this usually costs a great deal more than we ask. You will observe at once the many attractive features which we have designed for this low-cost bungalow, including the cobblestone foundation, solid brick porch, colonial columns and exposed rafters, blinds and trellis.

. . . .

Details and features: Five rooms and no bath. Front porch with hipped roof supported by wood columns; exposed roof rafter tails.

Years and catalog numbers:
1917 (2029, 029); *1918* (2029, 029); 1919 (2029, 029)

Price: $265 to $827

Locations: Dundee, Ill.; Worthington, Ind.; Alma, Mich.; Milbank, S.D.

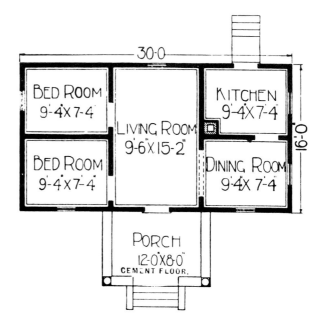

THE ROSITA

*A*lmost anybody can own a home when the materials are furnished for these remarkably low prices. This is particularly true when, as in the present instance, the material comes already cut and fitted. This reduces the cost of expert labor. Has good wood sheathing under the narrow beveled siding and when built according to our specifications will be warm enough for any climate. The trellised porch gives it a finished appearance, and the Fire-Chief Shingle Roll Roofing, which we furnish in either dark red or sea green color, gives you protection, either from paint or stain bills, for more than 17 years.

Details and features: Four rooms and no bath. Front porch with shed roof supported by tapered square columns.

Years and catalog numbers: 1917 (2036); 1918 (2036, 2043, 2044); 1919 (2043B, 2044B); *1921* (2043B, 2044B)

Price: $314 to $875

Locations: Hobart, Ind.; Soldier, Iowa; Milford, Neb.; Portland, N.D.; Dayton and Middletown, Ohio

Identical to: The Kimball

Years and catalog numbers: 1925 (6015); 1926 (P6015); 1928 (C6025)

Price: $625 to $638

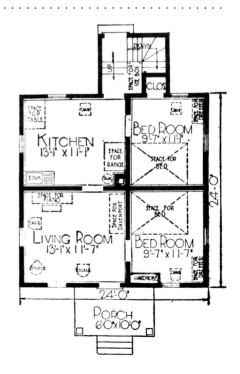

THE PINEOLA

*H*ere is an attractive and wonderfully well-constructed little home at a low price. Note the convenient porch, the colonial windows and the ornamental trellis. The dormer window and the Fire-Chief Shingle Roll Roofing, furnished in either dark red or sea green color, impart the correct distinction and color. A Pullman breakfast alcove in the kitchen will be found very convenient and is a feature of houses selling for more than four times the price of this one.

....

Details and features: Three rooms and no bath. Front porch with trellis; hipped dormer in front; glazed front door. Breakfast nook off kitchen.

Years and catalog numbers: *1918* (2098); 1919 (2098)   **Price:** $489 to $659

THE ADELINE

*T*here is something about this house that immediately secures your attention and admiration. Looking at the picture, you cannot help but admire the handsome porch with its square columns and ornamental trellis. The lines throughout are simple and dignified. The colonial windows and the dark red or sea green Fire-Chief Shingle Roll Roofing supply the touch of richness and color just needed to put this little home in a class of its own.

....

Details and features: Three rooms and one bath. Gabled front porch supported by tapered wood columns; glazed front door. Breakfast alcove off kitchen.

Years and catalog numbers: *1918* (2099); 1919 (2099); 1921 (7099); 1922 (7099)

Price: $696 to $971

Location: Norwood, Ohio

THE MT. VERNON

See page 106 for this design furnished in sections for Summer cottage use.

This four-room Simplex Sectional home includes many conveniences of a high-priced residence. The home comes in ready-made sections, using No. 1 yellow pine lumber and good-grade hardware.

. . . .

Details and features: Four rooms and one bath. Gabled front porch; window shutters and trellises on front; 1925 model has hipped and gabled screened front porch. Fireplace in living room; breakfast alcove off kitchen.

Years and catalog numbers: *1921* (55MH191); 1922 (55MH191); 1925 (55C1910)

Price: $851 to $1,221
. . . .

Similar to: The Betsy Ross

Differences: Open porch with gabled roof; different room arrangement

Years and catalog numbers: 1921 (3089); *1922* (3089); 1925 (3089); 1926 (P3089); 1928 (C3089)

Price: $1,412 to $1,654

The Betsy Ross

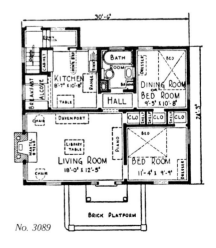

No. 3089

$\mathcal{H}$ ere is a house that is a real bargain in price. For industrial communities, mining towns or for farmers locating in new sections or on claims, this house stands without a peer. This house has been built several times with perfect satisfaction to the owners. We also recommend this design to subdivision owners who want to dispose of their property quickly at a fair price. In industrial centers, where large numbers of men are employed by manufacturing or farming concerns and where it is necessary that they should be located close to their work, a number of houses built according to our design illustrated on this page would sell quickly.

Details and features: Four rooms and no bath. Front porch with shed roof supported by square columns; gabled dormer in front; glazed front door. Pantry off kitchen.

Years and catalog numbers: 1921 (7004); *1922* (7004); 1925 (17004X)

Price: $923 to $1,083

Locations: Downer's Grove and Pekin, Ill.; Manning, Iowa; Harper, Kans.; Huntington, N.Y.; Fort Rice, N.D.; Stockport, Ohio; Willow Lake, S.D.; Clintonville, Wis.

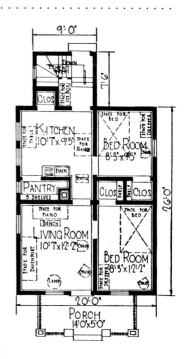

Living room

THE JOSEPHINE

*W*ith its four good-sized rooms, bath, large closets and many conveniences, you will like the Josephine more the longer you live in it. Through the San Jose door one enters a large square living room which will be very comfortable when furnished because of the nice long spaces along the walls. There is plenty of light for the porch does not cover the big front window, the door is glazed, and two small sash let in light on the side.

Details and features: Four rooms and one bath. Front porch with half-timbered and stucco gable supported by tapered wood columns; glazed front door.

Years and catalog numbers: 1921 (7044, 17044); *1922* (7044, 17044); 1925 (7044); 1926 (P7044); 1928 (P7044); 1929 (P7044)

Price: $998 to $1,464

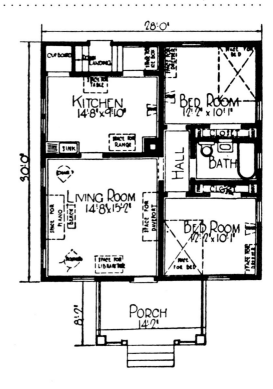

THE HAMILTON

The Hamilton bungalow fulfills all the promises of its handsome exterior. It is just as up to date and has as many good features in the interior. Just a glance at the floor plan will reveal the excellent arrangement of the rooms. Truly the Hamilton is a model of appearance, convenience and price.

Details and features: Five rooms and one bath. Front porch; hipped-gable dormer in front. Fireplace in living room; breakfast alcove and pantry off kitchen.

Years and catalog numbers: 1925 (3200X); *1926* (P3200); 1928 (P3200); 1929 (P3270)

Price: $2,084 to $2,124

Locations: St. Cloud, Minn.; Cincinnati, Ohio

Dining room

Bedroom

Living room

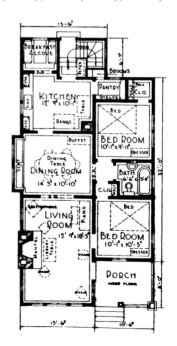

THE COLLINGWOOD

A most attractive, comfortable home with all such favored features as a porch, fireplace, dining room bay, breakfast alcove and refrigerator vestibule. One entire wall of the kitchen filled with twin windows, cabinets and sink. Two bedrooms, each with a closet and cross ventilation, open off the hall, as does the bathroom.

. . . .

Details and features: Five rooms and one bath. Wood siding exterior; front porch; hipped dormer in front. Fireplace in living room; arched opening between living and dining rooms; telephone nook in hall.

Years and catalog numbers: 1929 (P3280); 1932 (3280); *1933* (3280); 1934 (3280); 1935 (3280); 1937 (3280); 1939 (3280)

Price: $1,329 to $1,960

. . . .

Similar to: The Westwood

Difference: Brick exterior

Years and catalog numbers: 1932 (3299); 1933 (3299)

Price: $1,680

THE CARROLL

*T*he value in this plan has been studied by six prominent house architects who all voted it a success. A successful plan is one that gives the home owner convenience, beauty and comfort at the minimum cost. Study the floor plans of the Carroll and you will have to agree that it contains the maximum livable floor area and no wasted space.

. . . .

Details and features: Seven rooms and one bath. Stucco and clapboard exterior; vestibule with sloped curving roof; chimney with two pots; glazed front door with strap hinges. Fireplace in living room; sun room off living room.

Years and catalog numbers: *1931* (3344); 1932 (3344); 1933 (3344)

Price: No price given

THE MAYWOOD

SIX ROOMS, BATH AND PORCH

The Maywood two-story home bespeaks simplicity and worth. Designed after the finest in modern architecture, it makes an ideal home. The roof is of the cottage type, an effect produced by the projection across the middle and by the peak, attractively broken by the shingles to the front and the dormer at the side of the upper floor; combined with green shutters, a clever color contrast is obtained. The inset front porch with artistic seat and the large side porch with cement floor and pillars are features that surely please.

Details and features: Six rooms and one bath. Arched recessed entry; side porch. Fireplace in living room; arched opening between vestibule and living room.

Years and catalog numbers: *1928* (C3272); 1929 (C3272)

Price: $2,658 to $2,914

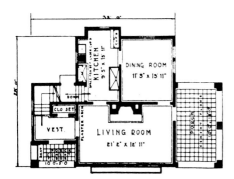

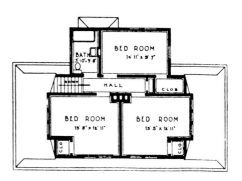

THE PLYMOUTH

The Plymouth, a typical American five-room bungalow with a well-proportioned roof, cottage-type windows and large front porch, was designed for the family of average size. Pictured with proper trees and shrubs, its walls painted white or ivory and its dark weathered roof, it surely is a home of which any American family of moderate means will be proud.

Details and features: Five rooms and one bath. Full-width front porch; hipped dormer in front; glazed front door. Arched opening between living and dining rooms.

Years and catalog numbers: 1933 (3323); *1934* (3323); 1935 (3323); 1937 (3323)

Price: $1,132 to $1,206

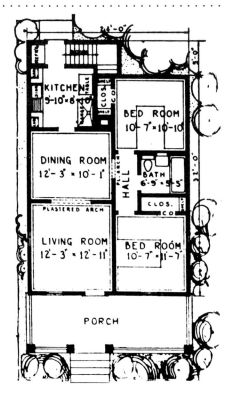

No. 52

A square concrete block residence with conveniently arranged rooms. Cement block houses can be constructed at about one-third less than stone construction and, if properly built and well furred on the inside to make a dead air space between the blocks and the plaster, will be perfectly dry and healthful.

. . . .

Details and features: Eight rooms and one bath. Concrete block exterior; full-width front porch with hipped roof; shed dormer. Sliding doors between living and dining rooms; open stairs.

Years and catalog numbers: 1908 (52); *1911* (52); 1912 (52); 1913 (209)

Price: $782 to $1,995

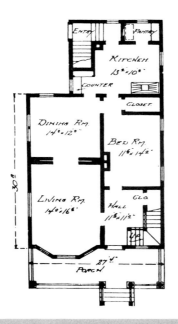

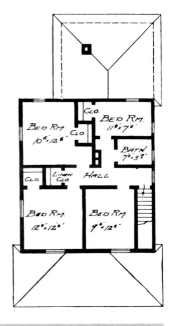

Hipped roof, two or more
stories

THE HAMILTON

*T*his square house is easy to build, as the design is simple. It affords a great deal of room and has a good appearance for the amount of money invested. Built in many places and is giving general satisfaction.

Details and features: Eight rooms and one bath. Full-width front porch with hipped roof supported by columns; hipped-gable dormer in front. Sliding doors between hall and parlor and living room.

Years and catalog numbers: 1908 (102, 150); 1911 (102, 150); 1912 (102, 150); 1913 (102, 150); 1916 (264P102, 264P150); 1917 (C102, C150); *1918* (102, 150)

Price: $1,023 to $2,385

Locations: New Haven and Norfolk, Conn.; Glencoe and Rockford, Ill.; Grand Rapids, Mich.; Belleville and Berlin, N.J.; Mingo Junction and Shelby, Ohio; Plainview, Tex.; Bedford City, Va.

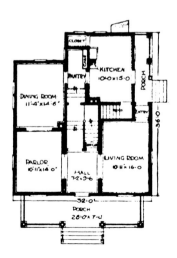

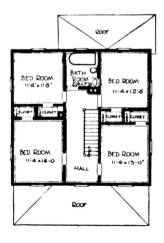

THE CHELSEA

*I*n demand for years, this conveniently arranged house is available at a very low cost compared with the accommodations it offers. A large front porch extends almost across the front of the house. If you are interested in this design, be sure to ask us for some names of people who have built it. We have a big list of satisfied owners.

Details and features: Seven rooms and one bath. Front porch with hipped roof and wood columns; hipped-gable dormer; glazed front door. Sliding doors between living and dining rooms; open stairs.

Years and catalog numbers: 1908 (111); 1911 (111); 1912 (111); 1913 (111); 1916 (264P111); 1917 (C111); *1918* (3027); 1921 (3027); 1922 (3027)

Price: $943 to $2,740

Locations: Roseville, Ill.; Solon, Iowa; Hudson Falls, N.Y.; Columbus, Sandusky, Warren and Wooster, Ohio; Youngstown, Pa.; Effington, S.D.; Terra Alta, W.Va.; Waukesha, Wis.

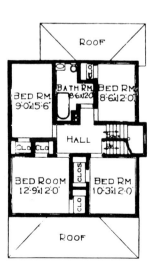

No. 112

*T*his house, which has been built in several states at a big saving to each builder, contains eight rooms, all conveniently arranged. Notice the wide panel cornice, which is very becoming to this style of architecture.

. . . .

Details and features: Seven rooms and one or no bath. Front porch with balcony above; projecting bay on second floor and dormer on third; corner pilasters. Sliding doors between dining room and hall; open stairs.

Years and catalog numbers: 1908 (112); 1911 (112); 1912 (112); *1913* (112); 1916 (112)

Price: $891 to $2,000

Locations: Birmingham, Ala.; Deer Creek, Ill.; Hartford City, Ind.; Ponea and Rushville, Neb.; Cohoes and New York, N.Y.; Granville, Ohio; Valley Springs, S.D.

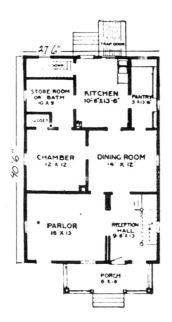

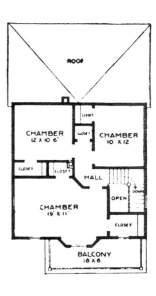

THE CLYDE

$\mathcal{T}$his Modern Home is a well-proportioned house, suitable for any locality. One is immediately impressed on approaching this house by its quiet dignity and air of comfort. The large, roomy porch seems to invite one to its cool shade. The builders report substantial savings and speak well of the high quality of material.

. . . .

Details and features: Seven rooms and one bath. Wraparound front porch with corner balcony above. Corner fireplace in sitting room; opening with columns between parlor and hall; sliding doors between dining and sitting rooms; open stairs.

Years and catalog numbers: 1911 (118); 1912 (118); 1913 (118); 1916 (118); 1917 (C118); *1918* (3033)

Price: $1,397 to $2,924

Locations: Oregon, Ill.; Dixon, Iowa; Detroit, Mich.; Canton, Mo.; Crafton, Neb.; Long Island City, N.Y.; Avon, S.D.; Rockwall and Terrell, Tex.; Watertown, Wis.

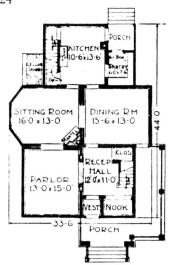

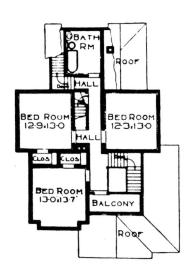

THE CLARISSA

This New England favorite has a large reception hall which is separated from the parlor by a colonnade. A colonnade separates the nook from the reception hall. Double sliding doors separate the parlor from the dining room. In the dining room there is a sideboard built into the pantry and a handsome oak mantel in the parlor. Note the stairs leading from the kitchen which connect with the main stairs, enabling one to go to the second floor from either the hall or kitchen.

. . . .

Details and features: Seven rooms and one bath. Front porch with hipped roof; hipped-gable dormers; shutters; bay window in reception hall and parlor. Corner fireplace in parlor; built-in console in dining room; open stairs.

Years and catalog numbers: 1911 (127); 1912 (127); 1913 (127); 1916 (264P127); 1917 (C127); *1918* (127)

Price: $1,357 to $2,670

Locations: Colorado City, Colo.; Tiskilwa, Ill.; Lansing, Iowa; Owingsville, Ky.; Wayne, Neb.; Demarest and Dunellen, N.J.; Kingston and Ossining, N.Y.; Connellsville, Pa.; Sioux Falls, S.D.

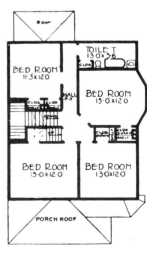

THE LAKELAND

A cozy double house for two families. Three rooms on the first floor and three rooms on the second floor for each family. Arrangement of rooms is exactly the same for both families.

. . . .

Details and features: Twelve rooms and two baths. Two-family house. Gabled front porch with wood columns; leaded window in living rooms; bay window in dining rooms; glazed front doors. Grille between living and dining rooms.

Years and catalog numbers: 1911 (129); 1912 (129); 1913 (129); 1916 (129); 1917 (C129); *1918* (129); 1921 (129); 1922 (129)

Price: $1,533 to $3,972

Locations: New London, Conn.; Kenilworth, Neb.; Oneida, N.Y.; Hartwell, Ohio; Racine, Wis.

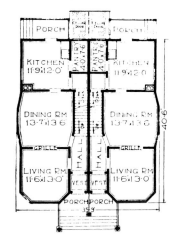

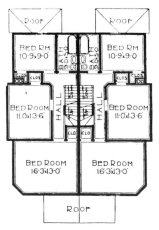

THE PALMYRA

A large, roomy house, well designed and suitable for a corner lot, having a large front and side porch.

Details and features: Ten rooms and one and a half baths. Wraparound front porch with balcony above; bay window in dining room. Corner fireplace and sliding doors in library; built-in sideboard in dining room with colored art glass window above; open stairs.

Years and catalog numbers: 1911 (132); 1912 (132); 1913 (132); 1916 (264P198); 1917 (C198); *1918* (198)

Price: $1,993 to $3,459

Locations: Colorado Springs, Colo.; Lincoln, Marseilles, Paxton and Ransom, Ill.; Rochester, Minn.; Port Union, Ohio; Frankfort, S.D.; Douglas, Wyo.

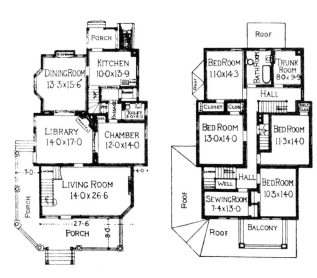

A well-proportioned and substantial city, suburban or country home with concrete porch. Our architects figured out the location and size of all doors and windows to come out just right by using full-size and half-size blocks, so that there will be no necessity of using any other size piece blocks. This makes the construction very easy and simple.

Details and features: Nine rooms and one bath. Concrete block exterior; full-width front porch with hipped roof and square piers. Cased openings in parlor; open stairs.

Years and catalog numbers: 1911 (143); 1912 (143); *1913* (143); 1916 (143)

Price: $712 to $896

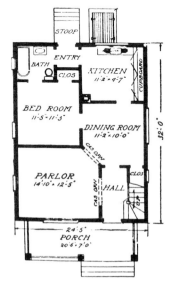

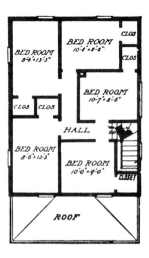

THE GLENDALE

This good, substantial house of nice appearance is suitable for suburban residence or country home. Every bit of space has been used to the best advantage, leaving absolutely no wasted space. A combination cupboard is placed between the dining room and kitchen, opening into both rooms. This arrangement makes all parts of the cupboard accessible from either the kitchen or dining room, saving many steps.

. . . .

Details and features: Seven rooms and one bath. Full-width front porch with hipped roof supported by wood columns; glazed front door. Built-in cupboard between dining room and kitchen; open stairs.

Years and catalog numbers: 1911 (148); 1912 (148); 1913 (148); 1916 (264P148); 1917 (C148, C2016); *1918* (2016); 1921 (7016)

Price: $916 to $2,188

Locations: Des Plaines and Kankakee, Ill.; Columbus, East Chicago and Elkhart, Ind.; Logan, Marion and Stanhope, Iowa; Akron, Cincinnati, Cleveland and Lorain, Ohio; Detroit and Grand Rapids, Mich.; Port Jervis and Verplanck, N.Y.; Bowbells, N.D.; Bellefonte, Connellsville and Kane, Pa.; Sioux Falls, S.D.

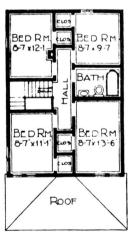

No. 157

A modern residence with an exceptionally large living room connected with the stair hall by means of a large cased opening and also connected with the dining room by a large cased opening. Every room is arranged to make the best use possible of all the available space. All the rooms on both first and second floors are large and well lighted and ventilated.

Details and features: Seven rooms and one bath. Stucco exterior; stepped dormer in front; side porch. Fireplace and beamed ceiling in living room; built-in wardrobe with leaded art glass doors in hall; open stairs.

Years and catalog numbers: 1911 (157); *1912* (157); 1913 (157)

Price: $1,521 to $1,866

No. 158

 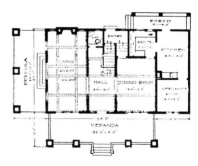

*T*his house is of a practically square design and can be built at a very reasonable price. The pergola is a popular feature in modern homes and in this case, being on the opposite side from the kitchen and servant's room, makes the house look well balanced.

Details and features: Eight rooms and one and a half baths. Front porch; balcony above; pergola on side; shed dormer. Beamed ceiling in living and dining rooms and hall; semiopen stairs.

Years and catalog numbers: 1911 (158); *1912* (158); 1913 (158)

Price: $1,548 to $1,845

*T*his house has two full stories and an attic. It is sided with Stonekote, more commonly known as cement plaster. It can be sided with clear cypress beveled siding if desired. A large front porch supported by massive Stonekote columns extends across the entire front. The balcony over the porch makes a very desirable place for an open-air sleeping porch when screened in.

. . . .

Details and features: Seven rooms and one bath. Stucco exterior; full-width front porch with shed roof supported by rectangular piers; balcony above. Sliding doors between parlor and dining room; mantel in dining room; semiopen stairs.

Years and catalog numbers: 1911 (163); 1912 (163); *1913* (163)

Price: $1,110 to $1,282

. . . .

Similar to: No. 120

Differences: Hipped-gable dormer; no front balcony; slightly different floor plan

Years and catalog numbers: 1911 (120); 1912 (120); 1913 (120); 1916 (264P120); 1917 (C120)

Price: $1,278 to $1,660

Locations: Edgemoor, Del.; West Springfield, Mass.; Long Island City, N.Y.

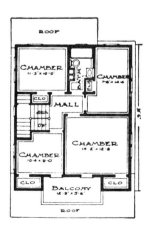

No. 174

$\mathcal{M}$odern Home No. 174 was designed particularly for a narrow lot. A large porch extends across the entire front of the house. Nearly all the windows are of colonial pattern. We particularly call your attention to the many nice features in the large dining room. Brick mantel and fireplace in the corner. A beautiful buffet is built in, with plate rail around the entire room. The window seat extends entirely across the bay. The kitchen is a small room, 10 feet 6 inches by 10 feet, having a fair-sized pantry and closet.

. . . .

Details and features: Five rooms and one bath. Full-width front porch with hipped roof; hipped-gable dormer; projecting corner windows on second floor; bay window in dining room. Sliding door between parlor and dining room; built-in window seat and corner fireplace in dining room; open stairs.

Years and catalog numbers: 1911 (174); 1912 (174); *1913* (174)

Price: $795 to $940

No. 176

$\mathcal{T}$his large modern type of square house offers an open-air dining porch in the rear and an open-air sleeping porch on the second floor. Note the Priscilla sash frames in each dormer which give this house a rich appearance and also afford a great deal of light in the attic, which is large enough for two small rooms.

. . . .

Details and features: Seven rooms and one bath. Full-width front porch with hipped roof supported by square piers; Palladian windows in gabled dormers. Fireplace in living room; open stairs and built-in seat in hall; sliding doors between living and dining rooms; built-in buffet and beamed ceiling in dining room; open stairs.

Years and catalog numbers: 1911 (176); 1912 (176); *1913* (176); 1916 (264P176)

Price: $1,455 to $2,141

No. 306

A large modern residence with a very large front porch with colonial columns. We have no doubt about pleasing the most critical with this large modern residence; it can save the builder a considerable amount of money.

. . . .

Details and features: Wraparound porch with wood columns; bay window in dining room; front door with oval window. Colonnaded opening between hall and living room; built-in bookcases with leaded glass doors in living room; china closet in dining room; semiopen stairs.

Years and catalog numbers: *1911* (306); 1912 (306); 1913 (215); 1916 (264P215); 1917 (C215)

Price: $1,363 to $1,561

Locations: Boston and Orange, Mass.; Buffalo and West Chazy, N.Y.; Connellsville, Pa.

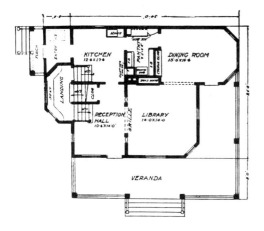

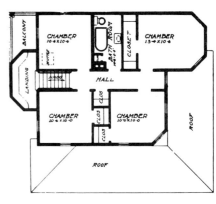

No. 179

*W*hile this house can be built for a very reasonable amount, it has the appearance of a $3,000 house, arranged to give an abundance of light and ventilation in every room.

. . . .

Details and features: Five rooms and one bath. Full-width front porch supported by paired columns; hipped-gable dormer; bay window in combination living and dining room; front door with beveled plate glass. Open stairs.

Years and catalog numbers: 1912 (179); *1913* (179)

Price: $939 to $1,003

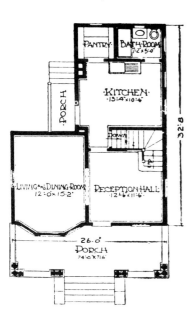

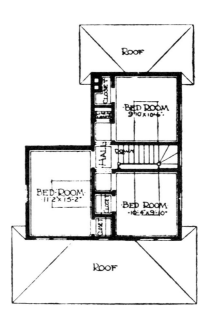

THE WHITEHALL

A neat and roomy house at a very low price. Was designed with two objects in view: economy of floor space and low cost. The dining room is connected with the living room by a large cased opening which practically makes one large room of these two rooms. Has a kitchen and good-sized pantry.

Details and features: Six rooms and one bath. Full-width front porch with wood columns; projecting two-story bay in front; front door with beveled plate glass. Cased opening between living and dining rooms.

Years and catalog numbers: 1912 (181); 1913 (181); 1916 (264P181); 1917 (C181); 1918 (3035); 1921 (3035); *1922* (3035); 1925 (3035); 1926 (P3035A)

Price: $687 to $1,863

Locations: Plainville, Conn.; Aurora, Ill.; Gary, Hammond and LaPorte, Ind.; Cresco and Davenport, Iowa; Morristown, N.J.; Eastwood, Hempstead and Richmond Hill, N.Y.; Allentown, Galeton, Hadley, Hellertown, McKeesport and New Castle, Pa.; West Point, Va.

THE CASTLETON

$\mathcal{A}$ well-designed house that will make a pleasant home. It is square in plan, giving the greatest amount of space for the least money. The exterior presents a dignified and substantial appearance. Beveled siding is used for the first story, Stone-kote or cement plaster for the second story.

. . . .

Details and features: Eight rooms and one bath. Full-width front porch with stucco piers; hipped-gable dormer; front door glazed with beveled plate glass. Fireplace in living room; pantry off kitchen.

Years and catalog numbers: 1912 (227); 1913 (227); 1916 (264P227); 1917 (C227); *1918* (227); 1921 (227); 1922 (227)

Price: $934 to $2,193

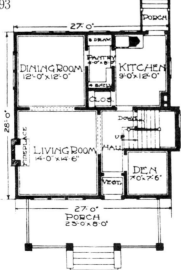

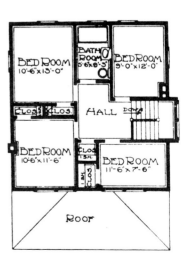

THE LANGSTON

A neat and roomy house, sturdy and attractive, at a very low price. Was designed especially with two objects in view: economy of floor space and low cost.

Details and features: Six rooms and one bath. Full-width front porch with hipped roof supported by brick and wood piers; hipped-gable dormer; exposed roof rafter tails; front door with beveled plate glass.

Years and catalog numbers: 1916 (181A, 2000); 1917 (C181A, C2000); *1918* (2000); 1919 (2000); 1921 (7000); 1922 (7000)

Price: $796 to $1,898

Locations: Washington, D.C.; Kankakee and Riverside, Ill.; Logansport, Fort Wayne and Roanoke, Ind.; McGregor, Iowa; Detroit, Mich.; Fort Plain, N.Y.; Dayton, Norwood, St. Bernard and Wellsville, Ohio; Chester and McKeesport, Pa.

Similar to: The Gladstone

Differences: Some models without dormer. No. 3315B has a different room arrangement and separate vestibule; No. 3414 has a small pedimented front porch.

Years and catalog numbers: 1925 (3222); *1926* (P3222); 1928 (P3222); 1929 (P3222A, P3222B); 1933 (3315A, 3315B); 1934 (3315A, 3315B); 1935 (3315A, 3315B); 1937 (3315A, 3315B); 1938 (3414A, 3414B)

Price: $1,409 to $2,153

The Gladstone

THE WOODLAND

The Woodland has an attractive stairway leading to the second floor. The bedrooms on the second floor have splendid ventilation, there being windows on two sides of the front rooms. No. 2007 plan has four bedrooms and balcony; No. 3025 has five bedrooms.

. . . .

Details and features: Seven or eight rooms and one bath. Full-width front porch with hipped roof supported by brick and wood piers; hipped front dormer; front door with beveled plate glass. Three floor plans; open stairs.

Years and catalog numbers: 1916 (264P179, 2007); 1917 (C2007, C179); 1918 (2007); *1921* (2007, 3025); 1922 (2007, 3025); 1925 (3025); 1926 (P3025); 1928 (C3025); 1933 (3025)

Price: $938 to $2,480

Locations: Antioch, Aurora, Glen Ellyn and Peru, Ill.; Geneva, Ind.; Bowen, Mich.; Athens, Cincinnati and Milton, Ohio

No. 2007

No. 2007

No. 3025

No. 3025

THE HILLROSE

*T*his modern country residence was awarded first prize in a contest participated in by 100 of our country customers. As can readily be seen, it is a house of which anyone can justly be proud, and yet our price for all the material required in its construction places it within the reach of the man of average means. Note how gracefully it is proportioned, how well lighted it is on all sides and how the massive porch adds to its appearance.

Details and features: Nine rooms and one bath. Full-width front porch with hipped roof; hipped-gable dormer; shed off kitchen. Built-in cabinet in living room; French doors between living room and parlor; china closet between pantry and dining room.

Years and catalog numbers: 1916 (264P189); 1917 (C189); *1918* (3015); 1921 (3015); 1922 (3015)

Price: $1,553 to $3,242

Locations: Waterman, Ill.; Griffith, Ind.; Stratford, Iowa; Houghton, N.Y.; Antwerp and Dixon, Ohio

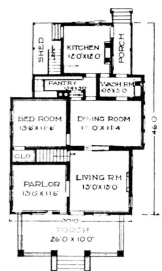

Hillrose farm buildings

THE CAMBRIA

*H*ere is a colonial house that is very popular. Note the triple windows, the ornamental trellis and the crescent blinds. The entrance is on the right side and is ornamented with flower boxes. A door opens into the reception hall, in which there is an open stairway to the second floor.

. . . .

Details and features: Seven rooms and one bath. Side front door; bay window in living room; shutters; glazed front door. Built-in window seat and fireplace flanked by bookcases in living room; open stairs.

Years and catalog numbers: 1916 (264P251); 1917 (C251); *1918* (251)

Price: $998 to $1,771

Location: West Acton, Mass.

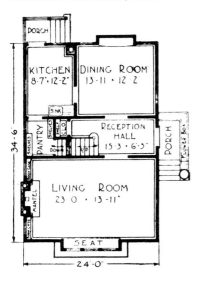

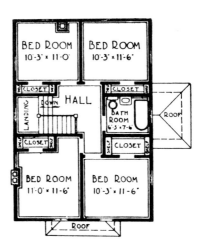

THE AUBURN

A large, modern type of square house, massive and ornamental, with an open-air dining porch in the rear and an open-air sleeping porch above. The dining porch and sleeping porch may be enclosed with screen during the summer months and with sash during the winter.

. . . .

Details and features: Seven rooms and one bath. Full-width front porch with brick piers; exposed rafters grouped in threes; hipped front dormer. Fireplace in living room; sliding doors between living and dining rooms; open stairs.

Years and catalog numbers: 1917 (C176, C2046); *1918* (2046); 1921 (2046); 1922 (2046)

Price: $1,638 to $3,624

THE MAGNOLIA

$5,140⁰⁰

From the days of George Washington to the present time, the colonial type of residence has always been popular. It has housed the greatest figures in American history, science and literature. Many will recognize a close resemblance in the Magnolia to the famous residence at Cambridge, Mass., where the poet Longfellow composed his immortal works. Leading architectural authorities declare that this type will continue to win favor for hundreds of years. There can be no question of its imposing appearance, graceful lines and other attractive features.

Details and features: Eight rooms and two and a half baths. Two-story portico with fluted columns; open terrace across front; side porte-cochere; decks and sleeping porch off second-floor bedrooms; glazed front door with sidelights and arched transom. Fireplace and nook in living room; French doors off hall; open stairs.

Years and catalog numbers: *1918* (2089); 1921 (2089)

Price: $5,140 to $5,972

Reception hall

Living room

THE ALHAMBRA

The Alhambra is an effective Mission style of architecture. Its exterior appearance, as well as the interior arrangement, will appeal to anyone who likes massiveness and plenty of room.

. . . .

Details and features: Eight rooms and one bath. Stucco exterior; curvilinear gables; overhanging eaves; open porch and terrace in front. Fireplace in living room; built-in sideboard in dining room; built-in seat in sun room.

Years and catalog numbers: 1918 (2090); 1919 (2090); *1921* (7080); 1924 (17090A); 1925 (17090A); 1926 (P17090A); 1928 (C17090A); 1929 (P17090A)

Price: $1,969 to $3,134

Locations: Norwood Park, Ill.; Dayton, Ohio

. . . .

Similar to: The Monterey

Differences: Different gable and porch designs

Year and catalog number: 1924 (3312)

Price: $2,998

The Monterey

THE AURORA

The Aurora is much favored by discriminating builders and is found in the most exclusive communities. Off the living room is a private veranda which can be screened in summer or enclosed with storm sash in winter.

. . . .

Details and features: Six rooms and one bath. Stucco exterior; side porch supported by rectangular piers; stringcourses; paired windows. Fireplace in living room; built-in buffet in dining room; open stairs.

Year and catalog number: 1918 (3000)

Price: $2,740

THE CARLTON

The Carlton is a prominent architect's conception of what a 20th-century residence should be. All rooms are large, light and airy. This is a house with individuality, and that will be a constant source of pleasure and pride to its owners.

. . . .

Details and features: Eight rooms and one bath. Stucco exterior; low-pitched hipped roof with wide overhangs; stringcourses. Fireplace in living room; semiopen stairs.

Year and catalog number: 1918 (3002)   **Price:** $5,118

Library

Sun parlor

THE GARFIELD

TEN ROOMS, BATH AND BIG PORCH FOR TWO FAMILIES

*T*he Garfield two-story twin-apartment home is considered a splendid investment opportunity. It can be sold at a handsome profit when built in a good locality. Sometimes the owner lives in one apartment and rents out the other to a tenant. Such rental usually pays the cost of the property. The first-floor apartment as well as the second-floor apartment has its own front entrance on the spacious front porch.

Details and features: Ten rooms and two baths. Two-family house. Full-width front porch with hipped roof supported by brick and wood columns; hipped-gable dormer. Cased opening between living and dining rooms.

Years and catalog numbers: 1919 (P3232); 1926 (P3232); *1928* (P3232)

Price: $2,599 to $2,758

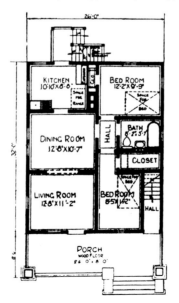

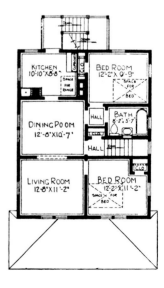

THE AMERICUS

$\mathcal{H}$ ere is a fine home that any American can be proud of and be comfortable in. It is a dignified, substantial house that will stand out among its neighbors and never go "out of style." The rooms are all good sized and well lighted and ventilated. Lots of big closets just where needed and a kitchen that will save a great many steps.

Details and features: Six rooms and one bath. Full-width front porch with shed roof supported by tapered stucco and wood piers; exposed roof rafter tails; glazed front door. Semiopen stairs.

Years and catalog numbers: 1921 (3063); 1922 (13063); *1925* (13063X); 1926 (P13063); 1928 (P13063); 1929 (P13063)

Price: $1,924 to $2,173

Locations: Fort Mitchell, Ky.; Collingswood, N.J.; Ossining and Yonkers, N.Y.; Cleveland, Norwood and St. Bernard, Ohio

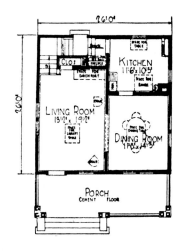

THE HAVEN

The last word in economy of space and material. Colonial windows, massive porch columns and attractive window boxes combine to make the exterior very pleasing. A modern grade entrance at the side of the house assures a clean and warm kitchen. Space provided for ice box at entrance with space above for shelves. Well-lighted inside stairway leads to basement under entire house.

Details and features: Seven rooms and one bath. Cypress siding exterior on first floor; cedar shingle exterior on second floor; front porch with hipped roof supported by brick and wood piers; window boxes in second-floor windows. Cased opening between living and dining rooms; semiopen stairs.

Year and catalog number: 1922 (3088)

Price: $1,584

Locations: Riverside, Ill.; Logansport, Ind.; McGregor, Iowa; Fort Plain, N.Y.; Cincinnati, Ohio; Chester, Pa.

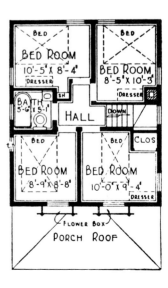

THE FULLERTON

This style of home has become very popular in the past few years. It adapts itself equally well to city lots or country estates, and in few other styles can you get so much space for such a small outlay of money.

Details and features: Six rooms and one bath. Full-width front porch with hipped roof supported by brick and wood piers; hipped-gable dormer; glazed front door. Fireplace in living room; open stairs.

Years and catalog numbers: *1925* (3205X); 1926 (3205X); 1928 (P3205); 1929 (P3205); 1933 (3205)

Price: $1,633 to $2,294

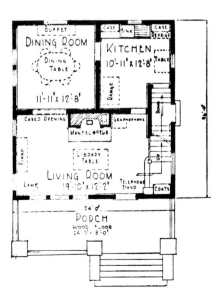

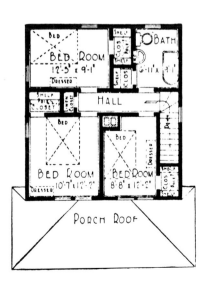

THE CORNELL

A 7-ROOM OR 6-ROOM HOUSE FOR A NARROW LOT

*I*magine this cozy home with the siding painted a dark tone color, with rich brown stained shingle for the second story, with window casings painted in pure white! It is a roomy house at a very low cost, because it is planned on square lines, permitting every square inch of space to be used to the best advantage. The large porch with its brick columns beneath and triple columns above, the wide trusses that support the porch roof and the numerous divided light windows make this house one of our most popular sellers.

Details and features: Six or seven rooms and one bath. Front porch with hipped roof supported by brick and wood piers; glazed front door. Two floor plans; cased opening between living and dining rooms.

Years and catalog numbers: 1925 (3226); 1926 (P3226); *1928* (P3226A, P3226B); 1929 (P3226A, P3226B); 1933 (3226A, 3226B); 1935 (3226B); 1937 (3226B); 1938 (3412)

Price: $1,360 to $1,785   **Location:** Avoca, Pa.

No. P3226A

No. P3226A

No. P3226B

THE ALBION

The Albion two-story residence has attractive qualities which reflect the most modern trend of architecture. These qualities include: utmost use of material and greatly lowered construction cost because the building is almost square. Every inch of floor space is available for living quarters. Painted pure white with contrasting green shutters and red or green roof and red brick chimney. Consider the large porch with its artistic columns, the numerous divided light windows and the wide beveled siding. Just study the floor plans and see for yourself how perfect in arrangement is the Albion Honor Bilt home.

. . . .

Details and features: Seven rooms and one bath. Front porch with hipped roof supported by wood columns; shutters in front; glazed front door. Mirrored closet door in vestibule.

Years and catalog numbers: *1925* (3227); 1926 (P3227)

Price: $2,496 to $2,515

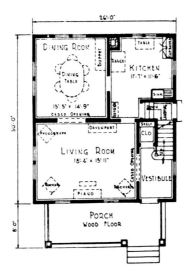

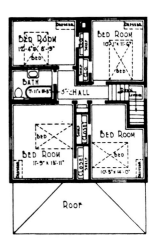

THE ROCKFORD

SIX ROOMS
AND BIG
PORCH

*T*he Rockford two-story home is finished with a veneer of brick. Substantial strength is expressed in its dignified exterior. The roof is of a hipped type, and any suggestion of plainness is eliminated by the use of a dormer in the front elevation, the tall brick fireplace chimney and the porch trellis for climbing plants. The solid brick rail gives the porch added privacy, thus increasing its usefulness to the family. The Rockford is conveniently planned to allow the greatest use of space consistent with good architecture.

Details and features: Six rooms and one bath. Brick exterior; full-width front porch with hipped roof and brick piers; hipped-gable dormer. Fireplace in living room flanked by windows; open stairs.

Years and catalog numbers: 1926 (P3251); *1928* (C3251); 1929 (P3251)

Price: $2,086 to $2,278

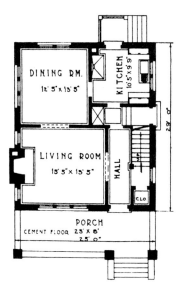

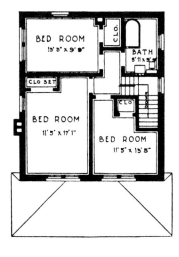

THE DAVENPORT

Designed for a narrow city lot, this comfortable two-story home offers many possibilities for the home owner who needs lots of room at low cost. Wide siding, which we suggest painting white or ivory, window shutters and also a comfortable front porch are a few of the noteworthy details of the exterior.

Details and features: Six rooms and one bath. Full-width front porch with hipped roof supported by brick and wood piers; shutters on front windows on second floor; glazed front door. Arched opening between living and dining rooms; open stairs.

Year and catalog number: 1931 (3346)

Price: No price given

THE DEXTER

  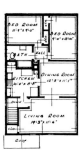

The Dexter "income bungalow" looks like a handsome single-family residence but actually contains two complete five-room apartments. Rental income from one apartment greatly reduces the owner's payments and may in time pay for the entire building. Good design happily combines face brick, stucco and stained shingles.

Details and features: Twenty rooms and two baths. Two-family residence. Brick exterior on first floor; steeply pitched, gabled vestibule; open front terrace; half-timbered front gable; arched front door.

Years and catalog numbers: *1931* (3331); 1932 (3331); 1933 (3331)

Price: No price given

THE BIRMINGHAM

$\mathcal{T}$he Birmingham is a two-story house designed for a narrow city lot but skillfully given the appearance of a handsome bungalow, having face brick walls and ornamental iron railing on a cement terrace.

. . . .

Details and features: Seven rooms and one bath. Brick exterior; steeply pitched, gabled vestibule; open terrace in front; arched front door. Dining alcove off kitchen; deck off second-floor rear bedroom.

Years and catalog numbers: *1931* (3332); 1932 (3332); 1933 (3332)

Price: No price given

No. 177

This combination of frame and cement plaster with wood panel strips, the latest style of construction, has proven a great success. The windows are of a design that is in harmony with the rest of the architectural scheme. A glance at the floor plans will show that all rooms are very large and well located.

Details and features: Six rooms and one bath. Stucco exterior; full-width front porch with hipped roof and stucco piers; half-timbered and stucco front gable; bay window in dining room. Fireplace flanked by colored art glass windows in living room; beamed ceiling and built-in buffet and window seat in dining room.

Years and catalog numbers: 1911 (177); *1913* (177); 1916 (264P177); 1917 (C177)

Price: $1,050 to $1,461

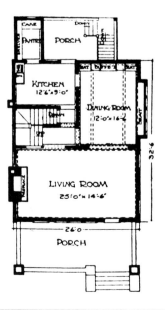

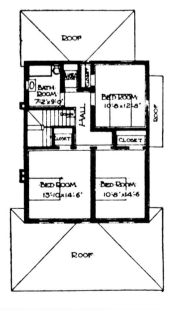

Hipped-gable roof

No. 101

*T*he rooms in this house are large and well proportioned. The front door enters directly into the living room. On the second floor is one large front chamber with two medium-sized side bedrooms, three closets and a large storeroom over the kitchen which can be used as a bedroom.

....

Details and features: Eight rooms and one bath. Side entrance; leaded glass window in parlor. Sliding doors between library and living room and parlor; pantry off kitchen.

Years and catalog numbers: 1908 (101); 1911 (101); 1912 (101); *1913* (101)

Price: $738 to $1,740

Locations: Ashland and Clifton, Ill.; Crown Point, Ind.; Wilton Junction, Iowa; Milford, Mich.; Plummer and Rogers, Minn.; Cortland, N.Y.

THE FLOSSMOOR

*A*s one enters the front door of this house, he immediately has a favorable impression from the large reception hall and the open stairway which leads to the second floor. The living room is directly off the reception hall and separated from the reception hall by a cased opening.

....

Details and features: Seven rooms and one bath. Full-width front porch with hipped roof and brick piers; triple window on second floor; glazed front door. Semiopen stairs.

Years and catalog numbers: 1912 (180); 1913 (180); 1916 (264P180); 1917 (C180); *1918* (3032); 1921 (3032); 1922 (3032)

Price: $838 to $2,124

Locations: Peoria, Ill.; Evansville, Ind.; Brainerd, Minn.; New York and Troy, N.Y.; Akron, Ohio; Duryea, Pa.

THE LETONA

This compact and inexpensive home has a large living room and an attractive open stairway. Each bedroom has a large clothes closet.

Details and features: Five rooms and one bath. Full-width front porch with wood piers; glazed front door. Open stairs; pantry off kitchen.

Years and catalog numbers: 1912 (192); 1913 (192); 1916 (264P192); 1917 (C192); *1918* (192)

Price: $619 to $1,215

Locations: Aurora and Galesburg, Ill.; Beech Grove, Ind.; Newburgh, N.Y.; Gibsonburg, Ohio

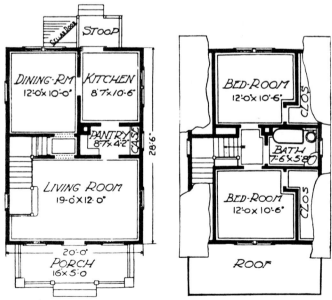

No. 264P159A

This house is well arranged, having no wasted space. The rooms are well lighted and ventilated with large windows. It makes a suitable suburban or country home and has been frequently built in large numbers.

. . . .

Details and features: Six rooms and one bath. Wraparound front porch; glazed front door. Open stairs.

Year and catalog number: 1916 (264P159A)

Price: $745

THE DELEVAN

You will look in vain elsewhere for a nicer appearing, more solidly constructed house of this size and character for less than $800. Note the substantial brick porch and the covered entrance over the front door. Fancy this little home painted pure white for the body and trimmed with a nice shade of green or dark red. The result is a little home worth much more as a selling or renting proposition than the original cost.

. . . .

Details and features: Four rooms and one bath. Front porch with brick walls and gabled roof supported by brackets; trellis.

Years and catalog numbers: 1917 (2028, 028); *1918* (2028, 028); 1919 (2028, 028); 1921 (2028, 028B); 1922 (2028B, 028B)

Locations: Fort Wayne, Ind.; Butler, Ky.; Hubbell, Mich.; Yardville, N.J.; Niles, Ohio; Grove City and Sellersville, Pa.; Milwaukee, Wis.

Price: $285 to $949

THE MADELIA

*H*ere is a house that industrial concerns like to provide for their managers and foremen. It makes a very classy dwelling with its colonial windows, private side porch and colored Fire-Chief Shingle Roll Roofing.

Details and features: Six rooms and one bath. Hipped roof over front door supported by brackets; side porch with wood columns; hipped-gable dormer in front. Semiopen stairs.

Years and catalog numbers: *1918* (3028); 1919 (3028); 1921 (3028); 1922 (3028)

Price: $1,393 to $1,953

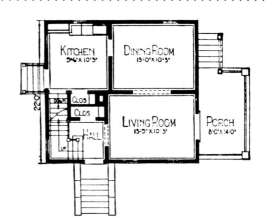

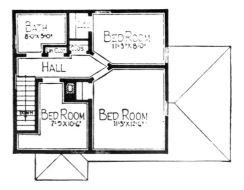

THE RODESSA

*I*t is hardly necessary to say that this is a most attractive little home. Furthermore, the price is also attractive. Much thought and expert advice have been expended in designing an exterior that will make this bungalow appeal to lovers of artistic homes, while the floor plan appeals to all people desiring the utmost economy in space. This plan has proved to be one of our most popular houses, and owners are delighted with it.

Details and features: Four rooms and one or no bath. Front porch with gabled roof; trellises; glazed front door. Roof and porch details vary slightly from year to year.

Years and catalog numbers: 1919 (7041); 1921 (7041); *1922* (7041); *1925* (7041, 3203); 1926 (P7041, P3203); 1928 (P7041, P3203); 1929 (P7041)

Price: $998 to $1,189

Location: Rocky River, Ohio

No. 7041 (1925)

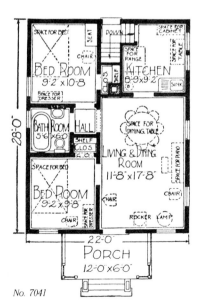

No. 7041

THE HATHAWAY

No. 3082

No. 3082

*A*merican tourists in Europe are always favorably impressed by the cottage homes of England. They speak enthusiastically of the appearance of solid comfort they convey and describe them as covered with vines and climbing roses. Most English homes are constructed of stone, brick or concrete. Here is a striking example of this style of architecture, in frame construction, made to closely resemble the original by the aid of stucco finish. The ornamental trellised porch is a typical English feature. It is cozy and graceful, and the colonial windows with their flower boxes make this type of house at home in any American community.

. . . .

Details and features: Four rooms and one bath. Stucco exterior; front porch with hipped-gable roof and trellis; window box in second-floor window; glazed front door. Breakfast nook off kitchen; semi-open stairs. The 1928 and 1929 models have six rooms and one bath and shingled exterior.

Years and catalog numbers: *1921* (3082); 1922 (3082, 3195); 1925 (3195); 1926 (P3195); *1928* (P3271); 1929 (P3271)

Price: $1,196 to $1,970

Location: Pelham Manor, N.Y.

No. P3271

No. P3271

No. P3271

THE IONIA

*H*ere you have comfort and convenience at small cost with attractiveness thrown in. There is a good front porch, three excellent rooms, a big attic, a basement under the entire house and an up-to-date grade entrance. All the windows in the house harmonize with the pretty bungalow door which leads to the combined living and dining room.

. . . .

Details and features: Three rooms and no bath. Front porch with hipped-gable roof supported by brick and wood piers; decorated bargeboards; glazed front door.

Years and catalog numbers: *1921* (7034, 17034); 1922 (7034, 17034)

Price: $695 to $1,038

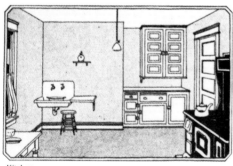

Kitchen

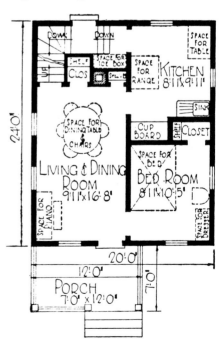

THE SALEM

*T*he Salem is a home combining character and loveliness. The top part of the house and porch gable is paneled on a stucco background. The balance of the exterior walls is finished with beveled siding. The front porch is a gem in the comfort it gives during the warm months. It can be glassed or screened in, making it usable the year around.

Details and features: Six rooms and one bath. Full-width front porch with gabled roof; half-timbered and stucco front gable; side porch with gabled roof; glazed front door. Fireplace in living room; semiopen stairs.

Years and catalog numbers: *1925* (3211); 1926 (P3211)

Price: $2,496 to $2,634

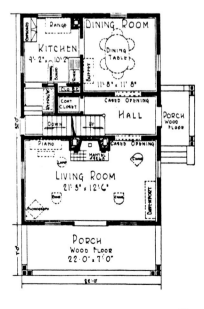

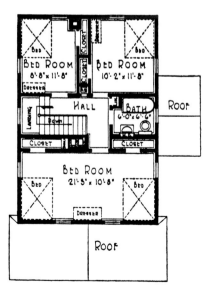

THE SOLACE

The Solace is a one-and-a-half-story bungalow type with a dormer on the rear. The exterior and interior have been carefully planned. Its six rooms and bath reflect modern comforts. In the Solace there is a great economy of floor space and low cost of upkeep. Every dollar's worth of material shows up to the best advantage. It has the same high-grade material as found in the higher-priced houses. The porch has a covered roof with pergola effect. This lends character and individuality.

. . . .

Details and features: Six rooms and one bath. Front porch with open slat roof; glazed front door. Cased opening between living and dining rooms.

Years and catalog numbers: *1925* (3218); 1926 (P3218); 1928 (P3218); 1929 (P3218); 1932 (3218); 1933 (3218)

Price: $1,476 to $1,581

. . . .

Identical to: The Waverly

Year and catalog number: 1933 (3321)

Price: $1,234

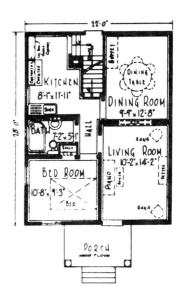

THE SUNLIGHT

*I*n this modern five-room bungalow the architects have carefully planned every detail so that every inch of space is used to the best advantage. The careful planning of the Sunlight relieves the usual household drudgery. Front and rear gables are ornamented with wood shingles, which can be stained a pleasing tone. The porch is an ideal place to enjoy the pleasant weather and a nice place for the kiddies to play. An enclosed rear entry is a feature.

. . . .

Details and features: Five rooms and one bath. Full-width front porch with hipped roof; exposed roof rafter tails; glazed front door. Cased opening between living and dining rooms.

Years and catalog numbers: 1925 (3221); *1926* (P3221); 1928 (C3221); 1929 (P3221)

Price: $1,499 to $1,620

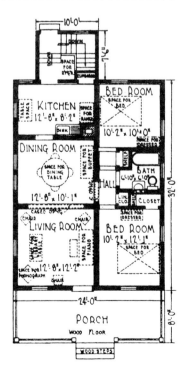

THE FOSGATE

The Fosgate Standard Built home readily meets with favor because it has an attractive exterior and a modern interior. It is made of good-quality material, ready cut and square. Priced on the bedrock of greatest value.

Details and features: Four rooms and one bath. Front porch with gabled roof; decorated bargeboards; glazed front door.

Years and catalog numbers: 1925 (6016); 1926 (P6016); *1928* (P6026)

Price: $616 to $722

THE FARNUM

The Farnum Standard Built home is patterned after the more expensive bungalow. It is well balanced in both exterior and interior. The material is a good grade; in fact, better than is usually found in this kind of a house.

Details and features: Five rooms and one bath. Full-width front porch with hipped roof and square columns; exposed roof rafter tails; glazed front door. Cased opening between living and dining rooms.

Years and catalog numbers: 1925 (6017); *1926* (P6017); 1928 (C6027)

Price: $917 to $942

THE CLEVELAND

he Cleveland has the outward appearance of a one-family residence, yet it has two apartments, each with its own entrance. Each apartment is a complete home in itself, enjoying every privacy, thereby making a very attractive investment. A porch on the first-floor apartment and a balcony on the second-floor apartment are features worth considering, not only because of their decorative value but especially because of the delightful afternoons and evenings that can be leisurely enjoyed during the warm season each year.

Details and features: Eight rooms and two baths. Two-family house. Full-width front porch with balcony and balustrade above. French doors between living room and bedroom.

Years and catalog numbers: *1926* (P3233); 1928 (C3233)

Price: $2,463 to $2,739

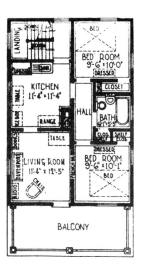

THE MANCHESTER

The Manchester home has the appearance of a one-family, two-story modern bungalow. Careful planning down to the smallest detail makes the Manchester a very good example of the so-called income bungalow. The first floor accommodates a five-room apartment with bathroom, and the second floor accommodates a four-room apartment with bathroom. This type of building not only provides a fine home for the owner but also furnishes a comfortable income by renting the other apartment to a tenant, whose rental usually pays for the cost of the investment. Again, the cost of constructing a home of this type is very little more than the cost of a one-story or a story-and-a-half bungalow.

Details and features: Nine rooms and two baths. Two-family house. Full-width front porch with hipped gable; front dormer with hipped gable. Fireplace in first-floor living room; arched opening between living and dining rooms.

Years and catalog numbers: *1926 (P3250); 1928 (C3250); 1929 (P3250)*

Price: $2,655 to $2,934

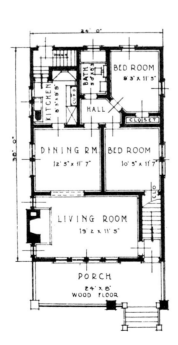

THE DOVER

*T*he Dover is an Americanized English-type colonial story-and-a-half cottage with a convenient floor plan. The massive chimney helps to "tie in" the front gable, and the cowled roof lines help to give a compact appearance. The exterior walls are planned for clear beveled siding but will look equally attractive if shingles are used.

Details and features: Six rooms and one and a half baths. Freestanding chimney; vestibule with sloping gabled roof; arched front door. Fireplace in living room; arched opening between living and dining rooms.

Years and catalog numbers: 1928 (P3262); 1929 (P3262); 1932 (3262); 1933 (3262); 1934 (3262); *1935* (3262); 1937 (3262); 1939 (3262)

Price: $1,613 to $2,311

Similar to: The Mansfield

Difference: Brick exterior

Years and catalog numbers: 1932 (3296); *1933* (3296)

Price: $2,292

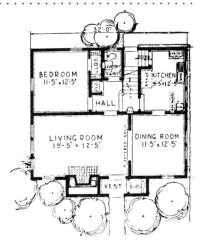

The Mansfield

No. 113

A modern house with a gambrel roof, large front porch and side porch. The side entrance makes it very convenient for a city or suburban residence or country home. The side porch could be very easily arranged to open up to a driveway which might be made directly at the side of the house. The rooms are very conveniently arranged.

. . . .

Details and features: Seven rooms and one bath. Full-width front porch with hipped roof supported by columns; side porch; bay window in front gable. Nook off hall; pantry off dining room; open stairs.

Years and catalog numbers: 1911 (113); 1912 (113); *1913* (113)

Price: $1,062 to $1,270

Locations: Dwight, Ill.; Springfield, Mass.; Dunbar and Harrisburg, Pa.

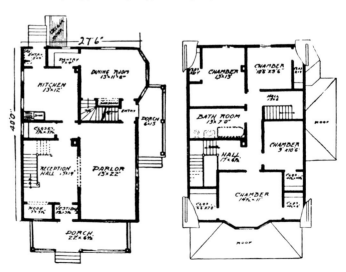

Gambrel roof

THE LUCERNE

A popular design—a two-story house with side dormer. Houses of this design are being built in very large numbers in several localities as they afford a great deal of room for the amount of money invested.

. . . .

Details and features: Five rooms and one bath. Full-width front porch with hipped roof and fluted columns; glazed front door. Open stairs.

Years and catalog numbers: 1908 (103); 1911 (103); 1912 (103); *1913* (103); 1916 (264P103); 1917 (C103); 1918 (C103)

Price: $582 to $1,390

Locations: Glenbrook and Waterbury, Conn.; Mason City and Rock Island, Ill.; Indianapolis, Ind.; Burlington and Davenport, Iowa; Boston, Mass.; Rockaway, N.J.; Elizabeth, Pa.; Milwaukee, Wis.

No. 122

A design that is popular in most all parts of the country. Having a gambrel roof, it is practical to build, as it can be built at a smaller cost than a full two-story house and yet contains practically the same amount of floor space. The open birch stairway in the reception hall is a little out of the ordinary. Instead of the usual newel and rail, it is paneled up three feet six inches high and finished with a wide ledge on top.

. . . .

Details and features: Six rooms and one bath. Corner front porch; two-story projecting bay; bay window in living room; glazed front door. Fireplace in living room; cased opening between living and dining rooms; pantry off kitchen; semiopen stairs.

Years and catalog numbers: 1911 (122); 1912 (122); *1913* (122)   **Price:** $915 to $1,043

*A*n attractive two-story house of frame construction with a gambrel roof with return cornices. Arranged to give plenty of light and ventilation in every room in the house. The front porch is covered by the projection of the second story and supported by extensive colonial columns with square paneled base. The projection on the porch is in harmony with the general lines of the house.

. . . .

Details and features: Eight rooms and one bath. Full-width front porch with portico supported by columns; bay window in dining room; glazed front door. Tile fireplace in living room; plate rail in dining room; open stairs.

Years and catalog numbers: 1911 (123); *1912* (123); 1913 (123)

Price: $1,163 to $1,404

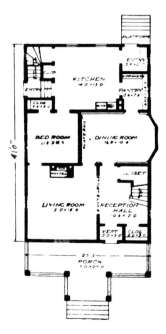

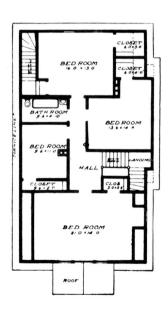

A modern residence of unique arrangement. The reception hall leads to all rooms, yet a view to the kitchen is excluded. The parlor has one of our oak consoles with a very large plate glass mirror.

. . . .

Details and features: Seven rooms and one bath. Full-width front porch with shed roof; gabled dormers with arched windows; bay window in parlor and sewing room; glazed front door. Console with mirror in parlor; fireplace in dining room; open stairs.

Year and catalog number: 1911 (153)

Price: $1,142

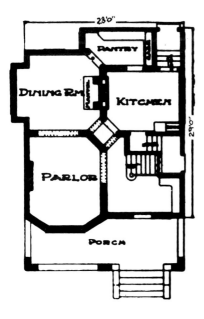

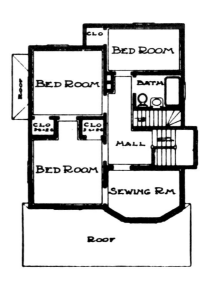

This is a double house built for two families. In this house we offer a very handy arrangement with a stair hall leading directly to the kitchen, dining room and parlor without having to pass through any of the other rooms. Each dining room contains a mantel, fireplace and buffet with French beveled plate mirror.

Details and features: Fourteen rooms and two baths. Two-family house. Wood siding exterior on first floor; stucco exterior on second floor; shingled gables; full-width front porch; two-story projecting center bay; dormers in front; glazed front doors with leaded glass transoms above. Fireplace and built-in buffet in dining rooms; open stairs.

Years and catalog numbers: 1911 (154); 1912 (154); *1913* (154); 1916 (264P154); 1917 (C154)

Price: $2,287 to $2,702

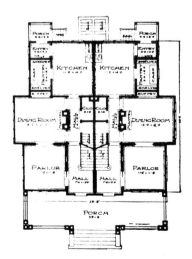

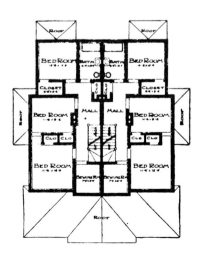

THE PHOENIX

A strictly modern Stonekote house with a front porch. The massive porch columns impart an air of strength and durability while the decorative effects and graceful lines make the whole structure very pleasing. Note the many possibilities for floral decoration. The lover of shrubs and flowers can make this house a bower of beauty.

Details and features: Seven rooms and one bath. Stucco exterior; front porch with shed roof supported by stucco piers; glazed front door with beveled plate glass. Fireplace in living room; sliding doors between living and dining rooms; console with mirror in parlor; open stairs.

Years and catalog numbers: 1911 (160); 1912 (160); 1913 (160); 1916 (160); 1917 (C160); *1918* (160)

Price: $1,043 to $2,077

Locations: Bradley and Norwood Park, Ill.; Detroit, Mich.; Long Island City and Saratoga Springs, N.Y.; New Oxford and Bethlehem, Pa.; Superior, Wis.

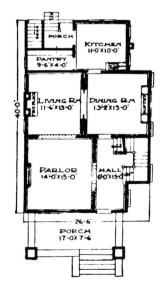

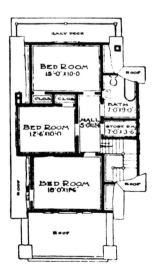

No. 164

A colonial two-story house with a gambrel roof, having a large front porch. On the same level with this porch there is an open terrace on the left elevation. The entire house, including the porch columns, is sided with shingles. Paneled lattice is provided under the porch, constructed with square porch balusters.

. . . .

Details and features: Eight rooms and one bath. Wraparound front porch supported by brick piers; shed dormer in front; glazed front door with sidelights. Built-in buffet in dining room; open stairs.

Years and catalog numbers: 1911 (164); 1912 (164); *1913* (164); 1916 (164); 1917 (C164)

Price: $1,259 to $1,623

Locations: Miami, Fla.; Beach Haven and Closter, N.J.; Dunkirk, New York and Rochester, N.Y.

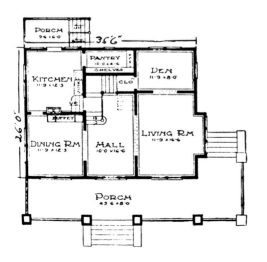

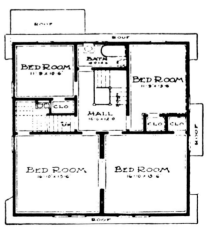

THE BONITA

    The Bonita is right for 25-foot lots. The front door opens into a large living room, which has an attractive open stairway.

Details and features: Five rooms and one bath. Full-width front porch supported by stucco piers; glazed front door. Pantry between living room and kitchen; open stairs.

Years and catalog numbers: 1912 (197); 1913 (197); 1916 (197); 1917 (C197); *1918* (197)

Price: $619 to $1,207

Locations: Kankakee and Rockford, Ill.; Waterloo, Iowa; Gibsonburg, Willoughby and Youngstown, Ohio

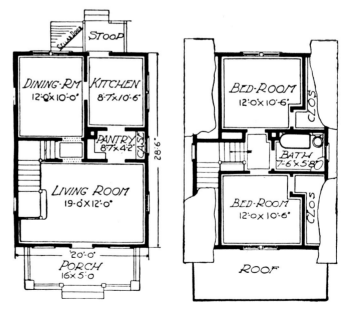

No. 138

*H*ouses like this with a cobblestone foundation, porch, piers and chimney are becoming quite popular. In many sections of the East and West, cobblestone of various tints can be procured at a nominal price (very often can be procured free of charge), and when used in a design such as our Modern Home No. 138 it adds a beautiful effect to the building. The manner in which the shingles are applied to take the place of siding on this house lends an additional charm to its appearance. Each alternate row of shingles is laid two and six inches to the weather. When stained a suitable color they look very beautiful.

. . . .

Details and features: Six rooms and one bath. Full-width front porch with cobblestone piers and open balcony above; two dormers in front; cobblestone chimney. Fireplace flanked by leaded glass windows in living room; semiopen stairs.

Year and catalog number: 1913 (138)

Price: $1,047

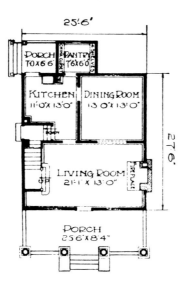

No. 264P252

*H*ere is a colonial home that is fast becoming popular. The entrance is on the right side. The design has a private porch on the front which is entered by French doors.

. . . .

Details and features: Seven rooms and one bath. Full-width front porch in front; hipped portico roof supported by brackets. Fireplace, bookcases and built-in window seat in living room; semiopen stairs.

Year and catalog number: 1916 (264P252)

Price: $998

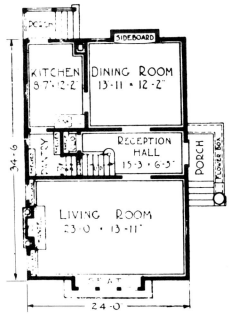

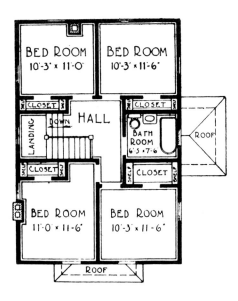

THE VERONA

The Verona is a high-class home of the Dutch type of colonial architecture. Here's an Honor Bilt home that always satisfies the owner and is adored by everyone in his locality. Its growing popularity is demonstrated by the ease with which it is sold after it is completed. Its simplicity and beauty make it a classic in architecture. Built many times in exclusive suburbs of New York, Chicago, Washington, Cleveland, Pittsburgh, Cincinnati and other large cities. Study its floor plans shown here. Could you desire more spacious rooms?

Details and features: Seven rooms and one bath. Full-width shed dormer in front; side porch; bay window in living room and dining room; front door flanked with sidelights. Fireplace and cove ceiling in living room; French doors in hall; breakfast alcove off kitchen; open stairs. Slight differences in exterior details between 1918 and 1926 models.

Years and catalog numbers: *1918* (2094); 1921 (7094); 1922 (17094); 1925 (13201); *1926* (13201)

Price: $2,461 to $4,347

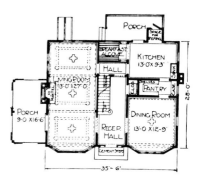

Living room

THE MARTHA WASHINGTON

The Martha Washington is a design that will delight lovers of the real colonial type of architecture. The entrance with its colonial columns, colonial door and sidelights is most inviting and attractive, flanked by the double colonial windows on either side. The view to the visitor or passerby presents a vision of hospitality and brightness that is characteristic of many famous historical homes. Fancy this commodious home set in a landscape as pictured in the illustration. The red tile approach to the brick porch ornamented with flowers and shrubbery will often prompt you to stand and admire this beautiful creation of the architect's skill.

. . . .

Details and features: Seven rooms and one bath. Full-width shed dormer in front; hood over six-panel front door flanked by sidelights. Fireplace and built-in window seat in living room; French doors between living and dining rooms; semiopen stairs.

Years and catalog numbers: 1921 (3030); *1922* (13080); 1926 (P13080A)

Price: $2,688 to $3,727

Location: Washington, D.C.

. . . .

Similar to: The Priscilla

Differences: Slightly smaller dimensions; gabled porch; different front window arrangement

Years and catalog numbers: 1925 (3229); *1926* (P3229); 1928 (C3229)

Price: $2,998 to $3,198

The Priscilla

THE ADAMS

*W*ith its seven rooms, each having windows at least on two sides, bath, numerous closets, grade entrance, large vestibule, popular long living room and numerous conveniences, the Adams will give you solid comfort. Standing on the brick steps you face a porch and entrance of pure colonial lines with front door and sidelights—all in spotless white. Lovers of colonial architecture will surely fancy this house.

. . . .

Details and features: Seven rooms and one bath. Front porch with curved roof; six-panel front door with sidelights. Fireplace in living room. No. 3059A has a gabled roof over the front porch.

Year and catalog numbers: 1920 (3059, 3059A)　　　**Price:** $4,721.

THE MARQUETTE

*I*n the Marquette the architect has very successfully applied the gambrel roof to a colonial type and added many attractive features. The front porch with its colonial columns worked in combination with trellises, the colonial attic windows and flower boxes produce a harmonious effect seldom obtained in this type of house.

. . . .

Details and features: Five rooms and one bath. Full-width front porch with hipped roof supported by trellised columns; round window in gable. French doors in living room; semiopen stairs.

Years and catalog numbers: *1921* (3046); 1922 (3046)　　　**Price:** $1,862 to $2,038

THE PURITAN

The Puritan is the most modern type of Dutch colonial architecture. Painted pure white with contrasting green shutters and the red or green roof with red brick chimney, it is an architectural masterpiece. Where will you find a more inviting entrance than this quaint colonial doorway with colonial hood, which can be ornamented by the colonial benches on either side of the doorway?

Details and features: Six or seven rooms and one bath. Full-width shed dormer in front; hood over six-panel front door flanked by porch seats. French doors between living and dining rooms; semiopen stairs. Two floor plans; larger model has sun room with balcony above.

Years and catalog numbers: *1922* (3190); 1925 (3190A, 3190B); 1926 (P3190A, P3190B); *1928* (P13190A, P13190B); 1929 (P13190A, P13190B)

Price: $1,947 to $2,475

Location: Washington, D.C.

No. P13190A

THE AMSTERDAM

*T*he dignity and beauty of the Dutch colonial exterior is combined in the Amsterdam with modern interior arrangement and conveniences. Each room has been carefully planned with a view toward providing generous space for the usual furniture and light on two sides.

. . . .

Details and features: Eight rooms and one and a half baths. Full-width shed dormer in front; window boxes; six-panel front door flanked by sidelights. Fireplace and French doors in living room; semiopen stairs.

Years and catalog numbers: 1925 (3196A); *1926* (P13196A)

Price: $3,641 to $4,699

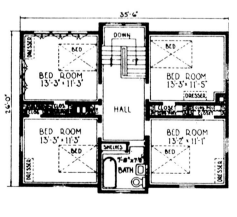

THE VAN DORN

The Van Dorn home is a fine example of modern Dutch colonial architecture. While its exterior reflects the classic of our historical colonial period, its interior has every advantage of our present-day superior arrangement. You approach the Van Dorn aware that here is a beautiful home. It is adorned with a true colonial entrance and windows. Green shutters contrast with the pure white siding, while below is the red brick foundation and buttress.

· ·

Details and features: Six rooms and one bath. Full-width shed dormer in front; portico with columns. Semiopen stairs.

Years and catalog numbers: *1926* (P3234); 1928 (P3234); 1933 (P3234)

Price: $1,576 to $2,249

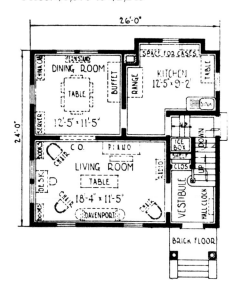

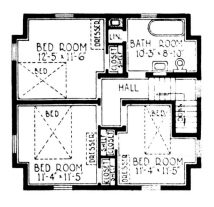

THE OAK PARK

SEVEN OR
EIGHT ROOMS
AND BATH

The Oak Park two-story home was designed to reflect the modern trend in Dutch colonial architecture. Here are the self-same beautiful lines that have won the admiration of all generations since Dutch colonial architecture was introduced. Here, too, you can choose from two of the newest and most approved modern interior arrangements. See the beautiful colonial entrance with its sidelights and fan over the door, hood and the brick porch Then again, the colonial windows and green shutters are offset by pure white siding. Its brick fireplace chimney overlooks the wide, overhanging roof.

. . . .

Details and features: Seven or eight rooms and one bath. Full-width shed dormer in front; front portico with gabled roof and wood columns. Two floor plans; fireplace in living room; French doors between living and dining rooms; semiopen stairs.

Years and catalog numbers: 1926 (P3237A, P3237B); *1928* (P3237A, P3237B); 1929 (P3288); 1932 (3288); 1933 (3288)

Price: $2,227 to $3,265

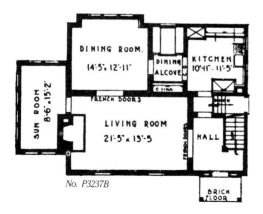

No. P3237B

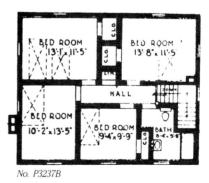

No. P3237B

THE VAN PAGE

The Van Page colonial two-story home is another splendid example of a modern adaptation of early Dutch architecture. All of the important features that are of Dutch-American ancestry are combined with modern ideas. For instance, the Van Page includes a variation from the regular hooded entrance, commonly associated with architecture of this kind. A modern front porch, cleverly adapted into the ensemble, takes the place of the decorative hood. Additional points of interest to the visitor are the gambrel roof and red brick fireplace chimney, the dark green shutters and flower boxes and the white or ivory body, below which is the colorful red brick foundation. The entrance includes beautiful colonial sidelights.

. . . .

Details and features: Six rooms and one bath. Front porch with pent roof and paired columns; full-width shed dormer in front. Fireplace in living room; arched opening between hall and living room; French doors between living and dining rooms.

Year and catalog number:
1926 (P3242)

Price: $2,650

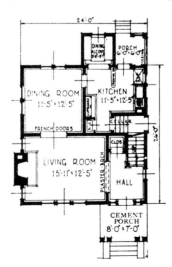

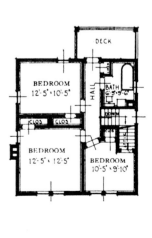

THE AMHURST

The Amhurst, a two-story quaint Dutch colonial home, is finished in brick veneer on the first floor and in wide siding on the second floor. It is greatly admired for (1) its picturesque and distinctive beauty, (2) Dutch colonial lines with modern interior, (3) substantial strength and permanence. The arrangement of the interior is a delight to its owner. Every room has been planned with careful thought to the other rooms, resulting in convenience, maximum livable space and cheerfulness.

Details and features: Six rooms and one bath. Brick exterior on first floor; siding on second floor; front porch; full-width shed dormer in front; glazed front door. Fireplace in living room; French doors between living and dining rooms.

Year and catalog number: 1926 (P3244)

Price: $2,825

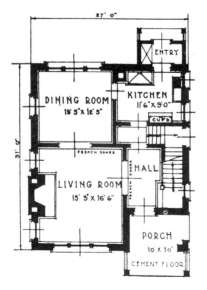

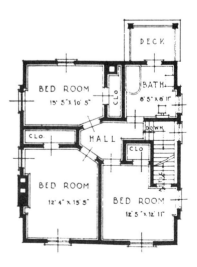

THE GLEN FALLS

NINE ROOMS
AND PORCH

he Glen Falls is an exclusive and pleasing Dutch colonial home. Picturesqueness, dignity and hospitality are three cardinal points that are outstanding characteristics. Comfortable and economical arrangement and strong and permanent construction are other important advantages to consider. Carefully planned to stress the harmonious lines are the colonial entrance door with its brick terrace and bench, the set-in porch with dignified wood columns, green shutters and flower boxes. Then, again, consider the wide siding, stucco fireplace chimney, topped with pots, through which the smoke rises from a crackling fire below.

Details and features: Nine rooms and one bath. Front porch with paired columns; two shed dormers in front; vestibule with steeply pitched roof. Fireplace and French doors in living room; dining alcove off kitchen; open stairs.

Years and catalog numbers: 1926 (P3245); *1928* (P3245); 1929 (P3245)

Price: $4,560 to $4,909

Bedroom

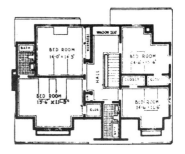

THE VAN JEAN

SIX-ROOM COLONIAL

*T*he Van Jean is an unusually well-arranged Dutch colonial house. It has many special features not generally found in houses of this price. It has a charming entrance that gives an atmosphere of welcome. It has colonial windows with divided lights above and one light below. Add to this the white siding and contrasting red or green roof with the red brick chimney, and you have a home that is sure to charm the most critical.

Details and features: Seven rooms and one bath. Full-width shed dormer in front; gabled portico; six-panel front door with flanking sidelights. Fireplace in living room; French doors in hall; semiopen stairs.

Years and catalog numbers: *1928* (P3267A, P3267B); 1929 (C3267A, C3267B)

Price: $2,499 to $2,899

Similar to: The Rembrandt

Difference: Portico detail

Years and catalog numbers: 1925 (P3215A, P3215B); *1926* (P3215A, P3215B)

Price: $2,383 to $2,770

No. P3267A

The Rembrandt

THE CHATHAM

The architecture of Holland has always been famous for its picturesque quality—and "blood tells," in art as well as in manner. Today this type of home is very popular. Its shape lends itself remarkably well to picturesque treatment in carrying the lines down to the ground. With the Chatham, careful thought has been given to the designing of the front vestibule entrance, window shutters and railing over the sun room addition.

. . . .

Details and features: Seven rooms and one bath. Full-width shed dormer in front; sun room on side with deck above; entry with trellises and six-panel door. Fireplace in living room.

Years and catalog numbers: 1934 (3396); *1935* (3396); 1937 (3396)

Price: $1,667

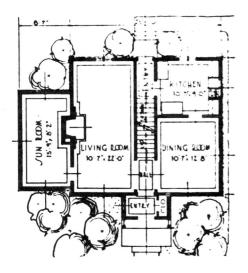

THE NEWBURY

D ignified in every line and proportion, this aristocratic member of the colonial period has many prototypes in all parts of the United States. Inviting, indeed, is the large front porch inset under the graceful sweep of the main roof. Well-proportioned square columns tie it in as a part of the main structure. Screened in summer, it forms a most popular place. The dormer shown on the front perspective is repeated on the rear and helps to break up the otherwise large roof area. The stone base of the chimney is an unusual and interesting detail. The front wall under the porch roof is planned to be covered with brick, while the balance of the walls is of wide beveled siding which we suggest painting white or cream.

. . . .

Details and features: Six rooms and one bath. Full-width front porch supported by paired columns; full-width shed dormer in front; six-panel front door. Fireplace in living room; rear porch off dining room.

Years and catalog numbers: *1934* (3397); 1935 (3397); 1937 (3397); 1939 (3397)

Price: $1,791 to $2,042

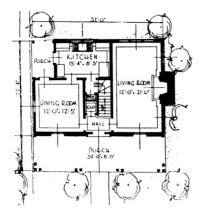

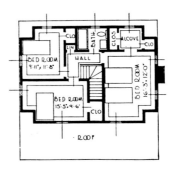

No. 130

A four-family apartment house with four rooms for each family that can be built at a very low cost and will make an exceptionally good paying investment. The building of this house at a low cost is made possible by the economical arrangement of the plans, such as our single stairway to be used for both families on the second floor, and with but one front door and one vestibule. Having the two bathrooms on the first floor adjoining the same wall and the bathrooms on the second floor directly over the bathrooms on the first floor makes it possible to use one set of plumbing pipes for all four bathrooms. One rear stair opening to each side to accommodate all the families in the building.

Details and features: Sixteen rooms and four baths. Four-family house. Front porch with balcony above; center gable; dentil cornice. Fireplace in living rooms.

Years and catalog numbers: 1911 (130); 1912 (130); *1913 (130)*

Price: $1,783 to $2,152

Locations: Boston, Mass.; Great Falls, Mont.; Woonsocket, R.I.; New Richmond, Wis.

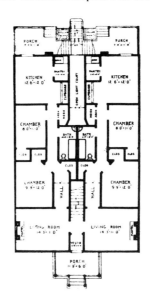

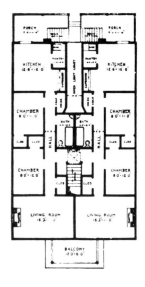

Flat or mansard roof

The flats in this two-family house are conveniently arranged so that the parlor and living room practically make one large room. The parlor in each flat contains a mantel, each dining room contains a china closet, and a large pantry opens into the kitchen.

Details and features: Twelve rooms and two baths. Two-family house. Front porch with balcony above; two-story projecting front bay. Fireplace in parlors; built-in china closet in dining rooms.

Years and catalog numbers: 1911 (131); 1912 (131); *1913 (131)*

Price: $1,491 to $1,870

Locations: Chicago, Ill.; Boston and Woburn, Mass.; New York, N.Y.

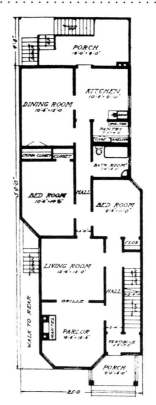

THE ATLANTA

A four-family apartment house with five rooms and bathroom for each family that can be built at a very low cost and will make an exceptionally good paying investment. A light shaft in the center gives light and ventilation for the halls and bathrooms. A private porch is provided for each family.

. . . .

Details and features: Twenty rooms and four baths. Four-family house. Two-story porches with gabled roofs; center gable with exposed roof rafter tails. Fireplace in living rooms.

Years and catalog numbers: 1916 (264P247); 1917 (C247); *1918* (247); 1921 (247); 1922 (247)

Price: $2,240 to $4,942

Locations: Derby, Conn.; Boston, Mass.; Great Falls, Mont.; Stouchsburg, Pa.

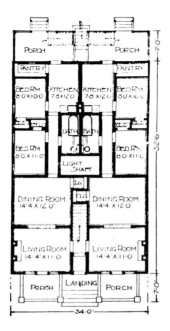

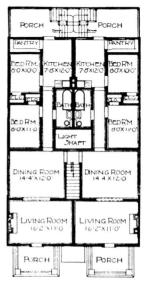

THE CALUMET

$\mathcal{B}$ uilt along Mission lines with Queen Anne windows and fancy doors, this 12-room, four-family flat building provides accommodation equal to a building containing 20 rooms. This economical feature is made possible by the provision for wall beds in the living rooms and dining rooms on both floors. The wall beds (to be provided by the builder), when opened, transform the dining rooms and living rooms into comfortable bedrooms.

Details and features: Twelve rooms and four baths. Four-family house. Stucco exterior; front porch with stepped parapet and balcony above.

Year and catalog number:
1918 (3001)

Price: $3,073

Wall bed

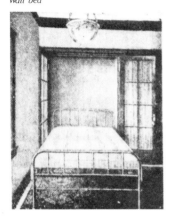

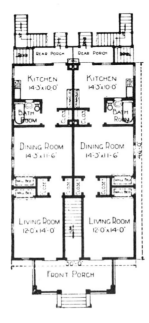

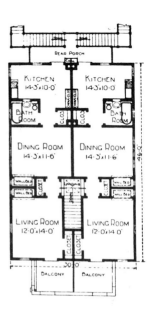

THE CHATEAU

*I*n almost every American city where new residential developments are under way, safeguarded by well-considered building restrictions, houses of this or similar pattern are always in excellent standing. Reserve and good taste are characteristics of this modern adaptation of the French-type home. With the common brick of the side walls painted white, with blue-green shutters and sash and soft brown roof, this home will stand out as an architectural gem in any neighborhood.

. . . .

Details and features: Six rooms and one bath. Brick exterior; panels under ground-floor windows; shutters; arched dormers; side gate to side entrance. Fireplace in living room; semiopen stairs.

Years and catalog numbers: *1934* (3378); 1935 (3378)

Price: $1,365

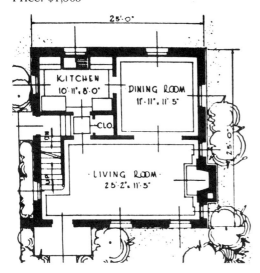

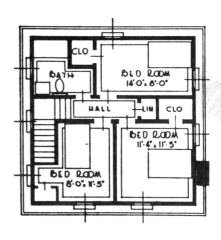

THE BRYANT

$\mathcal{N}$ot so long ago a valued customer presented us with the idea that one of our stepped-up level homes with a conventional exterior could be converted, with little effort, into one of a more modern aspect. Willingly, our designers set to work, and to their surprise produced the flat-roofed home illustrated herewith. It is a home that is far ahead in design, and yet it cannot be termed too extreme or severe in departure.

. . . .

Details and features: Six or eight rooms and one bath. Brick exterior; glazed front door with flat roof canopy. Split-level plan; optional fourth level; roof terrace off bedrooms.

Years and catalog numbers: *1938 (3411); 1939 (3411)*

Price: No price given

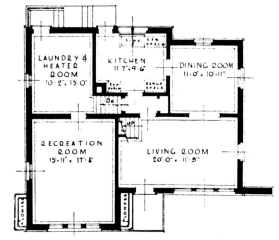

COTTAGES

*O*ur cottages show considerable architectural skill in their compact and practical interiors, suitable for the woods, lake or seashore. They make comfortable homes in which to live happily during vacation periods and weekends. They can be readily built during weekends without paid labor. Vacationists without previous experience have successfully erected our ready-cut cottages by following our simple plans and instructions.

. . . .

The following is a condensed list of Sears cottages, arranged by roof type, number of stories and location of entrance. Those that are Simplex Sectional—available packed and bundled in sections ready to bolt together—are so noted. Three of these cottages are featured as full entries.

Gabled roof, one story, end entrance
The Goldenrod: Three rooms and no bath. Simplex Sectional. 1911 (63B2); 1913 (55C22); 1918 (55MH122); 1921 (55MH122); 1922 (55MH122); 1925 (55C122). $210 to $462.
No. 63B4: Two rooms and no bath. 1911 (63B4). $146.25.
No. 55MH112: Three rooms and no bath. Simplex Sectional. 1918 (55MH112). $478.
No. 55MH118: Four rooms and no bath. Simplex Sectional. 1918 (55MH118). $558.
The Dells: Two rooms and screened porch. Simplex Sectional. 1918 (55MH121); 1925 (55C121). $235 to $337.
No. 55C1: Two rooms and no bath. Simplex Sectional. 1925 (55C1). $227.
The Clover: Four rooms and no bath. Simplex Sectional. 1925 (55C190). $761.
The Greenleaf: Four rooms and one lavatory. 1928 (P608). $513 to $539.

. . . .

Gabled roof, one and a half to two and a half stories, end entrance
The Silverhorn: Four rooms and no bath. Simplex Sectional. 1925 (55C186); 1926 (55P186). $478 to $680.
The Hillcrest: Four rooms and one lavatory. 1928 (P610). $698.

. . . .

Gabled roof, one story, corner entrance
The Lakeland: Four rooms and one lavatory. 1928 (P607). $598 to $635.

. . . .

Gabled roof, one story, side entrance
No. 55C17: Five rooms and no bath. Simplex Sectional. 1913 (55C17); 1918 (55MH117). $579 to $662.
The Yellowstone: Four rooms and one bath. Simplex Sectional. 1913 (55C38); 1918 (55MH138); 1925 (55C205); 1926 (55P205, 55P206). $465 to $811.
The Sunburst: Three or five rooms and one or no bath. Simplex Sectional. 1918 (55MH106); 1921 (55MH106); 1922 (55MH106); 1925 (55C106, 55C338); 1926 (55P106, 55P338). $405 to $1,084.
No. 55MH125: Three rooms and no bath. Simplex Sectional. 1918 (55MH125). $456.
The Alps: Five rooms and one or no bath. Simplex Sectional. 1921 (55MH188); 1922 (55MH188); 1925 (55C188, 55C337); 1926 (55P188, 55P337). $666 to $972.
The Adirondacks: Four rooms and one bath. Simplex Sectional. 1925 (55C192); 1926 (55P192). $1,091 to $1,146.
The Norbrook: Two rooms and no bath. 1928 (601). $297.
The Skywater: Four rooms and one lavatory. 1928 (C602). $690.
The Dove Haven: Five rooms and one lavatory. 1928 (P603). $837 to $879.
The Sunny Lane: Four or five rooms and one lavatory. 1928 (C605A, C605B). $583 to $758.

The Huntley: One room and no bath. 1928 (611). $197.

The Drake Woods: Five rooms and one lavatory. 1928 (P609). $664 to $697.

The Nipigon: Five rooms and one bath. 1939 (no number given). No price given.

. . . .

Intersecting gabled roof, one to one and a half stories

No. 125: Eight rooms and no bath. 1911 (125); 1912 (125); 1913 (125); 1916 (125); 1917 (125). $587 to $844.

The Strand: Five rooms and no bath. Simplex Sectional. 1921 (55MH187); 1922 (55MH187); 1925 (55C187). $876 to $1,058.

The River Grove: Four rooms and one lavatory. 1928 (P604). $795.

. . . .

Hipped roof, one to one and a half stories

The Washington: Four rooms and no baths. Simplex Sectional. 1918 (55MH136); 1925 (55C136); 1926 (55P136). $516 to $783.

The Bower: Five rooms and one bath. Simplex Sectional. 1921 (55MH189); 1922 (55MH189); 1925 (55C189). $895 to $1,089.

The Double-Duty: Four rooms and one bath. Simplex Sectional. 1924 (55C333). $617.

THE GOLDENROD

*T*his low-cost Simplex Sectional cottage, containing three rooms, has met with great popularity. It fills many a need for summer resort requirements. Ideal for industrial communities, such as mining districts, oil fields, etc., needing small cottages for immediate use.

. . . .

Details and features: Three rooms and no bath. Full-width front porch with shed roof; stickwork in gable; glazed front door.

Years and catalog numbers: 1911 (63B2); 1913 (55C22); 1918 (55MH122); 1921 (55MH122); 1922 (55MH122); *1925* (55C122)

Price: $210 to $462

. . . .

Similar to: The Dells

Difference: Two rooms and a screened porch; smaller dimensions

Years and catalog numbers: 1918 (55MH121); *1925* (55C121)

Price: $235 to $337

The Dells

THE SKYWATER

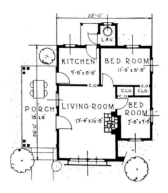

The Skywater summer cottage appeals to those who desire a distinctive style of English architecture. Here is convenience, quality and richness combined with economy. You have an investment in the Skywater summer cottage that is substantial and permanent; in fact, one that pays big dividends in health and that can always be sold at a profit. You can erect it yourself.

. . . .

Details and features: Four rooms and one lavatory. Steeply pitched roof; flat-roofed side porch (may be screened). French doors and fireplace in living room.

Year and catalog number: 1928 (C602)   Price: $690

THE DOUBLE-DUTY

A new and very popular idea, proved successful throughout the country. A substantial, comfortable Simplex Sectional home planned in such a way that when the owner builds a larger home he can convert this building into a two-car garage with very small expense. The partitions dividing the rooms come in sections and can be readily adjusted, without cutting, for use as partition walls in the garage.

. . . .

Details and features: Four rooms and one bath. Two glazed front doors opening onto terraces with trellis roofs.

Year and catalog number: 1924 (55C333)   Price: $617

FURTHER READING

· · · · · · · · · · · · · · SEARS MAIL-ORDER HOUSES · · · · · · · · · · · · · · ·

Bruce, Alfred, and Harold Sanbank. *A History of Prefabrication*. 1944. Reprint. New York: Arno Press, 1972.

Emmett, Boris, and John E. Jeuck. *Catalogues and Counters: A History of Sears, Roebuck, and Co.* Chicago: University of Chicago Press, 1950.

Gowans, Alan. *The Comfortable House: North American Suburban Architecture 1890–1930*. Cambridge, Mass.: MIT Press, 1986.

Halpin, Kay. "Sears, Roebuck's Best-Kept Secret." *Historic Preservation*, September–October 1981.

Holden, P. F. "Building Materials Department D/664: A History." Unpublished manuscript, 1918.

Schwartz, David M. "When Home Sweet Home Was Just a Mailbox Away." *Smithsonian*, November 1985.

Snyder, Tim. "The Sears Pre-Cut." *Fine Homebuilding*, August–September 1985.

Sorensen, Lorin. *Sears, Roebuck and Company: One Hundredth Anniversary, 1886–1986*. St. Helena, Calif.: Silverado, 1986.

Wheeler, F. K. "Recollection of 36 Years with a Fascinating Lumber Plant." Unpublished manuscript, undated.

Wilson, D. M. "Sears New Way of Selling Houses." Speech, Sears Annual Convention, Chicago, February 26–March 2, 1940.

· · · · · · · · · · · · AMERICAN DOMESTIC ARCHITECTURE · · · · · · · · · · · ·

Andrews, Wayne. *Architecture, Ambition, and Americans: A Social History of American Architecture*. 1955. Rev. ed. New York: Free Press, Macmillan, 1978.

Blumenson, John J. G. *Identifying American Architecture: A Pictorial Guide to Styles and Terms, 1600–1945*. Nashville: American Association for State and Local History, 1977. Rev. ed. New York: Norton, 1981.

Foley, Mary Mix. *The American House*. New York: Harper and Row, 1981.

McAlester, Virginia, and Lee McAlester. *A Field Guide to American Houses*. New York: Knopf, 1984.

Poppeliers, John C., S. Allen Chambers and Nancy B. Schwartz, Historic American Buildings Survey. *What Style Is It? A Guide to American Architecture*. 1977. Rev. ed. Washington, D.C.: Preservation Press, 1984.

Rifkind, Carole. *A Field Guide to American Architecture*. New York: New American Library, 1980.

Walker, Lester. *American Shelter: An Illustrated Encyclopedia of the American Home*. Preface by Charles Moore. New York: Overlook Press, Viking, 1981.

Whiffen, Marcus. *American Architecture Since 1780: A Guide to the Styles*. Cambridge, Mass.: MIT Press, 1969.

Whiffen, Marcus, and Frederick Koeper. *American Architecture, 1607–1976*. Cambridge, Mass.: MIT Press, 1981.

· · · · · · · · · · · · · · · HISTORIC PRESERVATION · · · · · · · · · · · · · · · ·

Derry, Anne, H. Ward Jandl, Carol Shull and Jan Thorman. *Guidelines for Local Surveys: A Basis for Preservation Planning*. 1977. Rev. ed. Washington, D.C.: U.S. Department of the Interior, 1986.

Hosmer, Charles B., Jr. *Presence of the Past: A History of the Preservation Movement in the United States Before Williamsburg*. 1965. Washington, D.C.: Preservation Press, 1974.

———. *Preservation Comes of Age: From Williamsburg to the National Trust, 1926–1949*. Charlottesville: University Press of Virginia, 1981.

Maddex, Diane, ed. *All About Old Buildings: The Whole Preservation Catalog*. Washington, D.C.: Preservation Press, 1985.

National Register of Historic Places. *How to Complete National Register Forms*. Washington, D.C.: U.S. Department of the Interior, 1979.

National Trust for Historic Preservation, Tony P. Wrenn and Elizabeth D. Mulloy. *America's Forgotten Architecture*. New York: Pantheon Books, 1976.

U.S. Conference of Mayors. Edited by Albert Rains and Laurence G. Henderson. *With Heritage So Rich*. 1966. Rev. reprint. Washington, D.C.: Preservation Press, 1983.

REHABILITATION

Morton, W. Brown, III, Gary L. Hume and Kay D. Weeks. *The Secretary of the Interior's Standards for Rehabilitation and Guidelines for Rehabilitating Historic Buildings*. 1979. Rev. ed. Washington, D.C.: U.S. Department of the Interior, 1983.

Old-House Journal. Brooklyn, N.Y.: Old-House Journal Corporation, monthly.

Poore, Patricia, and Clem Labine, eds. *The Old-House Journal New Compendium: A Complete How-to Guide for Sensitive Rehabilitation*. New York: Doubleday, 1983.

Reader's Digest Association. *Reader's Digest Complete Do-It-Yourself Manual*. New York: Author, 1973.

Stephen, George. *Rehabilitating Old Houses*. Information Series. National Trust for Historic Preservation. Washington, D.C.: Preservation Press, 1976.

———. *Remodeling Old Houses Without Destroying Their Character*. New York: Knopf, 1972.

Technical Preservation Services Branch, National Park Service. *Preservation Briefs*, nos. 1–13. Washington, D.C.: U.S. Department of the Interior, 1975–84.

———. *Respectful Rehabilitation: Answers to Your Questions About Old Buildings*. Washington, D.C.: Preservation Press, 1982.

Time-Life Books. *The Old House*. Home Repair and Improvement Series, no. 19. Alexandria, Va.: Author, 1979.

INFORMATION SOURCES

National Trust for Historic Preservation
1785 Massachusetts Avenue, N.W.
Washington, D.C. 20036

> Northeast Regional Office
> Old City Hall
> 45 School Street, 5th Floor
> Boston, Mass. 02108

> Mid-Atlantic Regional Office
> Cliveden
> 6401 Germantown Avenue
> Philadelphia, Pa. 19144

> Southern Regional Office
> 456 King Street
> Charleston, S.C. 29403

> Midwest Regional Office
> 53 West Jackson Boulevard
> Suite 1135
> Chicago, Ill. 60604

> Mountains/Plains Regional Office
> 511 16th Street
> Suite 700
> Denver, Colo. 80202

> > Texas/New Mexico Field Office
> > 500 Main Street
> > Suite 606
> > Fort Worth, Tex. 76102

> Western Regional Office
> One Sutter Street
> Suite 900
> San Francisco, Calif. 94104

Center for Historic Houses
National Trust for Historic Preservation
1785 Massachusetts Avenue, N.W.
Washington, D.C. 20036

National Register of Historic Places
National Park Service
U.S. Department of the Interior
P.O. Box 37127
Washington, D.C. 20013-7127

State Historic Preservation Offices
(Contact state government directories
or the National Register of Historic Places)

Technical Preservation Services Branch
Preservation Assistance Division
National Park Service
U.S. Department of the Interior
P.O. Box 37127
Washington, D.C. 20013-7127

MAIL-ORDER HELP

*S*ears provided the materials and plans to build 100,000 examples of the American dream. Today the National Trust for Historic Preservation provides the information and services to make possible another dream: preservation of all types of historic American buildings, including houses from Sears.

Owners and aficionados of Sears houses are especially encouraged to learn more about National Trust programs and membership as a means of helping preserve these special houses. To coincide with the publication of *Houses by Mail,* the National Trust is offering the following services:

Modern Homes, a periodic publication through which Sears house owners can share information, address common issues and explore the role of Sears houses in American social and architectural history.

Photographic prints of original Sears catalog pages for house styles featured in *Houses by Mail.* These are 8 by 10 inches and are suitable for framing. We will provide a reproduction of the complete catalog page for any house illustrated in the guide section, for the year indicated in italics. These pages (a sample appears here) include Sears's promotional copy, an exterior illustration, floor plan or plans and other specifications.

Photocopies of original Sears catalog pages for house styles featured in *Houses by Mail.* These are the same as above, except that they are photocopies rather than photographic prints.

Discounts on quantity purchases of *Houses by Mail* for special events, promotions and tours or for resale.

Membership in the National Trust carries many benefits for people interested in historic buildings and places, including the satisfaction of contributing to the preservation of America's past for future generations. Membership is open to all interested individuals, organizations, corporations, public agencies and libraries. Benefits include:

Historic Preservation, a four-color bimonthly magazine that presents lively features about restoration, architecture and the people active in preservation.

Preservation News, a monthly newspaper that keeps members up-to-date on new developments and issues.

Free admission to all National Trust house museums, which are located from Massachusetts to California.

10 percent discount on all books and merchandise ordered by mail from the Preservation Shop in Washington, D.C., or purchased at Trust museum shops.

Education and information services, including lectures sponsored by the Trust's Center for Historic Houses, an annual conference, and participation in study tours.

Special services and publications available under varied organizational memberships.

To obtain the special Sears house items and additional copies of *Houses by Mail* as well as to join the National Trust, photocopy the order form.

ORDER FORM

The Preservation Press
National Trust for Historic Preservation
1785 Massachusetts Avenue, N.W.
Washington, D.C. 20036
(202) 673-4058

Please send me the following items and quantities:

___ *Houses by Mail: A Guide to Houses from Sears, Roebuck and Company* ($24.95 each) $ _____

___ Information on quantity discounts for *Houses by Mail* $ ___Free___

___ Photographic Prints of Sears House Styles ($10 each): $ _____

Named Style(s) _____

Numbered Style(s) _____

___ Photocopies of Sears House Styles ($2 each): $ _____

Named Style(s) _____

Numbered Style(s) _____

___ *Modern Homes* (single copy free; additional copies, $1 each) $ _____

___ Other Preservation Press Books:

_____ $ _____

_____ $ _____

_____ $ _____

Subtotal $ _____

Less 10% for Trust members on purchases $ _____

Handling and shipping $ ___3.00___

Total Purchases $ _____

___ Please enroll me as a National Trust member:

__ Individual ($15)   __ Contributing ($50)
__ Family ($20)   __ Sustaining ($100) $ _____

Check (made payable to the National Trust) enclosed for   **Total** $ _____

. . . .

Name _____

Address _____

City/State/Zip _____

Telephone Number (_____) _____

___ I own a Sears house   Style or Number _____   Year: _____

Location of house if different from mailing address: _____

INDEX OF STYLES

*H*ouse styles are arranged by named styles and catalog numbers. Most catalog numbers with letters are listed by the numerals preceding the letters, and the letters themselves are alphabetical. Numbers that refer to the same style but that have different letters are grouped together under the primary entry; thus, Nos. 55MH136 and 55P136 are grouped with No. 55C136, and Nos. 2010A, C2010, P2010 and P2010B are grouped with No. 2010. Numbers that begin with the letters C or P and are not similar to other numbers are placed at the end of the list. Different styles of houses with the same name or number are listed with the years in which each was offered.

· · · · · · · · · · · · · · · · · NAMED STYLES · · · · · · · · · · · · · · · · ·

Adams, *38, 326*
Adeline, *255*
Adirondacks, *343*
Albany, *135*
Alberta, *250*
Albion, *293*
Alden, *187*
Alhambra, *42, 286*
Almo, *89*
Alpha, *97*
Alps, *343*
Alton, *70*
Altona, *111*
Americus, *289*
Amherst, *191*
Amhurst, *332*
Amsterdam, *328*
Arcadia, *84*
Ardara, *91*
Argyle, *45*
Arlington, *40, 119*
Ashland, *140*
Ashmore, *88*
Atlanta, *339*
Attleboro, *14, 149*
Auburn, *41;* (1925), *135;* (1933–35, 1937), *222;* (1917–18, 1921–22), *284*
Aurora, *32;* (1933), *162;* (1918), *287*
Avalon, *71*
Avoca, *197*
Avondale, *17, 242*

Bandon, *132*
Barrington, *154*
Bayside, *105*
Beaumont, *177*
Bedford, *139*
Belfast, *192*
Bellewood, *157*
Belmont (1932–33), *161;* (1916–18, 1921) *205*
Berkley, *193*
Berkshire, *186*
Berwyn, *215*
Betsy Ross, *256*

Birmingham, *296*
Bonita, *321*
Bower, *344*
Branford, *151*
Brentwood, *226*
Bridgeport, *102*
Bristol, *189*
Brookside, *90*
Brookwood, *158*
Bryant, *342*

Calumet, *340*
Cambria, *283*
Cambridge, *154*
Canton, *241*
Cape Cod, *103*
Carlin, *130*
Carlton, *32, 287*
Carrington, *185*
Carroll, *260*
Carver, *106*
Castleton, *279*
Cedars, *80*
Chateau, *341*
Chatham, *335*
Chelsea, *265*
Chester, *222*
Chesterfield, *79*
Chicora, *87*
Claremont, *156*
Clarissa, *268*
Cleveland, *309*
Clifton, *160*
Clover, *343*
Clyde (1921–22, 1925–26, 1928–29), *48;* (1911–13, 1916–18), *267*
Colchester, *101*
Colebrook, *150*
Collingwood, *260*
Columbine, *74*
Concord, *41;* (1933–35, 1937, 1939), *221;* (1911–13, 1916–18, 1921–22), *238*
Conway, *207*
Cornell, *10, 292*

· · · · · · · · · · · · · · · · · CATALOG NUMBERS · · · · · · · · · · · · · · · · ·

No. 3412, *292*
No. 3413, *227*
No. 3414A (3414B), *280*
No. 3415, *145*
No. 3416A (3416B), *102*

No. 3711 (3711A), *228*
No. 3721, *152*

No. 3979, *210*

No. 6000, *96*
No. 6001, *133*
No. 6002, *96*
No. 6003, *210*
No. 6011 (P6011), *99*
No. 6012 (P6012), *51*
No. 6013 (6013A, P6013), *52*
No. 6014 (P6014), *85*
No. 6015 (P6015), *254*
No. 6016 (P6016), *308*
No. 6017 (P6017), *308*
No. 6018 (P6018), *77*
No. 6019, *53*

No. 7000, *280*
No. 7002, *247*
No. 7004, *257*
No. 7006, *242*
No. 7008, *46*
No. 7009 (P7009), *248*
No. 7013, *211*
No. 7016, *272*
No. 7017, *62*
No. 7018, *45*
No. 7024, *129*
No. 7028, *46*
No. 7028A (C7028, P7028), *49*
No. 7030, *48*
No. 7031, *97*
No. 7034, *304*
No. 7041 (P7041), *302*
No. 7044 (P7044), *258*
No. 7080, *286*
No. 7094, *324*
No. 7099, *255*

No. 8013 (C8013A, C8013B, C8103X, P8013,
   P8013A, P8013B), *74*
No. 8040, *179*

No. 9030 (9030A, C9030A, C9030B, P9030A,
   P9030B), *48*

No. 12010A (12010B, C12010, C12010B), *68*
No. 12013, *251*
No. 12026, *123*
No. 12050 (C12050A, P12050A), *203*

No. 12069, *124*
No. 12087, *230*

No. 13039 (C13039, C13039X, P13039,
   P13039A, P13039X), *91*
No. 13045 (P13045), *178*
No. 13048 (P13048), *71*
No. 13049 (13049A, 13049AX, 13049B,
   C13049A, C13049B, P13049A,
   P13049B), *131*
No. 13050 (13050X, P13050), *72*
No. 13051, *92*
No. 13052A (13052B, P13052, P13052A,
   P13052B), *207*
No. 13053, *208*
No. 13056, *92*
No. 13058, *132*
No. 13063 (1922), *208;* (13063X, P13063)
   (1921–22, 1925–26, 1928–29), *289*
No. 13065 (P13065), *209*
No. 13078, *94*
No. 13080 (P13080A), *325*
No. 13084 (13084A), *95*
No. 13085 (P13085), *123*
No. 13086 (P13086A), *95*
No. 13192 (P13192), *251*
No. 13201, *324*
No. 13210 (C13210, P13210), *137*
No. 13282, *156*
No. 13283 (13283A), *216*
No. 13302, *165*
No. 13333, *145*
No. 13337A (13337B), *102*
No. 13354A (13354B), *103*
No. 13377X, *225*
No. 13379, *221*
No. 13384, *149*
No. 13393A (13393B, 13393C), *226*
No. 13394A (13394B, 13394C, 13394D), *226*
No. 13408, *106*
No. 13702, *194*
No. 13703, *151*
No. 13707 (13707A), *150*
No. 13712, *151*
No. 13716, *228*
No. 13718, *165*
No. 13719A (13719B), *152*
No. 13720A (13720B), *153*

No. 17002X (P17002), *247*
No. 17004X, *257*
No. 17006, *242*
No. 17013 (P17013), *211*
No. 17018 (17018A, P17018A), *45*
No. 17031, *97*
No. 17034, *304*
No. 17044, *258*
No. 17090A (C17090A, P17090A), *286*
No. 17094, *324*

THE AUTHORS

*K*atherine Cole Stevenson, an architectural historian, became interested in Sears houses when, as a staff member at the National Register of Historic Places, she came across a reference to mail-order houses and began independent research on this phenomenon, focusing on the houses produced by Sears, Roebuck and Company. She enlisted the aid of H. Ward Jandl, also an architectural historian, in collating the material, and *Houses by Mail* is the result. Stevenson is chief of the Technical Preservation Services Branch, Division of Cultural Resources, for the Rocky Mountain Regional Office of the National Park Service, Denver, Colo. The editor of *The Technology of Historic American Buildings* and coauthor of *Respectful Rehabilitation: Answers to Your Questions About Old Buildings*, Jandl is chief of the Technical Preservation Services Branch, National Park Service, Washington, D.C.

OTHER PRESS BOOKS

Respectful Rehabilitation: Answers to Your Questions About Old Buildings. Technical Preservation Services Branch, U.S. Department of the Interior. This primer answers 150 questions most frequently asked about rehabilitating old houses and other historic buildings. The answers are based on the Secretary of the Interior's Standards for Rehabilitation, which are reprinted in full. 192 pages, illustrated, bibliography, glossary, appendixes. $11.95 paperbound.

Fabrics for Historic Buildings. Jane C. Nylander. A catalog of 550 fabric patterns organized by period, type and manufacturer. Describes how to research, select and install modern reproductions to re-create period effects. 160 pages, illustrated, glossary, bibliography, appendixes. $10.95 paperbound.

Wallpapers for Historic Buildings. Richard C. Nylander. A catalog of 350 wallpapers organized by period, type and manufacturer. Describes how to research, select and install modern reproductions. 128 pages, illustrated, glossary, bibliography, appendixes. $10.95 paperbound.

What Style Is It? A Guide to American Architecture. John Poppeliers, S. Allen Chambers, Jr., and Nancy B. Schwartz, Historic American Buildings Survey. Building Watchers Series. One of the most popular, concise books on American architectural styles, this portable guidebook is designed for easy identification of 22 styles of buildings at home or on the road. 112 pages, illustrated, glossary, bibliography. $7.95 paperbound.

Master Builders: A Guide to Famous American Architects. Introduction by Roger K. Lewis. Building Watchers Series. Forty major architects who have left indelible marks on American architecture—from Bulfinch to Venturi—are profiled in this concise introduction. 204 pages, illustrated, bibliography, appendix, index. $9.95 paperbound.

Built in the U.S.A.: American Buildings from Airports to Zoos. Diane Maddex, Editor. Building Watchers Series. A guidebook-size history of 42 American building types, the book presents essays by noted authorities explaining the forms as a response to the functions. 192 pages, illustrated, bibliography, appendixes. $9.95 paperbound.

All About Old Buildings: The Whole Preservation Catalog. Diane Maddex, Editor. This fact-filled, catalog-style book offers a lively, readable mixture of photographs, drawings, resource listings, case histories, excerpts and quotations. It provides a wealth of information organized into 15 major subject areas. 436 pages, illustrated, bibliographies, index. $39.95 clothbound, $24.95 paperbound.

America's Country Schools. Andrew Gulliford. The first book to examine the country school as a distinctive building type, it captures the historical and architectural legacy of country schools (from dugouts and soddies to frame buildings and octagons) and provides ideas for preserving them. 296 pages, illustrated, appendixes, index. $18.95 paperbound.

America's City Halls. William L. Lebovich, Historic American Buildings Survey. Two centuries of municipal architecture are captured in this book featuring 500 photographs of 114 city halls in 40 states. 224 pages, illustrated, bibliography, appendix, indexes. $18.95 paperbound.

America's Forgotten Architecture. National Trust for Historic Preservation, Tony P. Wrenn and Elizabeth D. Mulloy. This overview of preservation surveys in 475 photographs what is worth saving and how to do it. 312 pages, illustrated, bibliography, appendixes. $14.95 paperbound.

With Heritage So Rich. New introduction by Charles B. Hosmer, Jr. This classic preservation book shows why America's architectural heritage should be preserved and helped spur passage of the National Historic Preservation Act of 1966. 232 pages, illustrated, appendixes. $18.95 paperbound.

Goodbye History, Hello Hamburger: An Anthology of Architectural Delights and Disasters. Ada Louise Huxtable. Foreword by John B. Oakes. These 68 pieces, most originally published in the *New York Times*, cover the classic urban confrontation of the 1960s and 1970s. Huxtable, winner of the first Pulitzer Prize for distinguished criticism, analyzes urban failures and successes, urging us to create more livable cities. 208 pages, illustrated, index. $14.95 paperbound.

Archabet: An Architectural Alphabet. Photographs by Balthazar Korab. Here is a new way of looking at architecture—through the eyes and imagination of an award-winning photographer in search of an alphabet in, on and around buildings. Juxtaposes dramatic photographs with quotations by architectural observers from Goethe to Wright. 64 pages, illustrated. $14.95 clothbound.